ADMINISTRATION OF WOMEN'S COMPETITIVE SPORTS

ADMINISTRATION OF WOMEN'S COMPETITIVE SPORTS

Dorothy Deatherage

California State University
Long Beach, California

C. Patricia Reid

California State University
Long Beach, California

Wm. C. Brown Company Publishers
Dubuque, Iowa

Consulting Editor

Aileene Lockhart
Texas Women's University

Copyright © 1977 by
Wm. C. Brown Company Publishers

ISBN–0–697–07136–7

Library of Congress Catalog
Card Number: 75–13165

Printed in the United States of America

Credits

The History and Functions of the National Section on Women's Athletics by Eline Von Borries. The National Section on Women's Athletics of the American Association for Health, Physical Education and Recreation, 1941. Reprinted by permission of publisher.

Division for Girls and Women's Sports Newsletter, May 5, 1971, by Edith Betts, DGWS Chairman. Division for Girls and Women's Sports, American Association for Health, Physical Education, and Recreation (National Education Association). Reprinted by permission of publisher.

Standards in Athletics for Girls and Women. National Section on Women's Athletics of the American Physical Education Association. Copyright 1937 by National Section on Women's Athletics of the American Physical Education Association. Reprinted by permission of publisher.

The Story of the National Leadership Conference on Girls and Women's Sports, National Section for Girls and Women's Sports of the American Association for Health, Physical Education and Recreation. Copyright 1956 by the National Section for Girls and Women's Sports of the American Association for Health, Physical Education and Recreation. Reprinted by permission of publisher.

Conduct of Intercollegiate and Other Extramural Sports for College Women. Approved by National Association for Physical Education of College Women, Athletic and Recreation Federation for College Women, Division for Girls and Women's Sports of the American Association for Health, Physical Education and Recreation. Reprinted by permission.

Commission on Intercollegiate Athletics for Women Operating Code by Division for Girls and Women's Sports, American Association for Health, Physical Education and Recreation, 1969. Reprinted by permission of publisher.

*"AIAW Handbook" of Policies and Operating Procedures 1974–75 by the Associa-*tion for Intercollegiate Athletics for Women, National Association for Girls and Women in Sport of the American Alliance for Health, Physical Education and Recreation. Copyright 1974 by the National Association for Girls and Women in Sport of the American Alliance for Health, Physical Education and Recreation. Reprinted by permission of publisher.

Commission on Intercollegiate Athletics for Women Newsletter, Sept. 15, 1971, by Lucille Magnusson, CIAW Chairman and Jo Anne Thorpe, DGWS Vice President. Commission on Intercollegiate Athletics for Women, Division for Girls and Women's Sports, American Association for Health, Physical Education and Recreation (National Education Association). Reprinted with permission of publisher.

"1970–71 NFSHSAA Handbook" National Federation of State High School Athletic Associations. Copyright 1970 by National Federation of State High School Athletic Associations. Reprinted by permission of publisher.

"Official Handbook" by National Federation of State High School Associations. Copyright 1974 by National Federation of State High School Associations. Reprinted by permission of the publisher.

"The Emergence of Sport in Physical Education," a paper presented by Betty Spears at AAHPER National Convention, April, 1973. Reprinted by permission of author.

The Life and Lights of the NAPECW by Elizabeth Halsey. National Association for Physical Education of College Women, 1962. Reprinted by permission of publisher.

Women and Athletics Women's Division, National Amateur Athletic Federation. A.S. Barnes and Company. Copyright by A.S. Barnes and Company, 1930. Reprinted by permission.

The Women's Board of the United States Olympic Development Committee: *Purpose — History — Accomplishments — Needs,* by the Women's Board of the United States Olympic Development Committee. Reprinted by permission of publisher.

HPER and the California Law prepared by Raymond A. Snyder and Donald T. Handy for the California Association for Health, Physical Education and Recreation. National Press Books. Reprinted by permission of the California Association for Health, Physical Education and Recreation.

Contents

Preface

The burgeoning of competitive sports programs for girls and women today emphasizes the need for organizing into a logical presentation the wealth of information about such programs that has been available only in fragmented form — to engender a full awareness of the enormous vitality of this entire area of competitive sports.

Although competitive sports for girls and women have existed in one form or another in the United States for years, the rapid increase in the number and scope of such programs at present at all levels has found personnel in schools and colleges unprepared to cope effectively with the many and diverse problems resulting from such unprecedented growth.

It is the intent of the authors to identify and explore, within the framework of organization and administration, the problems confronting competitive sports programs and the functioning of those programs — all in context with the historical background and philosophical concepts so necessary to a thorough understanding of the area.

The entire realm of competitive sports is becoming so highly specialized that the usual professional preparation courses in physical education do not provide the in-depth treatment necessary for personnel who will conduct highly organized competitive sports programs for girls and women in the schools and colleges. For this reason many professional preparation personnel feel the need to offer specific courses with sole emphasis in this area.

This book is provided as a text for specific courses in the organization and administration of competitive sports for girls and women within the school setting, but may be used equally well as a valuable resource in many other courses and seminars. It should prove particularly useful to those now in schools who find themselves directly involved in competitive sports programs.

The opening chapter, on basic beliefs, should provoke readers into giving thoughtful consideration to the impact and influence they have on youthful competitors. The chapters dealing with the administrative conduct of the program should be most helpful to those bearing a major responsibility in this area.

While changes are expected to result from Title IX, it is assumed that with few exceptions, mainly financial, the philosophy, standards, procedures, and so on will remain essentially the same.

A word should be said about the organization of the book. It does not follow the traditional pattern of historical background of the subject first, as an introduction to the main body of the book. The authors elected to place the historical development of competitive sports for girls and women toward the end because the primary emphasis of the book is on current *organization and administration* of these programs. This information is critically needed today. However, to be able to place the total subject in current perspective a knowledge of its long historical development is vitally necessary and should be read with interest and appreciation.

Although the *Division for Girls and Women's Sports* (DGWS) has recently become the *National Association for Girls and Women in Sport* (NAGWS), the term DGWS will continue to be used in this book when references are cited from publications that have not incorporated the recent change in name. It should also be noted that footnoted source citations are, in the main, elaborated upon in the "References" at the end of those chapters in which the footnotes appear.

The authors hope that wherever this book may find a use, whether as a text for students or as a reference book for those in the field, it will contribute to the development of high quality competitive sports for girls and women.

ADMINISTRATION OF WOMEN'S COMPETITIVE SPORTS

GO!
Photograph by Gary Moats
California State University, Long Beach

CHAPTER 1

Basic Beliefs

Topics involved in organization and administration of any given entity, whether it be a business, a hospital, a school, a government bureau or any subdivision of the above — a department, for example — include consideration of basic beliefs, budget, personnel, public relations, policies and procedures, lines of authority, and the like. These and other such items are explained here to the extent that they relate to the conduct of competitive sports programs for girls and women.

The central concern of the present chapter is to point out the critical importance of basic beliefs to the immediate and long-range effectiveness of competitive sports programs for girls and women and the necessity of their being consistent with educational goals in general. The process of identifying basic beliefs and of formulating philosophy, aims, and objectives will be explored; so also will be the resulting outgrowth of policies and procedures and their importance with reference to effective functioning of the total program.

IMPORTANCE OF BASIC BELIEFS

Basic beliefs are important because they are imperative "guides to action." No program can operate effectively without them. These beliefs should be solidly and consistently based and should stem from sound educational principles. They should provide the basis for an expression of the best potential values and purposes of the program and are a necessary prerequisite for the formulation of sound policies and procedures.

If a competitive sports program begins to operate without its leaders first having taken the all important step of identifying and scrutinizing basic beliefs, then it can fall into a number of pitfalls which may engulf it in a foment of problems that can, in turn, seriously impair its progress and success.

Historically competitive sports programs for American girls and women have operated on basic guidelines and standards which were

1

identified and are regularly reevaluated by leaders of such organizations as the National Association for Girls and Women in Sport. These guidelines are necessarily broad and general in nature, however, and were never intended to provide specific statements which would answer all questions for every competitive sports program in the country. They are nevertheless an expression of *basic* principles and should be used as a framework by those who are engaged in the process of initiating such programs.

It should be borne in mind that in some instances the process being discussed in these pages may refer to schools in a large public school district, while in others it may refer to specific institutions such as a particular college, a rural school, or a private school. Since there are great variations in size, geographic location, and environment, as well as specific uniquenesses in different situations, many factors may influence the formulation of specific beliefs. Factors which may definitely influence the thinking of groups facing such responsibilities are the kind of institution under consideration, the socioeconomic level of the students, the ethnic makeup of the community, and perhaps the religious climate of the comunity or school.

Variations among schools and colleges, other than size, might depend upon whether they are public or private, secular or religious, urban or rural, or coeducational or noncoeducational. Although all schools have much in common, they have, by the same token, many differences. The educational goals of private schools may vary somewhat from those of public schools. Certainly the educational philosophy of religiously oriented schools differs in many respects from that of secular schools. After all, that is why they have been established as religiously oriented schools. In the same way the educational philosophy of a wealthy, private girls' school might differ somewhat from the usual coeducational public school. These differences may have a definite impact upon the basic beliefs regarding a competitive sports program for girls.

The socioeconomic level of the students may or may not have implications for the development of basic beliefs about competitive sports for girls. It would seem, however, that the *principles* would not vary with this dimension. More than likely differences in socioeconomic levels would impose implications as far as the expense of the program is concerned, in terms of what the schools and/or parents might be able to afford. In lower socioeconomic areas one might expect to find less participation in the more expensive individual and dual sports and more participation in the less expensive team activities. Such items as special uniforms, travel, and awards might be expected to be restricted in those areas.

In religiously oriented schools one might find differences in basic beliefs among the various denominations themselves. Some parochial schools have highly competitive programs while others have very minor programs even for the boys, much less for the girls. These latter schools tend to embrace an intramural rather than an interscholastic or intercollegiate structure. The philosophies of parochial schools vary, obviously reflecting the religious attitudes, fundamental or liberal, of the various denominations concerned.

Even in large public school districts considerable differences exist among the various neighborhood schools. In some schools the student body may be composed almost entirely of one ethnic minority group. It is quite possible that the mores of such a group may so differ that attitudes may be affected. As a consequence, although a district philosophy regarding competitive sports for girls may be formulated, such schools may be expected to differ in the way they accept or apply the district philosophy.

The various factors which are being discussed here emphasize the fact that no one set of basic beliefs can serve all situations, nor would that necessarily be desirable.

The important fact to be remembered is that there are many pitfalls which may be encountered in the conduct of a competitive sports program. By establishing a consistent set of beliefs, based on principles, and by identifying and anticipating difficulties, one can usually avoid the traumatic experience of getting enmeshed in them. One can easily and innocently fall prey to a number of unanticipated problems from which she cannot easily extricate herself if she is not aware of their existence and if she does not have established policies and procedures to guide her actions.

FORMULATION OF BASIC BELIEFS

The personnel involved in formulating a statement of beliefs will vary in accordance with the educational level for which the statement is being sought. At the secondary school level one might expect to find some type of district committee, composed of administrators, supervisors of physical education and women physical educators. At the college and university level personnel from the women's physical education department usually constitute the committee. The administrative structuring of the latter level might require the approval of the dean of the school or of a specific dean of students or student activities. In men's intercollegiate athletic programs the administrative responsibility often goes from the athletic director directly to the president of the college. Highly organized women's programs, however, have not been in existence long enough for any real pattern of administrative channeling to have emerged.

In addition to the personnel mentioned at both educational levels it would be highly desirable to include student membership on the committees in question. Students not only may represent a different point of view but they are also quite capable of making constructive and significant contributions to the development of basic beliefs, goals and objectives of a program which, after all, is for them.

Regardless of the educational level the committee should first avail itself of existing and approved guidelines from such sources as the National Association for Girls and Women in Sport, and the Association for Intercollegiate Athletics for Women. There may also be similar statements from regional, state and local organizations that should be helpful for the committee to examine. (See Appendix — Example A for the constitution of a local conference.)

After a thorough study of such available materials the committee should be ready to begin the process of identifying and spelling out its own basic beliefs with regard to the specific program under consideration. These beliefs should be stated in broad, general terms and should be concerned mainly with what will be most desirable for those specific individuals for whom the program is being designed — the students. Following are two examples of basic beliefs, the first being from the Division for Girls and Women's Sports (DGWS), now known as the National Association for Girls and Women in Sport (NAGWS) which believes that:

> Sports are an integral part of the culture in which we live.
>
> Sports programs are a part of the total educational experience of the participant when conducted in educational institutions.
>
> Opportunities for instruction and participation in sports appropriate to her skill level should be included in the experience of every girl.
>
> Sports skills and sports participation are valuable social and recreational tools which may be used to enrich the lives of women in our society.
>
> Competition and cooperation may be demonstrated in all sports programs, although the type and intensity of the competition and cooperation will vary with the degree or level of skill of the participants.
>
> An understanding of the relationship between competition and

cooperation and the utilization of both within the accepted framework of our society is one of the desirable outcomes of sports participation.

Physical activity is important in the maintenance of the general health of the participant.

Participation in sports contributes to the development of self-confidence and to the establishment of desirable interpersonal relationships.[1]

The second is more comprehensive in scope and is a Statement of Philosophy developed by a large university.

The Women's and Coeducational Intercollegiate Sports Program is based on the belief that competitive sports contribute significantly toward the achievement of the goals of higher education. The intrinsic values to be derived from sports participation are recognized in current culture. Participation in intercollegiate sports affords opportunities for students to: (1) pursue excellence in performance; (2) attain personal growth, self-esteem, and self-realization; (3) participate in positive social interaction with teammates and opponents; (4) develop a level of fitness contributing to total well-being.

Ultimately, the realization of the purposes of a sound intercollegiate sports program in higher education is the responsibility of the leaders of the program. The administrators and coaches should be committed to fostering the goals designed for the entire program.

A well-balanced intercollegiate sports program shall be available to every full time university student possessing the level of skill to warrant the opportunity. The number of participants in each sport shall be based upon: (1) the number of highly skilled students interested; (2) the number of competent coaches to provide a feasible faculty/student ratio; (3) budget; and (4) staffing units provided.

The selection of sports to be included shall be based primarily upon student interest. A concerted effort shall be made to provide competent coaching, leadership, and budget to support any sport for which student interest exists.

The intercollegiate program shall be provided with the most highly qualified leadership available. Administrators shall work to promote the best interests of all sports. They shall have experience and competence in the various aspects of the position(s). Coaches shall have expertise in the sports to which they are assigned. In addition, they shall be positive examples to their team members in sportsmanship and shall have a primary commitment to the welfare of the participants in all facets of the competitive experience.

Competition, to be of value, shall be provided against opponents of relatively comparable ability. Where such competition is not

1. Division for Girls and Women's Sports, *Philosophy and Standards*, pp. 5 – 6.

available locally, every effort shall be made to schedule regionally, within the limitations of budget allocations among all sports. Each individual or team whose performance during the regular season demonstrates a high level of success shall be afforded every opportunity for regional and national competitive experiences.

Each student who participates shall accept the responsibility of representing the university by maintaining the highest standards of conduct and attitude. Participants shall follow established team policies and procedures in order to assure the continued privileges of competing. Consideration for regional and national competition shall be based upon full time participation on the university team. . . .

Though the basic purpose of the program is to provide maximum opportunities to as many students as possible, recognition of the outstanding athlete shall not be minimized. Every attempt will be made to recognize those individuals and teams whose excellence in performance warrants it. However, recognition shall include many performers rather than focus on the promotion of individuals. Publicity shall recognize performance and personal worth of the participants, avoiding the exploitation of the physical attributes of the performer.[2]

FORMULATION OF AIM AND OBJECTIVES

After basic beliefs have been identified and accepted the next step is to formulate the aim and objectives of the specific program. These stem directly from the statement of beliefs and although still stated in broad general terms they are more specific in nature. The "aim" of the program is long range and is the ultimate goal or purpose of the program. An example of an aim is, "to provide wholesome and enriching experiences for the skilled woman athlete through a carefully planned and conducted competitive sports program." The "objectives" are simply the stepping stones to the accomplishment of the aim. An example of an objective is, "to provide well-qualified coaches." Together the aim and objectives provide a framework for the design of the program. In essence they present a plan of operation for the entire project. They must be flexible enough to refrain from limiting or hindering the progress and expansion of the program while at the same time they should keep individuals from losing sight of what it is that they are committed to.

It is the firm belief of the present authors that the objectives of competitive sports for girls and women in schools and colleges should be

2. Statement of Philosophy, Women's and Co-educational Program.

consistent with educational goals in general. Indeed it would be paradoxical for any educational institutions to provide for their students programs whose objectives are inconsistent with the goals of the institutions themselves.

Although there are many academic expressions of educational goals and textbook definitions of such, suffice it to say that most concur in the proposition that "central to the goals of all education should be concern for the student." In other words what happens to the student as a result of the variety of experiences that she is exposed to, at any educational level, is of critical importance.

It has long been accepted that education in general has a concern for the individual, not only intellectually but also emotionally, physically, and morally as well. All educational experiences should in some way make desirable and worthwhile contributions to the total growth and development of the student.

With this point of view in mind it is the responsibility of those educators who have the task of formulating a philosophy (including aim and objectives) of competitive sports for girls and women to ensure that the program which emerges will indeed provide educational experiences which are consistent with the educational goals of the institution itself.

However, "paper goals" do not always develop into action. Therefore those who supervise and evaluate the program must assume the responsibility of ensuring that the goals originally set are consistently adhered to by all personnel involved in the conduct of that program. Personnel at whatever level of involvement should constantly evaluate the program in order to ascertain whether or not the experiences being provided the students remain in harmony with sound educational goals.

ESTABLISHMENT OF POLICIES AND PROCEDURES

The final step to be taken is the establishment of policies and procedures that will govern the conduct of the program. Up to this point the main concern has been that of building a strong foundation and of necessity it has been in rather broad, general terms. It is now time to become specific about exactly how the program will operate.

Policies are concerned with regulations that are accepted as necessary in order to ensure the effective functioning of the program. Procedures are simply those steps that are established to implement or facilitate the accomplishment of the purposes and adherence to the policies. For example, it probably will be a policy that each girl who participates in a competitive sports program must have a medical examination by a qualified physician. The procedures relating to this policy would state the way or ways in which it is to be accomplished. They would be concerned with arranging dates for examinations, developing necessary report forms, getting correct information to those faculty members coaching the teams, getting proper information to the participants, and other such items.

The policies which will be developed by a committee should be the expression of the beliefs, aim, and objectives that have already been established. It must be remembered, in addition, that all policies must be consistent from one to another of all governing groups having jurisdiction over the program at the local, state, regional, and national levels.

There are certain policies that will be basic to every program such as those related to the health and welfare of the participants, eligibility, number of games to be played, qualifications of the coach and the like. Highly developed programs that are broad in scope and involve not only local but regional and perhaps state and national levels of competition will need additional policies that govern travel, insurance, budget, scholarships, recruitment, and many other such pertinent items.

At this point a word of caution regarding the extensiveness of the policies and procedures should be expressed. Those responsible for policymaking ought to bear in mind that policies should be established upon the basis of the anticipated needs of the specific program, yet should not expect to anticipate every single need for every policy that will ever occur. Such action could so bind and limit the program that the worthwhile experiences one is trying to provide for the participants could instead become frustrating and unrewarding.

Although specific policies must be established at the beginning in order to permit the effective operation of a program, it should be remembered that policies can be added as real need for them is demonstrated. An in-depth discussion of policies and procedures common to most programs will be found in chapter 2.

As in every other educational endeavor one should provide for constant and periodic evaluation of the total program, and its procedures. From time to time those responsible for the organization and administration of the program should re-examine their beliefs, aim, and objectives in order to ascertain if these continue to be meaningful and to serve their purpose in our constantly changing society. It is not only desirable but necessary that this step be taken in order to ensure that the conduct of the program remains consistent with its stated basic beliefs. It is not beyond the realm of possibility, due to pressures of one kind or another, for programs to move very slowly away from what personnel involved sincerely think they believe. Without continual watchfulness and careful supervision on the part of those responsible for the program, a wide gap can develop between belief and practice. It is far easier to prevent the gap in the first place than it is to try to close it once it has occurred.

References

Division for Girls and Women's Sports. *Philosophy and Standards for Girls and Women's Sports*. Washington, D.C.: American Association for Health, Physical Education and Recreation, 1973.

Statement of Philosophy, Women's and Co-educational Intercollegiate Sports Program. Long Beach: California State University.

VOLLEYBALL: Serve and Return
Photograph by Dr. Richard Lussier
California State University, Long Beach

CHAPTER 2

Policies and Procedures

After basic beliefs have been identified, policies and procedures for the conduct of the program can then be developed. The purpose at this point is to put into perspective the policy-making roles of various governing organizations, to indicate the impact they have on the conduct of competitive sports at the institutional level, and to illustrate commonly accepted policies and procedures.

Ever since the turn of the century women physical educators have worked together within the framework of their national professional association to promote desirable sports programs for girls and women. The historical development of this organization, under the successive names of the Women's Athletic Committee, the National Section on Women's Athletics, the National Section for Girls and Women's Sports, and the Division for Girls and Women's Sports, will be presented in chapter 7. Yet another change in name, structure, and function occurred in 1974 when the American Association for Health, Physical Education and Recreation became the American Alliance for Health, Physical Education and Recreation, and the Division for Girls and Women's Sports became the National Association for Girls and Women in Sport (NAGWS).

In the process of developing policies and procedures for an individual institution, careful study must be made of regulations already established by organizations with authority to control interscholastic or intercollegiate competition. At the high school level, the state high school athletic or activities association has been granted this authority by the state department of education. Member schools must meet its minimum state regulations. Within the framework of the state association, institutions competing with each other frequently form an association, league, or conference to develop additional policies and procedures appropriate to the member schools. Policies and procedures developed by an individual institution, therefore, cannot be less stringent than regulations existing at the state and local level, but can be more inclusive and can reflect higher standards. Administrators and physical educators, responsible for the development of state, local, and individual school policies for competitive sports programs for high school girls, should be guided in their work by the *Guidelines for Interscholastic Athletic Programs for High School Girls.*[1]

Intercollegiate competition is controlled by policies and procedures established by the Association for Intercollegiate Athletics for Women (AIAW) at the level of regional and national championships, and by policies and procedures adopted by regional and local leagues or conferences composed of representatives of the various member schools. AIAW, an outgrowth of the Commission for Intercollegiate Athletics for Women (CIAW), is an official structure of the National Association for Girls and Women in Sport. AIAW and regional and local governing groups have utilized NAGWS guidelines and standards in the formulation of policies and procedures. Although these organizations have no direct control over local governing groups, institutions desiring to enter teams in regional and national championships must comply with policies and procedures established by AIAW for these events.

LEADERSHIP

Intercollegiate Sports

• ADMINISTRATION.   The administration of the women's intercollegiate sports program should be under the jurisdiction of women physical education teachers.

> The intercollegiate athletic program should be specifically designed for women, and its administration and organization should be the responsibility of the women in physical education. It is also the responsibility of the physical education faculty women to recommend and formulate policy for the expanded program to be submitted to the appropriate policy-approving authority of the institution.[2]

Thoughtful consideration needs to be given to the fundamental beliefs upon which such a policy is based. Of primary importance is the belief that the sports program should be developed to meet the needs and serve the best interests of highly skilled women students. Women physical education teachers are the most qualified members of the college faculty to make policy decision concerning the women's intercollegiate sports program. The administration of the women's intercollegiate sports program should therefore be under their jurisdiction —

1. DGWS, *Philosophy and Standards*, pp. 43 – 45.
2. Ibid., p. 47.

the final authority and responsibility resting with the chairperson. As the intercollegiate sports program expands, a director or coordinator of intercollegiate sports for women who is directly responsible for administering the program according to the policies established by the department, is customarily appointed.

Administrators of combined departments for men and women should delegate a woman faculty member to administer the women's intercollegiate sports program. A policy statement for women's intercollegiate sports should be recommended and approved by the women faculty members of the physical education department. The chairperson of the department, whether man or woman, has the final authority and responsibility, but should logically seek the counsel of the women with regard to the women's sports program.

Although in most institutions a woman directs the intercollegiate sports program for women, other patterns of organization do exist. Sometimes the administration of this program is under the jurisdiction of the association on campus designed to provide intramural and other activities for students. In still other situations, a department of intercollegiate sports is assigned the responsibility for control over athletics for both men and women. In all instances, it is extremely important that communication be well established between the women's physical education department and the administrator of the women's athletic program. Since the philosophy, purpose, and policies of women's intercollegiate sports may differ from those of men's intercollegiate athletics, it is vitally important that the administrator of the women's program be familiar with NAGWS and AIAW policies at the national level and with the policies of the regional and local governing groups.

• COACHING. DGWS has taken the position that " . . . qualified women should teach, coach, and officiate wherever and whenever possible, and in all cases, the professional background and experience of the leader must meet established standards of the physical education profession."[3] The qualified leader is defined as one who

> . . . meets the standards set by the profession through an understanding of (a) the place and purpose of sports in education, (b) the growth and development of children and youth, (c) the effects of exercise on the human organism, (d) first aid and accident prevention, (e) specific skills, and (f) sound teaching methods. . . . The leader should demonstrate personal integrity and a primary concern for the welfare of the participant.[4]

In addition to the above qualifications, it is strongly recommended

3. Ibid., p. 49.
4. Ibid.

that " . . . an official's rating be considered a prerequisite for coaching in order to enhance the coach's understanding of the official's role."[5] It is also desirable for the coach to have had prior personal experience in a competitive interschool sports program.

In situations wherein a nonstaff member is serving as the coach, DGWS guidelines state that " . . . a woman member of the physical education faculty should supervise the participants."[6] For participation in AIAW national championships, it is mandatory that the coach or a designate of the school be present; if the coach is unable to attend, the institution must arrange for the supervision of its team by a person designated in writing who is attending the event.[7]

An individual institution must of course establish its own specific policies regarding the qualifications and responsibilities of its coaches. It is considered most desirable to have activity specialists in the women's physical education department faculty serve as coaches for women's teams. It is assumed that such individuals have been selected for faculty status on the basis of their educational background, their understanding of the role of physical education in institutions of higher education, their ability to work with college students, and ther teaching/coaching skill. Since the women's physical education department is usually the administrative unit through which the women's intercollegiate sports program is conducted, faculty members in that department are in the best position to understand and carry out the philosophy and policies of the department because they have been involved in the development, evaluation, and revision of such policies.

• OFFICIALS.   DGWS specifies that "Intercollegiate events should be officiated by DGWS state or national officials. In those sports where DGWS does not rate officials, an equivalent rating is acceptable."[8] Regional and local governing groups also require the use of DGWS-rated officials, but sometimes vary in the level of rating required for officiating games and meets under their jurisdiction.

Interscholastic Sports

• ADMINISTRATION.   Whereas AIAW and regional and local governing groups have been developed to control intercollegiate sports for women, the growth of interscholastic programs for high school girls is under the direction of the well-organized state high school activities or

5. Ibid.
6. Ibid.
7. NAGWS. *AIAW Handbook*, p. 50.
8. DGWS, *Philosophy*, p. 49.

athletic associations. Delineation of the administrative organization is included in the *Guidelines:*

1. Existing legislative administrative bodies for interscholastic athletic programs will retain ultimate control of the total program for girls within the state. However, a women's advisory board composed mainly of women high school physical educators should be formed to propose policies to these administrative and legislative groups and to review policies approved by them.

2. Total responsibility for the administration and supervision of the local interscholastic athletic program is vested in the local school administration and the appropriate persons designated by the administration.

3. The responsibility for leadership of the local girls interscholastic program should be delegated to the women physical education teachers. The school administration should delegate to them the major responsibility for planning, organizing, coaching, and supervising the program with the understanding that the ultimate authority remains in the hands of the administration.[9]

High schools differ in their pattern of organization of interscholastic programs, depending upon the size of the institution and the number of women in the physical education department. Since the responsibility for the interscholastic program should be delegated by the principal to the girls' physical education department, the chairperson of that department may also serve as the coordinator for the interscholastic sports program, or she may appoint someone to carry out this responsibility. This person may also be in charge of the intramural program, or in larger schools, different individuals may direct these two programs.

• COACHING. DGWS has formulated the following guidelines concerning the leadership of the program:

1. The interscholastic program should be directed, coached, and officiated by qualified women whenever and wherever possible. No program should be expanded past the ability of the girls department of physical education to direct it.

2. All coaches should be certified teachers employed by the local board of education. If teachers other than trained women physical educators are used to coach, they should be qualified and work closely with the girls department.

3. A woman faculty member appointed by the principal shall accompany and supervise girls teams at all contests.[10]

The National Federation of State High School Associations

9. Ibid., p. 43.
10. Ibid., p. 44.

(NFSHSA) states that a school shall not "Permit coaching by anyone who is not a certified teacher regularly employed by the Board of Education and whose entire salary is paid by that body; or who has fewer than three regular periods of classes, gymnasium or study-hall duty per day."[11]

• OFFICIALS. Qualified women should be used to officiate whenever and wherever possible. "Officials should hold a current DGWS rating in the specific sport and should be registered with the appropriate administrative or regulatory bodies."[12] NFSHSA "Official Registration Rule" states that a school shall not "Use any paid athletic official who is not registered with the home high school athletic association and is not qualified according to the standards of such state association."[13] Because the quality of the competitive experience is directly related to the ability of the official, it is recommended that women advisory committees at the state and local level recommend the type of rating an official should have.

ELIGIBILTY

The rapid expansion in the area of competitive sports for girls and women has resulted in the need to establish eligibility requirements. Whereas the intramural program stresses participation for all, with a minimum of limiting regulations, intercollegiate and interscholastic competition requires students to meet certain eligibility standards.

The need for establishing eligibility requirements has at least a two-fold basis. First, and most important, is concern for the health and welfare of the individual students. The most obvious example of eligibility, based upon this concern, is verification through a medical examination that a student is physically able to participate in a rigorous sports program. Eligibility is also usually based on evidence that participants are full-time students and that they meet certain academic standards. Such requirements are opposed by some; nevertheless the intent is to place the sports program in proper perspective with the basic purpose of education. Students should be helped to understand that making normal progress toward an educational goal takes precedence over participation in the athletic program.

A second reason for establishing eligibility requirements is to ensure fairness in competition between teams from different institutions. Eligibility regulations are needed in order to standardize conditions

11. NFSHSA, *Official Handbook 1974–75*, p. 35.
12. DGWS, *Philosophy*, p. 44.
13. NFSHSA, *Official Handbook 1974–75*, p. 36.

of participation. One needs only to think about the hypothetical situation in which a "star performer" guides her team to victory through eight years of part-time college attendance to realize the importance of player eligibility regulations.

The actual establishment of eligibility regulations is the responsibility of each institution. However, it is vitally important that the eligibility standards already established by the group of institutions within which a school competes be included as minimum eligibility requirements. Furthermore, consideration should be given to standards established at each advancing level of competition (district, region, state, national) in order not to jeopardize the eligibility of students for competition at these levels. Because eligibility for intercollegiate sports differs from that of interscholastic sports, we will discuss each separately and indicate generally established criteria at each level of competition.

Intercollegiate Sports

• FULL-TIME UNDERGRADUATE STUDENT. In order to be eligible for participation in regional and national AIAW Championships, a woman must be

> presently enrolled as a full-time undergraduate in a college, junior college, or university. . . . However, a student in her final term who can graduate with less than a full load of course work shall be eligible to participate if she carries enough hours to graduate. If she has completed graduation requirements within the *preceding* semester, quarter, or trimester, has begun the sport season, and has met all other eligibility requirements for national championships, she shall be eligible. Also, if a student has completed her spring term within the *preceding* semester, quarter, or trimester and has met all other eligibility requirements for national championships, she shall be eligible in the summer.[14]

Since the structure of the curriculum has become increasingly different at the various institutions, governing groups at the local and regional levels have experienced difficulty in interpreting the meaning of "full-time student." Some have added the phrase "as defined by the institution," and others have included a specific minimum semester or quarter unit load requirement. Still others define a "full-time student" as one who has earned at least twenty-four semester, or thirty-six quarter credits between the beginning of one sport season and the start of the same season the next year.

• ACADEMIC AVERAGE. The AIAW has ruled that a student must

14. NAGWS, *AIAW Handbook*, p. 46.

maintain "the academic average required for participation in all other major campus activities at her institution"[15] in order to be eligible for regional and national championships. Some governing groups and institutions are more specific and state that the overall grade point average must be 2.0 on a 4.0 scale and that the student cannot be on academic probation.

• TRANSFER STUDENTS.   AIAW, regional governing groups, and individual institutions generally agree that transfer students should be immediately eligible to participate in intercollegiate sports following enrollment in that institution, providing all other eligibility requirements are fulfilled. In contrast to some men's programs, women students do not have to wait a semester or year before becoming eligible. It should be noted that a transfer student could have an overall grade point average above 2.0, but will be declared on academic probation if her grades fall below 2.0 at the institution to which she has transferred, in which case she is ineligible to participate in the intercollegiate program.

• AMATEUR STATUS.   AIAW has approved the following statement regarding amateur status:

> All participants must have amateur status. Amateur status is maintained in a sport if a player has not received and does not receive money other than expenses as a participant in that sport. These expenses include lodging, meals, transportation, and entry fee while participating in an intercollegiate event. Although the acceptance of officiating or coaching fees in excess of expenses has no effect on the eligibility for competition in AIAW events, these may jeopardize amateur status for open competition.[16]

The above statement defines amateur status for AIAW regional and national championships, and is thus accepted by regional and local governing groups for participation in intercollegiate meets and tournaments. However, each sport governing body also has its own definition of amateur status, and a highly skilled student who wishes to compete in "open" competition must meet the eligibility requirements for amateur status as defined by the governing body having jurisdiction over that sport (e.g., the United States Lawn Tennis Association, the United States Volleyball Association, etc). Students interested in "open" competition should therefore be advised to write to the governing body of the sport in question in order to become informed of qualifications for amateur status as a participant in that sport.

Although the position of AIAW with respect to athletic scholarships

15. Ibid.
16. Ibid., p. 45.

is discussed elsewhere, it should be noted here that "Acceptance of an athletic scholarship does not affect amateur status."[17]

• LENGTH OF PARTICIPATION. "A student may not participate in a national championship in any given sport more than four times. Futhermore, she may not have participated in more than four intercollegiate seasons of play in any one sport and remain eligible for an AIAW national championship in that sport."[18]

Individual institutions, however, need to further specify criteria which define what constitutes participation in any one year. Individual situations, such as illness, the need to work part-time, and changing majors may require a student to be in college more than the usual four years. If, during her first year, she participated in team practices but did not have the opportunity to play in any intercollegiate games, should she be allowed to participate for the next four years? Until that time when a national or league ruling is made, this is a decision which each institution will have to make based upon its own philosophy. Some institutions define participation in practice sessions as constituting one season of play whereas others state that a season of play is counted only when the student actually participates in intercollegiate games.

Inherent in any statement concerning length of participation is the concept that four seasons of play refers to the individual's total college attendance and not necessarily to the number of seasons at any one institution. Thus, a transfer student who has played basketball for two years at a junior college has only two more seasons of eligibility left at the four-year institution to which she transfers.

• PARTICIPATION REQUIREMENTS. Only students who have fulfilled practice requirements should be eligible to participate in intercollegiate competition. Such practice requirements are usually established by the coach of each sport, but some consistency of requirements among sports within an institution should be achieved. In order to protect the student from unrealistic demands from an overzealous coach, some institutions have established minimum and maximum number of hours per week for practice and/or game participation, and have further specified the number of practices required to become eligible for participation in intercollegiate events. Such standards prevent a highly skilled performer, who has not participated in team practices, from being allowed to participate in intercollegiate athletic events.

Institutions which are not able, because of lack of faculty, budget,

17. Ibid.
18. Ibid., p. 46.

or facilities, to provide an intercollegiate program in every sport, need to determine whether or not interested and qualified students should be allowed to enter intercollegiate competition in a sport in which the institution does not provide coaching. There is a general agreement that the requirement of regular practices under a qualified coach constitutes the most desirable program. However, institutions unable to provide such a program sometimes feel that their highly skilled students should not be deprived of the opportunity to compete. Other institutions, faced with the same limitations, have decided that they will provide competitive opportunities only in those sports in which they can provide a formally organized program. Such a stand could result in pressure being exerted by interested students on the college administration to provide the necessary increase in faculty, budget, and facilities so that the desired competitive program could be initiated. The position which AIAW has taken with respect to this issue follows: "A student is eligible if she has participated on her institution's intercollegiate team during the majority of its recent season which includes a majority of practices and a majority of events. However, if the institution does not have an intercollegiate team in this student's specific sport, and the institution approves her participation, she is eligible."[19]

• MEDICAL EXAMINATION. AIAW states that "Each student must have had a medical examination within the year of participation preferably immediately prior to participation in the sports season."[20] The necessity for meeting such a requirement is reiterated in similar eligibility standards at the regional and local governing committee levels, and in policies within individual institutions. The institution's health service is usually the final authority in determining whether or not a student is physically able to participate, based upon either medical examinations given by the health service or upon medical examination reports filed by individual physicans with the health service.

Each institution needs also to consider provisions it deems appropriate for students whose religious beliefs prohibit medical examinations. Practices existing for public school students and for men's athletics can provide suggestions relative to this situation. It is advisable to consult the insurance company covering women's intercollegiate sports to determine its position on liability coverage of students

19. Ibid., pp. 46 – 47.
20. Ibid., p. 49.

who object to taking medical examinations on the basis of religious belief.

• ATHLETIC SCHOLARSHIPS AND FINANCIAL AWARDS. Through the years, one of the most controversial subjects regarding eligibility has been whether or not students on athletic scholarships should be able to participate in the girls' and women's competitive sports program. Although DGWS was traditionally opposed to awarding of athletic scholarships, recent antidiscriminatory legislation has prompted it to modify its statement, and AIAW has voted to allow women on athletic scholarships to compete in national championships. Each institution must make its own decisions as to whether or not a scholarship program should be initiated. Because of the importance of this decision, it seems advisable to discuss this issue at further length.

Proponents of the scholarship system argue that since scholarships are awarded for high level skill in men's athletics and in such areas as music and art, the highly skilled woman athlete should not be discriminated against. If the attainment of skill is recognized by financial assistance in other areas, are we not diminishing the importance of achievement in women's sports when we oppose the awarding of scholarships to women athletes? Why should we deny a student who is gifted in sports the opportunity for a college education which she might not be able to afford without financial assistance? Interpretations made of the Civil Rights Act of the Fourteenth Amendment substantiate this point of view. As has been pointed out by legal authorities, women have the right "not to be treated differently than men." Therefore, since scholarships are offered for men, this argument goes, they should also be offered for women.

Among the most vocal opponents to the awarding of scholarships for women have been some men coaches and athletic directors with considerable experience in scholarship and financial aid programs which are such a vital part of men's intercollegiate athletics. If scholarships are given, they say, then an institution will naturally seek out the most highly qualified candidates, which in turn will be those students who will contribute the most toward winning teams for that insitution. Thus the awarding of scholarships cannot be divorced from recruitment, which is considered by many to be the root of many of the problems and unethical practices in men's intercollegiate athletics at the present time.

Educators who oppose athletic scholarships are committed to the point of view that financial aids programs and recruitment are not compatible with educational objectives. They believe that the goal of an intercollegiate sports program should be to provide competition for highly skilled students who have chosen to enroll in an institution for the educational opportunities which are available at that institution. Seeking out highly skilled players from among high school and junior college students with the intent of persuading them to enroll in an institution for the principal purpose of participating in sports is deemed by them to be inappropriate and detrimental to the best interests of the students involved. They warn that all precautions should be taken to avoid a "pay for play" situation from occurring in women's intercollegiate sports.

With the current emphasis on providing equal rights and privileges for women, and with law enforcement agencies focusing on discriminatory practices, women physical educators have been forced to reevaluate their position on scholarships. Since the major criticism leveled against the awarding of scholarships has been based on the evils associated with recruitment, AIAW has revised its position statement to allow the benefits of a scholarship program for students while attempting at the same time to control the abuses by developing regulations restricting to some degree the awarding of financial aid and the recruitment of athletes. "Athletic ability is one of the talents which can be considered in the awarding of financial aid to students. However, students should be free to choose the institution on the basis of curriculum and program. Staff time and effort should be devoted to the comprehensive program rather than to recruiting efforts."[21]

The AIAW Regulations for the Awarding of Financial Aid to Student Athletes became effective August 1, 1974, following approval by a mail vote of the AIAW member institutions in May of 1974. These regulations state that: "Financial aid may be awarded for only tuition, fees, room, and board."[22] The Regulations further specify that "All financial aid for student-athletes must come from and be awarded through the appropriate institutional aid office and/or agency after the student has been admitted to the university. Recommendations for such aid must come from the administrator for women's intercollegiate athletics."[23] Also that

> All financial aid for athletes shall be awarded for a maximum of one academic year. Such aid shall be renewed yearly if the student maintains academic eligibility, makes normal progress toward a degree as determined by the institution, observes conduct as defined by the Code of Ethics for Players, realizes successful progress

21. Ibid., p. 32.
22. Ibid., p. 37.
23. Ibid., p. 34.

toward athletic potential through participation on the intercollegiate team in which the financial aid is awarded. If a student athlete is injured and as a result cannot participate in the sport season for which financial aid is awarded but is otherwise eligible, the student shall not be denied financial aid for athletes.[24]

Institutions in the process of developing programs of financial aid for student athletes should refer to the current AIAW Handbook of Policies and Operating Procedures for a listing of all regulations relating to financial aid, which include: administration; eligibility for those receiving financial aid for athletes; limitations of financial aid for athletes, including schedule for number of student athletes who can be on financial aid; and recruitment of athletes when financial aid is a factor. Notable among the recruitment regulations is the following:

> Active recruitment of prospective student-athletes may not include a member of the university or its delegate being paid or given release time for the purpose of athletic recruitment. Illegal recruitment practices include sending students to recruit athletes, or contacting high school coaches, players or other personnel to solicit names of prospective student-athletes.[25]

The attempt which NAGWS has made to keep the focus of financial aid in perspective should be noted. It should also be understood that NAGWS does not recommend the awarding of financial aid, but that such is now permitted by this organization.

Decisions being made now by individual institutions concerning procedures for granting financial aid and recruitment will greatly influence the future growth and direction of the women's intercollegiate sports program. It is to be hoped that decisions will be consistent with the purpose of fostering "development of sports programs for the enrichment of the life of the participant,"[26] and [fostering] broad programs of women's intercollegiate athletics which are consistent with the educational aims and objectives of the member schools, and in accordance with the philosophy and standards of the NAGWS."[27]

• PARTICIPATION ON MEN'S TEAMS. The equal rights for women movement has also been influential in changing traditional patterns of team membership. With increased pressure from highly skilled young women desiring to compete on men's teams, and with some legal decisions being made in their favor, men's athletic organizations in many instances are now rewriting their eligibility regulations to avoid dis-

24. Ibid., pp. 34 – 35.
25. Ibid., p. 41.
26. DGWS, *Philosophy,* p. 5.
27. NAGWS, *AIAW Handbook,* p. 8.

crimination. High school and college women are breaking the barrier and earning the right to compete on men's teams.

Although allowing women to compete on men's teams may temporarily solve the legal requirements of providing equal opportunities for women, a more careful analysis suggests an alternative solution of providing separate but equal sports programs for men and women.

Women do not have the physical capacity in strength and endurance that men at the same skill level have. An examination of sports records shows that women's records reach only to within 60 to 90 percent of those of men. Therefore, the best male performer in the world will consistently be better than the best female performer in the same sport, if that sport puts a premium on strength and endurance. It is only the exceptional female athlete who is able to compete successfully against highly skilled males. Therefore should not separate but equal programs be provided to ensure that all highly skilled girls and women have opportunities for competitive sports experiences equal to those offered for men?

An analysis of the structure of competitive sports in our culture supports the principle of offering separate competitive sports programs for males and females. Olympic competition provides equal opportunities for both men and women to compete, but primarily against their own sex. At most levels of professional and amateur competition in both team and individual sports, women compete against women and men against men, except for those sports, such as tennis, wherein mixed doubles competition is held in addition to separate men's and women's competition. It is significant that no sport group sponsors athletic events in which men compete against women, except in sports specifically organized on a coeducational basis.

A concern expressed by many women physical educators is that some administrators may feel justified in financially supporting just one "school team" if the team is open to both men and women. This could result in reducing the women's program to only those sports not included in the men's program. Although there is no indication that such an action may be taken, the pressure on administrators to meet the demands imposed on school budgets might force them to examine this action among the numerous possibilities for reducing present budget allocations.

Still another implication of recent legislation allowing women to compete on men's teams involves the possibility that men, not able to make the men's team, will demand the right to try out for the women's team. If women are allowed to compete on men's teams, then justice to all would mandate that men could compete on women's teams. Because of the differences in strength and endurance of men and women, men could squeeze out women for positions that women would ordinarily have qualified for on women's teams. Such a situation would make a farce of the competitive sports programs for both sexes.

Those who support the position that women should be allowed to compete on men's teams point out that highly skilled women should not be denied the benefits of being able to compete against those with comparable skill. Since women's competitive sports programs are of fairly recent origin and therefore do not carry the prestige and status of men's programs, it is understandable that some very highly skilled women desire to participate on men's teams. In institutions where no women's program is offered, the only way to compete is through making the men's teams.

NAGWS has taken the position of encouraging the development of women's teams but not preventing women from competing on men's teams where a comparable program does not exist for women:

> teams for girls and women should be provided for all girls and women who desire competitive athletic experiences. While positive experiences for the exceptional girl or woman competitor may occur through participation in boys' or men's competitive groups, these instances are rare and should be judged acceptable only as an interim procedure for use until women's programs can be initiated.[28]

At colleges having teams for both men and women, women competing on men's teams have been declared not eligible to compete in AIAW national championships. This rule forces the student to make a choice, and prevents her from competing on both teams. As the opportunities for women's competition increases, and as women become better coaches, it is to be hoped that women students will choose to participate with the women's teams.

The above discussion on regulations for men's and women's teams does not apply to those sports in which an institution may have coeducational teams. Because the men's intercollegiate program usually does not offer competitive opportunities for men in such activities as archery, fencing, and badminton, the women's intercollegiate sports program frequently sponsors coeducational teams in these sports. Competition is so organized that women compete against women and men against men, with mixed doubles being included for dual sports. Where the coeducational program is under the jurisdiction of women's intercollegiate sports, eligibility standards for men are the same as those established for women. Governing groups which offer com-

28. Ibid., p. 33.

petition for coeducational teams should establish standards for the conduct of these events. At the present time, AIAW does not offer national championships for coeducational teams, but the CIAW did sanction the 1972 United States Intercollegiate Archery Tournament, an event for men and women.

• LIMITATIONS OF PARTICIPATION. *Guidelines for Intercollegiate Athletic Programs for Women* recommends that

> intercollegiate participation should not interfere with primary educational objectives. (a) A girl should participate on only one competitive team during a season. (b) Participation on more than one team includes participation on an additional team within an institution or participation on an additional team outside an institution. In unusual circumstances such participation may be permitted provided it contributes to the welfare of the participant and does not place excessive demands and pressures upon her.[29]

Such an eligibility statement is frequently found in boys' and men's athletics, but has not been universally adopted by women's athletic groups. The intent is to protect the student from neglect of educational responsibilities. Exploitation of student athletes by outside organizations is prevented by institutions with such a ruling. While some women's athletic programs have adopted such a ruling, as is true also for some governing groups, others have avoided including it for several reasons. Some feel that a problem does not exist at the present time, and that the enactment of such a regulation could create difficulty in interpretation and in the checking on the outside participation of their student athletes. Others express the point of view that a woman college student is mature enough to judge for herself whether or not she has the time and energy to keep up with her academic work, participate on a college team, and also play on an outside team. As more opportunities for intercollegiate competition at local, regional, and national levels are provided for highly skilled girls, it could be anticipated that their needs will be met through the college program, since the practice and play schedule will be expanded. Women will be forced to choose between participation on a college or outside team. The most recent eligibility criteria adopted by AIAW do not mention the subject of participation on more than one team, whether one or both are within or outside the institution.

Interscholastic Athletics

Eligibility requirements for high school students are determined by respective state high school athletic or activities associations and

29. DGWS, *Philosophy,* p. 49.

therefore differ. High school administrators and coaches should become familiar with all regulations concerning the organization and administration of interscholastic sports in their states. Handbooks containing this information are available through the state high school activities or athletic association.

The National Federation of State High School Associations has included the following statement on eligibility of players in its By-Laws:

> To represent a school in any interstate athletic contest, a pupil must be eligible under the following rules:
>
> Section 1.   His school shall be a member of the state athletic association of his home state and he must comply with all eligibility rules of such association.
>
>   If his school is not eligible to membership in his home state association, it must be an affiliated member if the state has provision for such affiliation.
>
> Section 2.   He shall be an amateur in accordance with the amateur rule as formulated by his home state athletic association.[30]

In addition, the NFSHSA has established minimum eligibility requirements which are recommended to but not required of state high school athletic associations. These are included below as examples of eligibility requirements which are followed by many of the state associations.

1.   19-Year Rule: Students become ineligible when they reach their nineteenth birthday.

2.   8-Semester Rule: In a four-year high school, students may participate for eight consecutive semesters, or in a three-year senior high, for six consecutive semesters. Attendance of 15 days of any semester shall count as a semester of participation.

3.   Semester Scholarship Rule: Students are required to do passing work in at least fifteen periods (three full credit subjects) per week. Failure to earn passing semester marks in three full credit subjects shall render a student ineligible for the following full semester. The record at the end of the semester shall be final and scholastic deficiencies may not be removed for the purpose of meeting minimum eligibility requirements.

4.   Amateur Rule: Students become ineligible for participation in all sports if they violate the following Amateur Rule in any sport:
     (a) Participating under an assumed name.
     (b) Competing on a team on which one of the players was paid.

30. NFSHSA, *Official Handbook 1974–75*, pp. 14 – 15.

(c) Entering into a playing contract with a professional club or agent.

(d) Using athletic skill for financial gain.

(e) Accepting a fee for officiating or for working as an instructor in other than a recognized recreation program. (Working as a registered official is a violation.)

5. Awards Rule:

(a) Accepting cash or any merchandise award. All awards shall be symbolic in nature with no intrinsic value.

(b) Accepting a symbolic award, from any source, in excess of the amount established by the state association.

(c) Accepting a trip to a University contest which is not within the standards contained in the Recruiting Code of Good Conduct.

(d) Accepting expenses for attending a summer athletic camp from any person (other than parents or legal guardian) or organization.

A state association may adopt provisions for reinstating a student who has violated the Amateur and Award Rules provided there is at least one year of ineligibility from the date of the violation.

6. Non-School Participation Rules: Participation on a non-school team in a sport during the same season athletes are representing their school in that sport shall cause them to become ineligible. Each state association shall establish seasons of competition during the school year for out of season participation.

7. Transfer Rule: An athlete who transfers enrollment corresponding with a change of residence of parents or legal guardian shall be considered eligible as soon as properly certified. Students transferring schools without a corresponding change of residence of the parents or legal guardian from a district where they have been in attendance to the new district, or if there has been no change of residence, shall attend one calendar year from the date of enrollment at the school to which they transferred in order to establish eligibility.

8. Recruiting Rule: Transfer from one school to another for athletic purposes because of undue influence by anyone connected with the school shall cause a student to forfeit remaining high school eligibility.

9. Enrollment Rule: In order to establish eligibility, a student must enroll not later than the beginning of the eleventh school day of any semester.

10. Grade Rule: To be eligible, a student must be in 9th grade or above and not graduated from high school.

11. Physician's Certificate Rule: A student must present, during the year and, prior to competition, a physician's certificate of physical fitness for athletic participation.

12. Specialized Camp Rule: A student shall become ineligible in a sport for one calendar year from the date of last offense if participating in a specialized camp, school clinic or other similar program involving coaching and instruction in that sport unless the program and participation meet the following requirements;

    (a) It has been presented to and approved by the Board of Control of the state high school association.

    (b) The camp program does not include any type of competition other than customary practice situations.

    (c) The fee (tuition) is provided by the student or student's parents.

    (d) No school uniform or equipment shall be used.

    (e) Participation in a specialized athletic camp, school clinic or similar program in any one sport shall not be longer than 2 weeks in any calendar year.[31]

Guidelines for Interscholastic Athletic Programs for High School Girls parallel the above eligibility recommendations as follows:

1. Participants must be bona fide students of the high school which they represent. They shall not have attended high school for more than eight semesters after entering the ninth grade. They must be successfully carrying full academic loads. Students under temporary suspension or probation for disciplinary reasons should not be allowed to participate.

2. Participants must have amateur standing in the interscholastic sports in which they participate.

3. Written permission of the parent or guardian is required for all participants.

4. A physician's certification of a girl's fitness for participation shall be filed with the administration prior to the first practice in a sport. The examination must have been made within the time period specified by local regulations. Written permission by a physcian should be required for participation after a serious illness, injury, or surgery.

5. Participants should carry some type of accident insurance coverage that protects them during athletic competition.[32]

HEALTH AND SAFETY

Medical Examination

Both high schools and colleges should include in their policies a statement requiring a medical examination for participants prior to their engaging in the interscholastic or intercollegiate sports program. " . . .

31. Ibid., pp. 34 – 35.
32. DGWS, *Philosophy*, p. 44.

Where health examinations are done by the family physican," DGWS recommends, "a covering letter explaining the program of activities and an examination which would include the information needed are suggested."[33] In case of illness or injury, it is deemed advisable to secure written permission from the physican before the student is allowed to return to active participation.

Emergency Care

Policies should be established by each institution with respect to care of students injured (1) during practice sessions, (2) during contests held at the home institution, and (3) during contests held away from the home institution. Ideally all coaches should have a fundamental knowledge of first aid procedures and should have a first aid kit available for use at all practices and contests. High school and college policies should be followed with respect to securing emergency medical care and the filing of appropriate accident reports. Since practice sessions and contests are frequently held after school hours (late afternoons and evenings) it is especially important that policies be established with the high school nurse or college health service concerning emergency care of students injured when health personnel may not be available. DGWS recommends that "First aid services and emergency medical care should be available during all scheduled intercollegiate athletic events,"[34] and for high schools, that "A doctor should be on call for all contests, and someone who is qualified in first-aid procedure should be in attendance."[35]

Insurance

It is essential that high school and college students be covered by some type of accident insurance during practice and athletic competition. Some states have even established legal provisions which require participants on interscholastic and intercollegiate teams to have accidental death insurance and insurance for accidental bodily injuries. For example, state law in California requires that the governing bodies of the State Colleges and the State Universities

> shall provide accidental death insurance in an amount of at least five thousand dollars ($5,000) for each member of an athletic team and shall in addition provide insurance protection for medical and hospital expenses resulting from accidental bodily injuries in an amount of at least five thousand dollars ($5,000) for all such

33. Ibid., p. 50.
34. Ibid., p. 48.
35. Ibid., p. 44

services for each member of an athletic team . . . for the death or injury to members of athletic teams arising while such members are engaged in or are preparing for an athletic event promoted under the sponsorship or arrangements of the educational institution or a student body organization thereof or while such members are being transported by or under the sponsorship or arrangements of the educational institution or a student body organization thereof to or from school or other place of instruction and the place of the athletic event.[36]

Governing boards of school districts in California are likewise responsible for providing accidental death insurance in an amount of at least $1,500 for each member and at least $1,500 insurance protection for medical and hospital expenses resulting from accidental bodily injuries under the same conditions listed above. Further, "The governing boards of the various school districts shall require that each member of an athletic team have insurance protection . . . to be paid either out of the funds of the district, the funds of the student body, or by any other persons on behalf of, the individual team members of students covered by such insurance."[37]

Some state high school associations sponsor and administer a comprehensive athletic protection plan, whereas other state associations work out a protection plan in conjunction with insurance companies which are then administered by such companies.

Since state laws regarding insurance vary, it is up to the individual in charge of interscholastic or intercollegiate sports at each institution to investigate the type of insurance coverage needed and the procedures which should be followed to secure and utilize it.

FINANCING

The development and maintenance of an interscholastic or intercollegiate sports program depends upon the availability of financial support. No institution should initiate such programs until funds have been allocated for them in the total school budget.

At the college level, DGWS guidelines state that

The budget for women's intercollegiate athletics should be part of the budget of the institution so that the program is assured. A separate budget item should be specifically designated for this program. (This does not preclude the use of state monies, student fees, gate receipts, and other sources of income, but the program should not depend solely on fluctuating sources of income.) The budget

36. Snyder and Handy, HPER and California Law, pp. 79 – 80.
37. Ibid., p. 80.

should be administered by the appropriate personnel in women's physical education.[38]

Further discussion of financing and budgeting will be found in chapter 5.

TRANSPORTATION

Policies regarding transportation vary among school districts and among institutions of higher education. For this reason, associated student body officials should be consulted regarding policies in effect for extracurricular and/or athletic team transportation. With such regulations being considered as a minimum, the women's physical education department needs then to determine if and what additional policies should be established in order to insure the safest conditions possible for the transportation of their students to athletic events.

Following are some questions which might serve as a guide to a school in the process of establishing policies regarding transportation.

1. Does the school district or institution have busses, station wagons, or cars available for transportation of students? Is there a charge for use of such vehicles? What requirements are established for drivers of school cars (passing of a test in addition to driver's license, minimum age, department of motor vehicles record of accidents and moving violations, etc.)?

2. If the institution does not provide use of vehicles for transportation, does the budget allow for rental of busses, station wagons, and cars? What insurance coverage does the rental agency provide? What requirements should be established for drivers of rental cars?

3. If the budget does not allow for the expense of renting vehicles, and individual cars must be utilized as a last resort, what regulations should be considered minimal concerning the car and the driver? Should the car be inspected, and by whom, to determine that it is in safe condition? What type of insurance coverage should be minimal? Should drivers be limited to faculty members, or can students with driver's licenses qualify? What about using parents and/or interested parties (friends, husbands, boy friends, alumnae, etc.) as drivers? What requirements should the driver have to meet — ownership of a driver's license, age limitation, satisfactory accidents and moving violations record, written and/or practical driving test? By whom should tests be given? If owner of car is not the driver, should approval of the owner for use of car for transportation to athletic events be secured? Can interested students not on the same team travel with the team?

38. DGWS, *Philosophy*, p. 47.

4. In cases where individual cars are utilized, what regulations need to be established with respect to traveling together as a team? Does the faculty member have to travel with the team? Do all cars have to leave and return to the institution together? Can students living near the location of the scheduled event provide their own transportation to and from the event? If an independent travel is authorized, should students be reimbursed for their mileage expenses? Who determines which students are to ride in which cars?

5. If teams are traveling to events taking place a great distance from the institution, what provisions should be established relative to airline travel? Must regularly-scheduled airline flights be used, or can an institution make arrangements for chartered flights? Should teams be allowed to take night flights, which are sometimes cheaper, or travel on standby which is least expensive (though very uncertain)? What arrangements should be made to transport students to the airport, to their destination upon arrival, and return? Do students have to travel on the same flight?

6. If overnight accommodations are necessary, what are desirable arrangements for housing? Should the advisor have a separate room? How many students per room?

In all of the above considerations, attention should be focused on: (1) meeting any and all legal requirements necessary for maintaining adequate insurance coverage; (2) meeting all regulations imposed by the state code, the school district, and/or governing bodies of institutions of higher education, and of each individual institution; and (3) establishing additional requirements necessary to insure the health and welfare of the participants. Institutions not having adequate financial support to meet what they deem to be desirable standards for the health and welfare of their participants should limit participation to only those events for which financial support is adequate. In no case should the health and welfare of the students be jeopardized in order to allow the students the opportunity to participate in athletic events.

SEASONS

The establishment of sport seasons (fall, winter, spring) should be primarily the responsibility of the immediate local or regional governing group to which an institution belongs. Such decisions will be based upon the operational schedules of the institutions involved (beginning and end of semester or quarter, final exam period, holidays,) weather, availability of facilities for practice and competition, and the number of other sports activities to be scheduled during the same time period. Local and regional governing groups on the college level may also wish to consider the schedule of regional and national championships.

For colleges it is recommended that:

a. The length of the season and the number of games should be established and agreed upon by the participating schools.

b. The length of the season will vary according to the locale and sport and should not be so long that the educational values for the student in terms of the total program are jeopardized (approximately 12–14 weeks). This season should include conditioning and instruction.

c. The season may be lengthened to include opportunities for participation in state, regional or national tournaments or meets for which individuals or teams qualify.[39]

A similar length of season and period of conditioning is recommended for secondary schools, with the additional proviso that ". . . An extended season should be limited to a postseason tournament which should not exceed the area or state level."[40]

The end of a sport season ordinarily comes at the conclusion of league play and/or at the time of the culminating tournament. Governing groups need to establish the time period within which interschool competition in each sport is to be scheduled. Governing groups may also wish to determine the date when initial practice begins, or they may decide to leave this decision up to each member school.

SCHEDULING

Primary to the establishment of policies regarding scheduling should be concern for the welfare of the student participant. As stated by DGWS, "We believe that the *scheduling* of sports activities for girls and women should be in accordance with their needs and that their schedule should not be required to conform to a league schedule established for boy's and men's sports."[41]

At the high school level, provisions to protect the girl from missing classes should be established by the development of policies concerning the distance within which contests should be scheduled and the timing of such contests. "Competition should be limited to a geographical area which will permit players to return at reasonable hours. Safe transportation should be assured."[42] Insofar as possible the timing

39. Ibid., p. 50.
40. Ibid., p. 45.
41. Ibid., p. 31.
42. Ibid., p. 45.

of events should be such as to avoid or minimize absence from regular school classes.

At the college level, "The athletic schedule should not jeopardize the student's class and study time."[43] Individual institutions should establish minimum and maximum lengths of practice periods per week, maximum number of contests per week, and maximum amount of time to be devoted to a combination of practices and games per week. Both the time needed by the full-time students for study and the practice time necessary to prepare students for the calibre of competition involved should be considered. Every attempt should be made to schedule contests in such a way that students will not have to miss classes in order to participate, and that they can return from events at a reasonable hour.

The level of competition should be commensurate with the skill and experience of the players. "Contests should be scheduled among schools having players of comparable ability in order to equate competition. In order to make this possible, scheduling in each sport need not be with the same institutions each season."[44] Governing groups may wish to develop criteria for leagues based upon expectation of team performance as decided by the individual institution and/or the governing group. Teams might be classified as "A," "B," "C," and competition could be scheduled in keeping with this classification. Such procedures do much to avoid the undesirable outcomes resulting from a very highly skilled team playing against a team with much less experience.

References

AAHPER. "Policies on Women Athletes Change." *Update,* May 1973.

NAGWS. *AIAW Handbook.* Washington, D.C.: AAHPER. 1974–75.

Division for Girls and Women's Sports. *Philosophy and Standards for Girls and Women's Sports.* Washington, D.C.: AAHPER. 1973.

National Federation of State High School Associations. *Official Handbook 1974–75.* Elgin, Ill.: NFSHSA.

Snyder, Raymond A., and Handy, Donald T. *HPER and the California Law.* Palo Alto, Calif.: National Press Books.

43. Ibid., p. 50.
44. Ibid., p. 48.

TOUCHÉ
Photograph by Dr. Richard Lussier
California State University, Long Beach

CHAPTER 3

Coaching Personnel

When planning a competitive sports program there are numerous problems that must be dealt with, not the least of which are those relating to personnel. The preparation, in-service education, orientation, and evaluation of coaching personnel are discussed in the following pages. The problems of the lack of specific preparation of women coaches is explored, with some suggestions for "self improvement," and the question of remuneration for coaches is presented.

PREPARATION OF COACHING PERSONNEL

Perhaps one of the most critical problems encountered in this area is that of providing *adequately prepared* personnel to coach the various teams. Many women physical educators fear becoming involved because they do not feel adequately prepared. This fear, or lack of confidence, is not entirely without cause. Competitive sports programs in many parts of the country are a fairly recent innovation at both the secondary and collegiate levels. Most of those involved in the conduct of such programs are graduates of professional preparation programs in physical education and until recently little was included to prepare persons for coaching. The focus of these programs has been and still is on the preparation of teachers. What coaching preparation students have received has been cursory at best and in most instances the coaching skills that a physical education major has are "caught" rather than "taught." Most women's physical education departments in colleges and universities are now beginning to realize that they have a responsibility not only in the area of teacher preparation but in the area of coaching preparation as well. If high level competitive sports programs for girls and women are to be developed along sound lines personnel must be adequately prepared to conduct them. Certificate programs and specializations in coaching are beginning to make their appearance as elective options in conjunction with the regular teacher preparation programs; as yet, however, there are not too many graduates who have participated in them.

The term "adequate" can mean different things to different people. What is adequate preparation? Is one adequately prepared to coach a sport if she played on a high school team or must she have competed in college? Must she have been on a team that played in regional and national tournaments? Or would it suffice if she played on an intramural team in college? How well skilled must a person be in order to be adequately prepared to coach? Most coaches agree that the more playing experience an individual has in a given sport, at all levels, the more desirable it would be. However, they also agree that one does not necessarily have to be a champion in a sport in order to be adequately prepared to coach it. According to Dr. Reuben Frost, a coach should be well skilled in the sport which he coaches. He states:

> A coach who does not have considerable expertise in the sport which he is coaching will always be handicapped. Young people recognize very quickly a lack of knowledge about, and a lack of skill in, what is being taught. While there are exceptions, it is true that student athletes will listen more closely, observe more carefully, and accept advice more readily when they are fully aware that the coach has a depth of knowledge and experience in what he is teaching.[1]

It has often been said that a good coach must be a good teacher. Good teaching includes mastery of the subject matter. By the same token, good coaching must include mastery of the sport to be coached. Good coaches, in the highest sense of this term, are almost invariably very good teachers.

Are knowledge and experience the sole criteria of adequate preparation? If they were, the problem of selection of coaching personnel would be considerably simplified. Another criterion, and perhaps the most important one, concerns itself with the kind of person the prospective coach is and the quality of her influence on young girls and women. The controversy over whether or not participation in competitive sports can instill a set of standards or values in the participant or help her develop desirable personality and character traits, will continue indefinitely. However, in the event that these results are attainable, and many people believe they are, there is no question as to the importance of the leadership in helping to

---

1. American Association for Health, Physical Education and Recreation, *Secondary School Athletic Administration: A New Look* (Washington, D.C.: AAHPER, 1969), p. 28.

bring them about. Quoting Dr. Frost again, "all attest to the importance of the right kind of leadership, the personality and actions of the coach, as being the critical factors."[2]

In evaluating the leadership qualities of the prospective coach the one in charge of selecting coaching personnel will have to answer the following questions: What kind of influence will this person have on the participants? What is her philosophy of coaching? Is it consistent with that of the program in question? Will her main concern be to win the league championship or will it be to provide the most educationally sound experience possible for the participants? It may not be possible to find answers to all such questions until the coach has been seen in action over a period of time. However, regardless of the difficulties inherent in selection, every effort should be made to ensure that those individuals who are chosen to coach in girl's and women's competitive sports programs will provide the kind of leadership that will result in desirable social and moral influences on the participants.

In discussing the area of preparation one should not fail to mention the importance of in-depth knowledge of the general principles of coaching. The concern here is not for any particular sport but for all sports. There are certain principles that thread themselves through the entire spectrum of activities to be coached. Examples of such principles include those related to (1) ways of organizing for practice, (2) motivational techniques, (3) player selection, (4) player discipline, (5) standards of conduct, (6) coaching psychology, (7) analysis of problems, (8) team morale, (9) coach-player relationships, and (10) public relations.

In considering the criteria that have been suggested for adequate preparation of coaching personnel it becomes readily apparent that to fulfill such criteria to the letter would impose extreme hardship on many departments, especially those with limited personnel. It becomes particularly difficult if such departments attempt to compete in the total spectrum of sports common to programs in their respective geographical areas. The difficulty lies in the fact that schools and colleges within close proximity to each other may vary tremendously in size and means. Within a thirty-mile radius there may be five colleges ranging in enrollment from one thousand to twenty-five thousand students. One institution may have a physical education department faculty of twenty, while another may have only three or four. Yet it is entirely possible that both institutions

2. Ibid., p. 27.

may compete in the same league or conference. It might pose no problem at all for the larger school to provide adequately prepared personnel to staff a ten-sport competitive program within which no single individual would be required to coach more than one or two sports. However, in the institution having the smaller department, each faculty member would have to coach three or four sports, a next-to-impossible situation.

One can only come to the conclusion that the problem is complex, and that there are no easy solutions. There are many fine women coaches today who do fulfill the criteria that have been mentioned; some of them are "born" but most of them are "made." Many have developed themselves through a variety of techniques discussed in the next section. It is to be hoped that with the coaching "certificate program" the problem of adequately prepared women coaches will soon disappear.

REMUNERATION FOR COACHING

One of the questions currently under discussion at educational institutions is, "Should women coaches be paid, and if so how much?" Some individuals still hold to the conservative point of view that faculty should be so dedicated to their profession that to accept pay for coaching would border on the unethical; others believe that women coaches should be given pay equal to that received by men coaches.

Additional remuneration for such extra-curricular activities as GAA is not without precedent. Many school districts have subscribed to this practice for a number of years. Whether or not women coaches receive extra pay or some type of remuneration for their coaching duties depends upon a number of factors, not the least of which is the institutional budget for faculty salaries. Another factor of course is the attitude of the institution or school district toward the value and importance of the women's competitive sports program.

The climate relative to this issue is today much more favorable than it was a few years ago. The nondiscriminatory legislation is making an impact and will continue to have an even greater influence as time goes on.

It seems only fair to accept the point of view that women coaches, as well as men, should receive some form of extra remuneration for work done over and above their prescribed duties. Remuneration should bear relationship to the amount of time and preparation spent in the activity, and in the case of college staffing formulas, it should be consistent with remuneration provided for other similar activities.

There are three commonly accepted methods of providing remuneration for coaching: namely, extra pay, released time, and teaching units.

Extra pay seems to be the most commonly accepted remuneration for coaching at the secondary level. The amount of money received depends upon school district policy. Occasionally released time is given along with, or as a substitute for, extra pay. This simply means that a coach is given additional periods without instructional assignments. Instead of teaching five periods a day she may teach only four. Most coaches, however, prefer extra pay to the released time, mainly because the released time is usually spent in planning for coaching activities anyway. Women coaches, for the most part, do not receive the same amount of extra pay that men coaches do. The rationale for this is that men spend a good deal more time in their coaching duties (resulting to a considerable extent from their recruiting activities) than do women.

At the college level the most common type of remuneration for women and for many men is based on the staffing formula. In other words a coaching assignment is assessed to be the equivalent of so many units or credits of equated time based on the activity. The activity might be assessed at three units of teaching time, for example. This then would equal three units of the faculty member's total teaching load. If she should coach a sport each semester, she would receive six units per academic year on her total teaching load. The number of units a coaching assignment receives will vary from one institution to another but will usually be based upon a formula of some type. It should be mentioned that the coaching activity is considered to be the conduct of an advanced class under this procedure, and students in this system will therefore receive academic credit for participating in the activity.

To further clarify: where the system is based on units or credits, equated teaching load is often expressed in terms of percentage of teaching load. For example, if the staffing formula called for a twelve-unit teaching load and the equated coaching assignment was three units, the coaching load would be 25 percent of the total teaching assignment.

Because staffing formulas and teaching loads differ greatly from institution to institution and are expressed varyingly in units, credits, or even number of classes assigned, it is desirable to express assignments in terms of percentages. In men's athletics, depending upon the type of assignment, a coach's load may vary from full time (head coach of the major sport, football), to a possible 25 percent of the total teaching load (coach of a so-called "minor sport" such as tennis). In general, women's programs have not arrived at the point where "head coach" receives a full-time teaching load. The coaching assignment might vary from 25 to 50 percent of the total teaching load. It would probably be not over 50 percent in most instances, but might conceivably be less than 25 percent.

To establish or recommend what percentage of the total teaching load coaching should be would hardly be desirable since it would be only a matter of opinion or personal judgment. Such a decision would have to be made at each institution based on the type of staffing formula in use at that institution. Certainly the percentage of the load should be commensurate with the duties performed and time spent. An inherent problem in combining coaching and teaching in one load is that often the coaching is so demanding that the teaching aspect might suffer, especially in the area of preparation time. Another problem can be the missing of classes due to game trips. These are problems that must be anticipated and dealt with by those who are responsible for both the coaching and teaching programs. In view of such problems certainly no one should carry more than one coaching assignment at a time, and every effort should be made to schedule the coach's teaching load in such a way as to provide for preparation time, and to minimize possibilities of missing classes. If the coach's schedule can be arranged so that her teaching classes come in the morning, the possibilities for missing classes will be largely eliminated. Also concern should be given to the avoidance of the kind of schedule that spreads the coach from early morning to late at night, giving her no time for other activities or adequate rest and relaxation.

The importance of public relations cannot be overemphasized if women coaches are to expect remuneration for their coaching responsibilities. The wholehearted support of the student body, other faculty, administration and community will be needed if this issue is to be resolved to the satisfaction of all concerned.

IN-SERVICE PREPARATION

For the individual who feels that she needs to upgrade her coaching skill or to become highly specialized there are a number of avenues available. There are numerous coaching workshops presented every summer and university extension courses are offered during the academic year which are staffed by experts in the various activities. Because these workshops are usually of short duration (one to two weeks) the emphasis is usually on coaching methods and techniques rather than on personal skill improvement. These workshops provide an excellent opportunity for participants to learn more about how to coach, to learn new styles of play, and to get a better understanding of rules changes and their interpretation.

In addition to summer workshops there are short clinics and mini-workshops held during the year for the purpose of upgrading coaching. These often concentrate on one aspect of an activity such as offensive or defensive techniques, or new rule changes and interpretations.

One other excellent opportunity open to the woman coach who wants to improve her coaching skill is as close as her male colleagues in the men's physical education department. Simply by observing the basketball, tennis, or swimming coach, for example, one can learn a considerable amount about how to coach such an activity. These men are usually experts and are generally more than happy to be of assistance to a female colleague whether or not she really needs help or is only trying to add some polish to her coaching technique.

Until and unless teacher preparation departments begin to place more emphasis in their curriculum on preparation for coaching, those who must assume responsibility for coaching assignments must continue to rely upon the knowledge and experience which they have gained by participating in the sports to be coached, and upon participation in the in-service activities suggested in the previous paragraphs. One should not necessarily wait until she becomes an "expert" before she is willing to accept a coaching assignment. Were this attitude to prevail one of two things might happen. Either many girls and women would not have the opportunity of participating in competitive sports experiences at all, or women physical educators might lose their "Golden Opportunity" for controlling and conducting their own programs.

ORIENTATION OF PERSONNEL

One might legitimately ask, "Why must coaching personnel be oriented?" It could well be assumed that if a person were given a coaching assignment, and were qualified to fulfil it, she ought to be able to do it without going through some type of orientation process. The best answer is that there is more to coaching than producing winning teams.

Every department that provides a competitive sports program has, or should have, a philosophy which sets guidelines for the conduct of that program. These guidelines should be consonant with the well-considered aim and objectives of the program, the established standards for both coaches and participants, and the policies and procedures which are unique to the program in that department; in keeping too with the policies and procedures of organizations which will govern play, such as school districts, leagues, conferences, and federations.

Regardless of the expertise of the coach it is vital to the conduct of the program that she participate in a carefully planned and well-organized orientation program designed specifically for the institution in which she will coach. The orientation should be designed not to limit or inhibit the coaches' actions in carrying out their duties, but rather to familiarize them with philosophy, policies, and procedures under which they will be operating. Obviously it should be extremely informative and should aim at minimizing the occurrence of unforeseen problems. It should provide the individual coach with a frame of reference from which to operate, and should enhance her effectiveness in the conduct of the program.

The orientation itself may be in the form of an initial meeting for new coaches with perhaps several follow-up meetings which would include all coaching faculty. The meetings should be conducted by the director of the program if there is one. If not, either the department chairperson or an experienced member of the coaching faculty might conduct them. In any event the department chairperson should be present as the administrator who is ultimately responsible for all departmental programs.

An important adjunct to any such orientation program and a necessity for an effective competitive sports program is a written handbook or policy manual which incorporates an explanation of the departmental philosophy of competition supplemented by all the pertinent policies and procedures under which the specific program operates. Channels of authority should be clearly stated and although there should be a degree of flexibility, they should be so stated as to allow little room for misinterpretation. Pertinent items to include in such a handbook are: basic beliefs, leadership (including duties of the program director, coaches, student leaders), administration (including financing, budget, scheduling, health policies, housing facilities, travel insurance), eligibility, recruitment and scholarship policies, standards (including dress and general deportment of both participants and coaches), scheduling and care of facilities and equipment, maintenance policies and procedures and special policies relating to the school, the district, the league and/or conference. (See Appendix—Example B for policy manual.)

It might also be desirable to provide the participants with a student handbook which would contain information about the scope of the program and some of the areas listed above which would have pertinence for them, such as philosophy, standards, health policies, use of facilities and equipment, eligibility, duties of student leaders, and similar items. (See Appendix—Example C—Student Coordinators Manual.)

Such handbooks are not only important for orientation purposes but also for the use of those who are continuing members of the program. They are also an excellent public relations medium that should be in the hands of appropriate members of the school or college administration.

In summary, orientation is a necessary and ongoing procedure for both new and continuing personnel which can contribute to the effectiveness of a competitive sports program by providing pertinent information to both coaches and participants, which should, in turn, minimize unforeseen problems, undesirable behavior, and poor public relations.

EVALUATION OF PERSONNEL

One of the most difficult and often touchy duties that an administrator has to perform is that of evaluating personnel. The evaluation problem often has it roots in the administrative function of original selection of personnel. Although careful and refined selection techniques cannot guarantee success in performance, wise original selection can often preclude difficult situations from presenting themselves. Meticulous screening for procurement of qualified coaching personnel plus well-planned and carefully conducted orientation procedures can certainly minimize the sometimes unpleasant aspects of evaluation.

One might conceivably ask, "Why evaluate?" If the coach produces winning teams isn't that all the evaluation that one needs? The question is valid, if producing winning teams is the major goal of the competitive sports program. It may seem naive to believe that there are still other important objectives besides winning but fortunately most coaches and participants will agree that winning is but one of the many desirable outcomes of sports competition.

It is not only desirable but necessary to periodically evaluate coaching personnel. Such evaluations are not limited to the problem of retention but are also for the purpose of helping coaching personnel to know how well they are fulfilling their function, not only that of a coach but also that as representative of a program with certain standards and values, and as a person who is in a position to have considerable influence on the standards and behavior of young girls and women.

In order to evaluate the performance of any individual for whatever purpose, standards of performance must first be developed. These standards or criteria must already be in effect, understood and subscribed to by the individual when she accepts the assignment to coach. It is highly desirable that these criteria have been set by the department faculty as a whole. They should be an integral part of the total philosophy of the competitive sports program and should be realistically designed as behavioral concepts which are specific in nature. There are any number of evaluative criteria which could be developed. Each tool must be designed in terms of the individual program with all the uniqueness that is implied. However, items common to most coaching situations are: (1) knowledge of and skill in the sport, (2) organizational ability, (3) rapport with participants, (4) ethical behavior, (5) adherence to department philosophy, policies and procedures, (6) adherence to policies and procedures of governing agencies at the local, regional, state and national levels, (7) leadership, (8) standards of student conduct, (9) relationship with other coaches, (10) management of the sport budget. These are examples of broad general categories which could be broken down into numerous sub-items comprising a very comprehensive evaluation device.

It cannot be too strongly emphasized that the coaching personnel should thoroughly understand the criteria by which they will be evaluated before they begin their coaching assignments. This should be part of the orientation process and such criteria should be included in the policy manual for the conduct of the competitive sports program.

Designing the evaluation tool is by no means the most difficult part of evaluating coaching performance. The difficult part comes in the actual process. The first concern is who should evaluate and the second is how to ensure that the evaluation procedures used are valid and reliable; that is to say, as valid and reliable as a fallible human being can make them. It seems desirable for those who have the ultimate responsibility for the program to do the evaluating. In most instances these persons are the department chairperson and the director of the competitive sports program (if these are not one and the same individuals). Who these responsible persons are vary depending upon the policies of the district or institution.

Obviously those who do the evaluating should be knowledgeable regarding the goals of the program and the evaluation criteria. They should also be somewhat knowledgeable about the sport being coached. Perhaps most important of all, these individuals should be particularly perceptive as to the changes in human behavior that are taking place in the young people as a result of their unique relationship with the coaching leadership. Such behavioral changes are sometimes so subtle that it is most difficult, if not impossible, to discern them in cursory evaluation sessions.

Students' evaluations should not be overlooked as an important source of feedback inasmuch as students are the direct recipients of the coaching impact. They are in a very good position to know if the coach is well organized, if she is knowledgeable in the sport, if she holds high standards, if she is providing them with rewarding experiences, if she communicates well, and if she motivates them to learn and to give their best.

The more evaluations there are the greater the chance of reliability. Time, then, becomes an important factor because most department chairpersons are far too busy to be able to observe individuals several times in their capacities as teachers and coaches. This is the point at which the entire evaluative process often breaks down. To base evaluative judgments on only one observation would be presumptuous, to say the least. Those who evaluate must rely on many sources of evidence. In all fairness to those being evaluated the techniques used must be as valid and reliable as the variables of the situation allow.

Implicit in the evaluation process is feedback to those being evaluated. Each individual being evaluated should know the result of the evaluation, preferably in a face-to-face conference with the evaluator(s). Both strengths and weaknesses should be discussed with an in-depth exploration of areas of concern. Reinforcement should be given where appropriate and suggestions made where problem areas are found to exist. The environment of the conference should be productive rather than destructive, positive rather than negative. The one thought that should be paramount in the minds of all concerned should be the welfare of the students and the providing of a good competitive sports program.

ACTION IN SPACE
Photograph by Dr. Richard Lussier
California State University, Long Beach

CHAPTER 4

Administrative Organization

The type of administrative organization of competitive sports programs for girls and women differs according to the size of the department, number of sports offered, number of students involved, and administrative structure of the institution and department. And even though a program may have a beautifully designed administrative structure, the total success of the program itself rests with the people who function within the administrative framework. Each individual from the director to the student sport coordinator has an important function to perform. A breakdown at any point along the line may have an unfavorable effect unless it is compensated for by an increase of responsibility and work on the part of someone else. It is therefore extremely important for each individual to know her role or responsibility and understand completely her relationship to the success of the total program. A description follows detailing the type of responsibilities which could be delegated at each level of operation of the competitive sports program.

FACULTY

Since the organization and administration of the competitive sports program is usually under the jurisdiction of the women's physical education department, it follows that the faculty of that department should be involved in developing the philosophy and goals of the program, and should approve of the policies which are established for its conduct. As the department faculty make policy decisions on other curriculum offerings, so too should they approve the policies governing the growth and development of the competitive sports program at their institution.

WOMEN'S COMPETITIVE SPORTS COUNCIL

It is suggested that within the committee structure of the department, a Women's Competitive Sports Council be established, to consist of the department chairperson and all coaches, with the director serving as chairperson of the council. Such a Council can develop the procedures for the conduct of the program, explore problems arising from it, make recommendations for policy revision, and initiate new policies. The actions and recommendations of the Council could then be communicated through the director to the total department faculty for their information or approval, as may be appropriate.

Meetings of such a council can provide an opportunity for the director to keep the coaches informed of any changes in institutional procedures emanating from the health service, associated students, and records office, which directly relate to the conduct of the program. Such meetings can also be utilized by the director to communicate to the coaches current information from local, regional, and national governing groups, and to seek their coaches' advice concerning important issues to be voted on by these governing groups. The sharing of ideas among the coaches about their individual sports programs can also be a valuable outcome of such meetings.

Since the competitive sports program is designed to serve women students, it would seem entirely logical and proper to include students on the Council. With students actively seeking representation on faculty committees at the present time, the inclusion of a representative from each sport, such as a student sport coordinator would seem desirable for this reason also. Students serving on a Competitive Sports Council should have the opportunity to express their ideas concerning how the program might be improved. Student opinion can indeed serve to promote a better program for all involved. During this process the student would also benefit by gaining more insight into, and a broader perspective of, the purposes and values of the program, and at the same time develop a deeper understanding of the need for adhering to established policies and procedures.

FUNCTIONAL PROCEDURES

The Department Chairperson

What the role of the department chairperson will be in the organization and administration of a competitive sports program for girls and women depends upon her role in the total department organization. Considerable variation occurs in how schools and colleges function — even in how segments within given institutions operate. Because of such variability it would be neither possible nor desirable to suggest specifically how all departmental chairpersons should fit into the organization of the competitive sports program. However this does not preclude the mentioning of several functions of the department chairperson which might be common to a variety of organizational patterns. A number of these functions follow:

1. Selection and appointment of the director of the competitive sports program.
2. Selection and/or appointment of faculty personnel to serve as coaches.
3. Participation in the development of the philosophy, policies, and procedures of the program.
4. Scheduling of classes or time for competitive sports activities.
5. Scheduling of facilities for practice sessions and games.
6. Approval and allocation of department budget for the purchase of equipment needed specifically for the program.
7. Supervision of coaching faculty if there is no director of the program.
8. Evaluation of coaching faculty if there is no director of the program, or assisting her if there is one.
9. Submission of maintenance requests for service required specifically for the program.
10. Coordination with the men's athletic personnel on facility usage and other problems.
11. Coordination with maintenance in relationship to the servicing of the total program.
12. Attending meetings of groups that govern the conduct of the program at the institutional level and possibly outside the institution.
13. Helping to maintain effective public relations at all levels pertaining to the program.
14. Cooperation with and being supportive of the program director.
15. Facilitation of the effective conduct of the program in every way possible.
16. Being constantly aware of the direction the program is taking relative to the established goals and objectives.

The Director of Competitive Sports

The role of the competitive sports director or coordinator will vary according to the level and type of institution, number of sports offered, and the degree to which the institution participates in interschool competition. The position of the director varies from that of coordinating activities in a small high school with no administrative released time to that of a full-time administrative position in a large university.

The list of functions below is illustrative of the type of responsibilities being assumed by directors in departments with expanding competitive sports programs.

1. Orientation of coaches to the institution's competitive sports program; to include philosphy, purposes, policies, and procedures of the institutional program, and of the league or conference.

2. Communicating to students pertinent information regarding opportunities available for participation in the competitive sports program, including sports offered and qualifications for team membership.

3. Preparation of the annual budget request, based upon anticipated needs for each sport as submitted by the coach for that sport.

4. Justification of annual budget request before the treasurer and/or student body group(s) responsible for allocation of student-body funds.

5. Allocation of funds received from the student body (or whatever source may be involed) based upon policies developed and approved by the coaches.

6. Administration of expenditures from the budget based upon coaches' requests for funds within their budget allocation.

7. Preparation and submission of the annual equipment budget request to the department chairperson, based upon requests submitted by coaches.

8. Coordination with the health service in scheduling physical examinations for participants, notification of examination schedule to coaches, and subsequent verification of health clearance of students to coaches.

9. Maintaining liaison with the health service concerning policies and procedures in handling student injuries, approval of return to participation by students following injury or illness, and follow-up of students with special health problems.

10. Filing accident reports with the health service and other personnel concerned for the prompt initiation of appropriate insurance claims.

11. Determination with the records office of academic eligibility of participants.

12. Verification of student eligibility on official entry forms for league or conference competition, and for regional and national events.

13. Recommending to the department chairperson the schedule of sports to be offered and, if requested, the assignment of faculty to coaching positions.

14. Compilation of the master calendar of competitive events, based upon sport schedules submitted by coaches, and distribution of such to all personnel involved in or related to the competitive sports program.

15. Coordinating publicity in cooperation with sport coaches and student sport coordinators.

16. Conducting meetings of the Competitive Sports Council to clarify policies and procedures, to consider proposals for their revision, to discuss problems concerning the program, and to make recommendations for the improvement of the program.

17. Serving as a consultant to coaches in answering questions concerning interpretation of policies and procedures, preparation of budget and travel requests, scheduling, and handling of problems arising in their sports within the institution and/or with other institutions.

18. Serving in an advisory capacity in the organization and conduct of all intercollegiate tournaments and meets sponsored by coaches at her institution.

19. Supervising faculty assigned to coaching positions, if so delegated by the department chairperson, and assisting the department chairperson in the evaluation of faculty having coaching assignments when so requested.

20. Informing the department chairperson and faculty members concerning all aspects of the competitive sports program.

21. Representing the program within her institution, within the community, and at league or conference meetings; and serving as voting representative for regional and national governing groups if so delegated by the president of the institution and/or department chairperson.

22. Compiling annual report of the year's activities, based upon reports received from coaches.

Coaches and Their Responsibilities

In addition to the primary function of coaching her team, each coach has a number of responsibilities relating to the organization and conduct of her sport. Responsibilities frequently assigned to coaches are as follows:

1. Orientation of students to goal and purposes of program, to eligibility requirements for participation, and to participant responsibilities and desired conduct of team members.

2. Forwarding list of all students participating in sport to director for verification of academic eligibility and health clearance.

3. Informing students of date, time, and place of physical examination for clearance by the health service.

4. Submitting to the director proposed sport budget covering anticipated schedule of events for following year, and needed financial support.
5. Submitting written requests to the director for expenditures covered by allocated budget.
6. Scheduling all competitive events for her sport and submitting season's schedule to the director, keeping her informed of any changes which may occur.
7. Arranging for facilities and equipment as needed for events scheduled in her sport at her institution.
8. Securing officials as needed for events scheduled at her institution.
9. Organizing and supervising all practice sessions and competitive events held at the institution, and attending and supervising her team at all events in which the team participates at other institutions.
10. Providing immediate care for participants injured during team activity, and following established procedures for emergency treatment if such is deemed necessary.
11. Completing accident reports and filing with the director.
12. Organizing and conducting culminating meets and tournaments within the sport held at her institution.
13. Reporting outcomes of league or conference meets, matches, tournaments to the appropriate league or conference official.
14. Publicizing the events in which her team participates — to include announcement of such events and results of events, through appropriate news media.
15. Serving as the official representative of the institution at coaches' meetings for her sport held by the league or conference to which the institution belongs.
16. Filing an annual report at the conclusion of each season with the director.
17. Adherence to policies and procedures established by her institution, by the league or conference to which her institution belongs, and by the league or conference organization of coaches in her sport.

The Athletic Trainer

Athletic trainers have been an integral part of men's intercollegiate athletics for many years, but only recently have the competitive and skill levels of women's intercollegiate sports developed to the point where the services of an athletic trainer have become as necessary for the women's program as for the men's. Indeed, many institutions justify the need for an athletic trainer available to women on the premise that failure to provide women athletes with appropriate preventive and rehabilitative care for injuries incurred in intercollegiate sports could be construed as negligence on the part of the institution and discriminatory against women if the services of a trainer are available for men. Among the functions of an athletic trainer are the following:

1. Supervising the conditioning and equipping of all women athletes.
2. Carrying out instructions given by the team physican regarding routine procedures in the treatment of athletic injuries.
3. Supervising treatment and rehabilitation of all injured women athletes in collaboration with the team physician.
4. Screening all sports candidates for physical eligibility based on results of the annual physical examination administered by the team physician.
5. Maintaining all necessary medical records of all women athletes.
6. Filing reports of injuries for insurance purposes.
7. Requesting all necessary training supplies.
8. Determining physical readiness of athletes to return to competition based on consultation with the team physician.
9. Maintaining regular training room hours.

The Student Sport Coordinators

The opportunities for student leadership have long been claimed as one of the values of intramural and extramural programs. As institutions expand their programs of interscholastic and intercollegiate sports, opportunities for student leadership still continue to be available through the development of positions such as student sport coordinators or managers who serve as assistants to coaches. The growth of the competitive sports program has created many more duties and responsibilities for coaches. Capable students can greatly assist coaches in the performance of their responsibilities and can, at the same time, gain invaluable experience in the organization and conduct of a sport. Among the duties and responsibilities of the student sport coordinator the following are commonly noted:

1. Checking out equipment and setting up facilities for practices and games.
2. Completing forms necessary to request expenditures from budget allocation.
3. Serving as hostess to visiting teams.
4. Assisting the coach in publicizing the competitive events within her sport through appropriate news media.
5. Assisting the coach in compiling the list of players and in hav-

ing the players complete appropriate forms necessary for participation in the program.

6.   Keeping individual and team records of participation as deemed
appropriate for her sport.

7.   Serving as student representative on Competitive Sports
Council.

8.   Assisting the coach whenever and wherever possible.

It should be noted that in view of the rapidly developing competitive sports programs in colleges and universities, and recent federal
legislation which will enable these programs to have greater resources
and status, various trends in organizational patterns different from the
traditional design just discussed are emerging in some institutions.
Such patterns involve an expansion of the governance of the program
beyond the women's physical education department into institutional
athletic boards of control comprised not only of appropriate department personnel, but all-institutional personnel at the administrative,
faculty, and student levels. Such boards assume certain of the policy-
making functions and oversee that part of the program which relates
to the interests of the institution.

Due to the uniqueness of institutions in terms of size, philosophy,
financial status, type of student, private or public, etc., each will
inevitably have to determine its own organizational pattern or structure for the governance and conduct of its women's competitive
sports program.

RACING
Photograph by Dr. Richard Lussier
California State University, Long Beach

CHAPTER 5

Administrative Functions

Administrative functions refer to those actions, tasks, or duties that characteristically demand some type of action on the part of an individual who supervises or administers a program. The complexity of these functions are in direct ratio to the size of the program. The effectiveness of the program depends to a considerable extent upon how carefully these functions are planned, and how successfully they are accomplished. The major responsibility rests with those who are in charge of the program; however maximum cooperation of the coaching personnel is necessary in order to facilitate successful completion of these functions.

FISCAL PROCEDURES

Financing

If competitive sports programs are considered to be educational in nature it follows that they should be financed on the same basis as other educational endeavors. In other words they should be financed by the instructional budget. However, competitive sports, being somewhat dichotomous in nature, are also viewed as part of "student activities," which are extra-curricular in nature, much as are debating, some musical activities, and drama. These activities are often classified as "student body" or "associated students" activities. As such they have historically received some financing from student body or associated student funds.

The term "student body" is usually applied at the secondary level, while "associated students" is commonly used at the college level, but each designates the total student population and its governmental structure. In this section "student body" will be used to refer to *both* levels of education (for the sake of simplified terminology).

Usually a student body fee is paid by each student who is enrolled in an institution. The total of these fees becomes the operating budget for student activities that are financed in whole or in part by this student organization. Traditionally student body funds have contributed substantially to the men's athletic program although they have by no means financed the entire cost. Normally these funds are used for such items as game uniforms, officials' fees, travel expenses, entry fees, and league and conference fees. How this money is used varies considerably, depending upon school district policies, institutional policies, and even upon legal restrictions (as in the case of state colleges and universities).

Women's competitive programs have normally been financed by the physical education department. This fiscal situation posed no major problem before the programs began to expand into highly organized interscholastic and intercollegiate activities. There was really no need for game uniforms in a typical "GAA" (intramural type) structure, nor were there travel expenses and a variety of fees relating to leagues and conferences. However, the picture is changing quite drastically now, and the women are finding that financing an interschool program is a real problem.

In a fairly recent conference on Sports Programs for College Women a variety of patterns of financing seemed to be emerging with no real agreement on what approach to financing should be taken.[1] Some persons felt that the women's programs should be financed entirely by the departmental budget while others felt that student fees were a legitimate source to tap for aid in support of women's interschool program activities. Phebe Scott felt that inasmuch as the general principle of using student fees for such purposes was well established on most campuses it should be a valid source of support for women's interschool program activities.[2]

Another possible source of income might be gate receipts. Many feel that there are too many problems inherent in this particular method to utilize it. Realistically, most women's competitive programs have not yet reached the point at which gate receipts, if employed, would bring in much revenue. Perhaps in the future this situation may change. Even in men's programs, with the exception of the "big time" schools, gate receipts do not begin to finance the total athletic program.

Two valid sources exist from which to seek financial support for the women's competitive sports program: the physical education departmental budget, and student body fees. Departmental budgets vary

1. Division for Girls and Women's Sports. *Sports Programs for College Women* (Washington, D.C.: AAHPER, 1970), pp. 25 – 30.
2. Ibid., p. 28.

greatly among secondary schools as they do among colleges and universities, with the obvious result that some departments can support their competitive programs to a much greater extent than others. The department chairperson has the responsibility of ensuring that the instructional program does not suffer at the hands of the competitive sports program. For this reason budget priorities, which are based on sound educational philosophy and which are in keeping with funds available, must be planned and adhered to.

Although women's athletic programs historically have received little or no student body funds there is no reason why such financial support should not be sought. There is ample justification even if tradition is lacking. A very carefully prepared justification should be presented including all pertinent facts and figures if one is to expect any consideration of such a request. One should certainly not expect to receive any large appropriation the first time such a request is made. However, even a minimal allocation is a beginning which can consistently be increased if the growth and benefits of the program are made obvious, and those in charge of its conduct are patient. It must be remembered that this money is paid by the students and they will allocate it to those activities that seem important to them. Here again is where good public relations pays off. As was previously mentioned, many attitudes are changing regarding the importance of women and women's activities, thanks to anti-discrimination legislation. It would not be surprising to see such attitudes reflected in the amount of funds allocated to women's competitive sports programs. Suffice it to say that the financial future of such programs seems much brighter than it did even in the not-too-distant past.

Budgeting

Before the budget can be prepared it must first be determined what constraints exist relative to the utilization of funds. The use of student body funds in particular is circumscribed by certain restrictive fiscal policies, and it is quite possible that there may be certain restrictions placed upon the use of departmental funds also.

There are several steps to be taken in preparation of the budget, five of which seem to be basic. These are (1) realistic assessment of needs, (2) projection of needs into a preliminary budget, (3) review of proposed budget, (4) revision of proposal if necessary, and (5) submission of final budget to the funding body for consideration and approval.

Realistic assessment of needs means ascertaining what is necessary in the way of financial support in order to conduct the program. It does not mean necessarily what one would "like to have," or what would be "nice to have." It does mean what, in the opinion of those in a position to know, is really needed to effectively accomplish the purposes of the program.

The question may legitimately be asked, "Why not ask for everything one wants because the budget will be cut back anyway?" It is true that budgets are usually, if not always, pared down. The main reason for this is that seldom, if ever, is there enough money to fulfill the budgetary requests of all units. The game of "pad the budget/pare the budget because it is padded" really accomplishes no purpose and is not an administratively effective procedure. An honest and realistic budgetary submission soon becomes recognized for what it is, especially if the budgetary unit has established a reputation for ethical practices. Budgetary cuts will still occur; however they will not be based on the philosophy of "pad and pare" but rather on demonstrated need and the amount of resources available to be shared.

Assessment of needs varies in accordance with the budget that one is preparing, that is, student body or departmental. The departmental budget is usually concerned with equipment and supplies. Assessment of needs for this budget depends mainly on three factors; namely, a current inventory of available items, purchasing records of such items for the past year or two, and the number of participants anticipated. Ignoring the current inventory when estimating needs is inefficient and wasteful. In an ongoing program there are always used items which can still be utilized to good advantage the next season. The items referred to here are usually expendable, such as balls, bats, and arrows. Often referred to as supplies, they usually require a high rate of replacement. Other items, such as golf clubs, bows, rackets, foils, and sabers, have a long life and can be used for perhaps several seasons. These are sometimes referred to as nonexpendable and take a lower replacement rate than the above items.

The inventory records serve the purpose of not only making one aware of what items are on hand for use (both new and old) but also what the wearability or "use performance" of such items is. An accurate inventory, therefore, gives one a clue as to what the future needs will be.

Purchasing records also provide helpful clues insofar as they show what the actual purchasing pattern has been for the past two or three seasons. This information may reinforce what has been learned from the inventory, and it can also be especially helpful in indicating desirable replacement rates for nonexpendable items.

Anticipating the number of participants is obviously pertinent to the estimating of need. Whether an activity is a developing one or one that has become stabilized as to numbers is important. A sport that is new to a program may have comparatively few participants the first season but may grow considerably in numbers by the second or third season. A sport that is well established and has been in the program for several seasons will probably not vary too much from season to season in number of participants. If the activity in question requires individual equipment for each player, as do tennis, badminton, or golf, the factor of anticipating participants becomes even more important to the process of estimating budgetary needs.

Other items of need commonly supplied by the departmental budget are first aid supplies such as tape, ankle wraps, bandage, antiseptics and other solutions, ice packs and other drug sundry items. In a large program, especially at the college level, the costs for these items can add up to a considerable sum which must necessarily be included in the total budget to be submitted.

The departmental budget is usually developed by the director of the program (with the aid of the coaches) and is then submitted to the department chairperson in an acceptable format. These two individuals usually confer on the budget, at which point it is either accepted as presented or is revised in accordance with resources available. After this budget has been approved it is usually incorporated as a unit into the entire departmental budget and is supervised accordingly.

The development of the budget to be submitted to the student body is usually a much more complex procedure than the one described above. As was previously mentioned, there are usually rather stringent policies governing ways in which the student body's monies may be expended and also how its budget is to be developed. Commonly the student body budget funds items that are "game-related" — budget categories that are involved when a competitive match or tournament is being played: game uniforms, officials' fees, travel expense including meals and housing, awards, and membership fees.

Because there is so much variation in budgetary procedures among school districts, and between the secondary and college level, it is impossible to describe a budget design that would fit all situations.

All the factors mentioned above may not be applicable in every school. Some schools may travel and some may not. Some programs may give awards while others do not. The length of seasons vary as well as number of games played. The numbers of participants differ. Each of these variations in programs will obviously have an impact in the estimating of budgetary needs.

Assessment of needs for the student body budget should first be made at the grass-roots level — by the coaches who will be responsible for coaching a given sport. They should be responsible for estimating what the cost of conducting their activity will be. The estimate should be based on a number of factors, among the most common of which are: (1) number of games to be played, (2) length of season, (3) amount of travel, (4) number of meals, (5) cost of housing, (6) number of awards needed, (7) officials' fees, (8) number of tournaments (local and regional), and (9) number of special replacement items needed.

After needs have been assessed by the coach of each activity they must be projected into a preliminary budget. This will usually be a "working format" and will include specific items with estimated costs based on current price quotations from appropriate sources. The working format is for the purpose of review before all of the budgetary requests are compiled into the final approved format for submission to the funding agency. This preliminary review occurs at the departmental level and is usually done by the director of the program, if there is one, and/or the department chairperson. The purpose of the review is to ascertain whether requests are realistic in relation to those of the other sports and to ensure equitability among the sports in relationship to need. After the review has been satisfactorily completed and any necessary adjustments made, the various budget requests are compiled into a final format which is submitted to the treasurer of the student body or designated group.

There are a variety of budget formats, one of the most common being the "line item" budget. In this format the budget is divided into specific categories each of which is called a line item. Each line item has a number for reference purposes. When the budget is finally approved and is allocated to the budgetary units, each line item is allocated a certain amount of money. This format is somewhat inflexible because the expenditures must be consistent with the amount listed for each line item. The line items are not interchangeable, so that in the actual spending of the budget, if one finds that more money is needed on one line item and less in another, she must obtain special permission to transfer funds from one line to another. Naturally this involves a certain amount of paper work and is time-consuming. The flexibility of the line item format depends to a considerable extent upon how definitive the breakdown is. If it is fairly broad there obviously will be more flexibility than if it is very narrow.

Another budget format, one which provides for flexibility but perhaps requires more supervision, is the "lump sum" budget. In this format one is allocated a given amount of money for the total expenditures of the program. It is then left up to the supervisor of the budget to apportion it fairly and equitably to the various sport units. She must also keep very accurate records of expenditures to ensure (1) that each area does not exceed its allocation and (2) that the total expenditures do not exceed the total allocation. Student body budgets are more apt to be of the line item type, while departmental budgets may tend toward the lump sum type. (See Appendix, Examples D and E, for sample budgets.)

Once the budget has been allocated for the competitive sports program through the student body, these funds need to be re-allocated to sport activities. Coaches need to know the exact amount of funds available to them for their respective competitive seasons. If the total budget which has been allocated does not cover the budget requested, then a method of re-allocation must be developed, based upon the stated needs of each sport activity, and it must be fair to all concerned. Standardized procedures for "trimming" budgets should be adopted by mutual consent of the coaches, and the director of the program then makes the final allocation to each sport activity.

With the advent of "national tournaments" a new dimension has been introduced into the problem of budgeting. The already strained student body budget is now saddled with a new demand. In some cases the cost of sending a team to a national tournament comes close to the total budget allocation for the entire intercollegiate sports program. The crisis becomes even more critical if several teams from the same institution qualify to enter national championships. In such cases a strong appeal must be made to the student body for additional financial support. A carefully prepared statement with appropriate facts and justifications should accompany the request if any consideration of it is to be hoped for. Should the request not be approved the women's physical education department or an appropriate group within the department must consider the various alternatives available to them.

Some institutions have approved procedures for fund-raising projects which places the responsibility on the team participants to decide whether or not they desire to finance their own trip. Such projects must be carefully planned and supervised to ensure that the health and welfare (including academic status) of the students are not jeopardized in their zeal to earn the needed amount of money. It will also be necessary to ascertain if such fund-raising projects are within the approved policies of the institution and the department as well. The question will probably arise as to whether or not solicitation of contributions, or the development of a booster club are acceptable methods of fund procurement. In considering this question the long-range implications and possible ramifications should not be ignored in the interest of the immediate concern. A careful exploration of all avenues should be made, including the effects of similar fund-raising activities on the men's athletic program, before such a decision is made.

Another alternative for funding national tournaments may be that of reducing the budget allocation of the various sports in order to provide monies for the more successful teams to go to national tournaments. Such a decision must be based upon the purpose of the women's competitive sports program. Most institutions subscribe to the philosophy that support of a variety of intercollegiate sports on the local level of competition should have priority over opportunities for national competition for a few highly skilled individuals or teams if such a choice must be made.

Still another alternative is that of deciding that participation of teams in national competition must wait until support of such teams is allowed for in the student body budget. This may be slow in coming because the burden of proof that such support is merited must be accepted by the program itself. This will depend to a great extent upon public relations, and upon continued attempts to create an awareness upon the part of the student body (especially its officers), of the values and benefits of the programs, not only to the participants but to the institution as well. The present climate of non-discriminatory practices toward women should improve the situation.

Whereas the first National DGWS tournaments were open to all institutions who wished to enter, the more logical trend now is to require teams to qualify on a regional level (as in basketball), and/or to establish national minimum standards (as in swimming). Allowing only the winning teams at the local or regional level to continue on to national championships should reduce the budgeting problems that arose when all teams in an institution could request entry into national championships whether or not they were of proven national caliber.

As soon as the budget allocation is received it is urgent that some type of bookkeeping procedures be put into practice regarding the expenditure of funds. Purchasing policies must be established that will lead to effective supervision of the budget including approval procedures and accurate records of expenditures.

Approval for expenditures varies from the secondary to the college level and there are also variations within these levels. Policies are often set by the administration of the various institutions. It can be said that, generally speaking, departmental expenditures at the college level require less administrative approval than they do at the secondary level. At the college level, once the departmental budget has been allocated, requisitions usually go directly from the department chairperson to the purchasing office whereas at the secondary level they might be channeled through the principal's office to purchasing. Requisitions for expenditures from the student body budget normally go directly from the department to the student body office for approval.

Purchase requisitions should be initiated either by the department chairperson or the director of the program, depending upon which budget is involved, and on the administrative structure of the department. This procedure clearly identifies those individuals who are responsible for the supervision of the budget, promotes consistent and efficient record keeping and strictly minimizes the problems of accountability.

COORDINATION PROCEDURES

Coordinating with Student Body

• EXPENDITURES FROM BUDGET: Institutions will vary considerably with respect to procedures to be followed in submitting requests for funds which have been approved and allocated. The director of the competitive sports program needs to understand all such procedures, and to conscientiously follow all instructions in order that a cooperative relationship can be established between her and student body budget personnel.

Student body budgets involve considerable amounts of money, and thus accounting procedures are likely to be very specific and rigid. Such information as the following is customarily required when requesting funds for travel: type of event, date and time, location, number of students and faculty involved, and method of transportation. It is then necessary to specifically request the amount needed for meals (number involved and cost per meal[s]), amount needed for transportation (number of cars, rate, and estimated mileage), and amount needed for lodging if overnight trip. Additional items which may or may not pertain to the request include entry fees, officials' fees, practice fees, and so on.

In order to expedite communication between the coach requesting funds and the director, forms can be utilized by coaches in providing the above information to the director (see figs. 5.1 and 5.2). The director then writes up the official request on forms provided by the student body office (see fig. 5.3). By having the coach submit duplicate copies of her request, the director can retain one copy to file in the budget folder for that sport, and return the duplicate to the coach to indicate that the request has been processed. This procedure also provides the coach with an accurate accounting of the funds remaining in her budget.

The director should also establish a bookkeeping system through which she can deduct all expenses and add funds which have been returned. In addition to keeping accurate records for the total budget, she should maintain an up-to-date record of the amount remaining in the allocation for each sport activity. Toward the end of each academic year, it may be necessary to review the status of the budget in order to ascertain if it is necessary to transfer unused funds from one account to another where needs have not as yet been met.

Of fundamental importance to the successful operation of accounting procedures is complete understanding by the coach of her responsibility in turning in required receipts and verification of expenditures upon her return to the campus. If funds have been advanced to her prior to leaving campus, then receipts and necessary forms accounting for her expenditures must be completed and returned to the student body office (see fig. 5.4 for trip expense report; fig. 5.5 for mileage expense form; and fig. 5.6 for meal expense form). If, instead, the institution utilizes the reimbursement method, then funds can only be claimed for those expenditures for which the coach submits receipts.

In the case of expenditures for such items as trophies and equipment, it is customary for the student body office to require that a purchase order be submitted and approved prior to placing an order for such items. The signed purchase order is then exchanged for the

```
Women's Physical Education          Previous Balance_____
Women's and Coed Intercollegiate    Adjustments_____
    Sports                          Balance_____
                                    Amount of this Request_____
                                    New Balance_____

            INTERCOLLEGIATE EVENTS HELD AWAY FROM S.U.

To be submitted in duplicate with Travel Request to Director of
Women's Intercollegiate Sports at least one week in advance of
event.

    Sport_____Date submitted_____ Request number_____
    Event_____ Place _____
    Date & Time of Leaving_____Date & Time of Return_____
    Number of students_____ Number of Faculty_____Total Number_____

ENTRY FEES (Please specify number and amount
per person or team .........................     TOTAL_____
_____
_____

Check to be made out to: _____ Deadline Date_____
Address_____

TRANSPORTATION...............................     TOTAL_____
    Number of miles_____@ 10¢ a mile;_____
    Number of cars_____ cost per car_____
    Total cost_____
    Drivers (must carry $25,000-$50,000
        insurance)
    _____  _____
    _____  _____
    _____  _____

MEALS (only for tournaments, includes tax and
tip).........................................     TOTAL_____
    Number of breakfasts____@ $2.50 cost_____
    Number of lunches   ____@ $3.00 cost_____
    Number of dinners   ____@ $5.50 cost_____

LODGING (maximum of $9.50 per person).........     TOTAL_____
    Number of nights_____Rate_____
    Check to be made out to_____
    Address_____Amount_____

OFFICIALS....................................     TOTAL_____
    Names_____ @ Rate_____
          _____ @ Rate_____
          _____ @ Rate_____

EQUIPMENT RENTAL, GREEN FEES, ETC. (Please be
specific)....................................     TOTAL_____
    _____
    _____
    _____
    Check to be made out to_____
    Address_____Amount_____
..............................................................
Eligibility?  All okay_____Students not eligible:
```

FIGURE 5.1

```
Women's Physical Education         Previous Balance_____
Women's and Coed Intercollegiate   Adjustments_____
   Sports                          Amount of this request_____
                                   New Balance_____

                INTERCOLLEGIATE EVENTS HELD AT S.U.

To be submitted in duplicate to Director of Women's and Coed Inter-
collegiate Sports one week in advance of event.

Sport_____Date submitted _____Request number_____

Event_____ Opponents _____ Facility_____

Date_____Starting Time_____Ending Time_____

Has reservation of facility been approved?_____

Names of students participating:

_____

_____

_____

_____

_____


EXPENSES:

   Officials........................................TOTAL_____

        Names_____ @ rate_____

              _____ @ rate_____

              _____ @ rate_____

Equipment Rental, Green Fees, etc. (please be
specific).....................-.......................TOTAL_____

_____

_____

_____

   Check to be made out to_____

   Address_____Amount_____
........................................................................

Eligibility: All okay_____Students not eligible:
```

FIGURE 5.2

Requests accepted on this
form only. Submit to
A.S. Business Office.

Associated Students
State University

Request for Payment or Purchase

(This is not a purchase order)

Previous Balance _____

Add: Increases or Adjustments _____

Less: Decreases or Adjustments _____

Less: This request _____

New Balance _____

Request No. _____

TO: (Name) _____ Date _____ Account No. _____

(Address) _____ Account Name _____

_____ Check _____ Purchase Order ____ Mail ___ Hold ___

Wanted Quantity Unit	Decription (Give complete description and dates)	Unit Price	Cost*
	Sub-Total		
	Tax		
	Total		

INSTRUCTIONS

1. AVOID RUSH ORDERS. Anticipate your needs. Order far enough in advance so that P.O. or checks may be processed. We will ask for at least two bids on items over $200.00. Normally a minimum of 48 hours should be allowed for issuance of any check or P.O.

2. Number RPP serially for each account.

*3. Cost must be shown, including tax. Check whether cost is estimated _____ or actual quotation _____ .

4. Give *complete* description of articles wanted, ONE VENDOR ONLY PER REQUEST.

5. Indicate whether check or P.O. and whether to mail or HOLD.

6. Submit pink and yellow copies to A.S. Business Office. Retain blue copy. Original invoice must be forwarded if request is for a check to a vendor.

7. When purchase order has been typed, the pink copy will be returned to you. When articles have been received, please come to the A.S. Business Office to approve payment.

Bids Attached: Yes ____ No _____

Needed by: _____

Approved by: _____

Merchandise or Services
Accepted by: _____

Signature

Missing, Defective Items,
Comments: _____

_____

_____

_____

_____

BUSINESS OFFICE USE ONLY

Paid by Check No. _____ Date _____

FIGURE 5.3

```
                    ASSOCIATED STUDENTS
                    STATE UNIVERSITY

                    TRIP EXPENSE REPORT
                                          ADVANCE #_____
                                                  $_____

ACTIVITY_____ EVENT _____ DATE _____

DEPARTURE_____.M._____RETURN_____.M._____
            Time          Date              Time          Date

NO. OF PARTICIPANTS: STUDENTS_____FACULTY_____OTHERS_____TOTAL_____
```

DATE	MEALS			HOTEL	CAR	TAXI	OTHER*	TOTAL
	Bkfst.	Lunch	Dinner					
TOTAL								

```
*EXPLAIN                          AMOUNT RETURNED $_____

REMARKS (Be explicit):_____   I certify that the above is a true
                                    statement of expenses rendered for
_____       official Associated Students acti-
                                    vities.
_____

_____   _____
                                          Signature
_____
```

FIGURE 5.4

ASSOCIATED STUDENTS

REQUEST FOR MILEAGE REIMBURSEMENT

NAME_____ ACTIVITY
TO CHARGE_____

( ) Advance   ( ) Reimbursement_____19____

Date	From	To	Total Miles	Amount	Remarks

Activities may set mileage rates according to their budget needs, however,
the maximum reimbursement rate allow-   _____
able is 10¢ for first 150 miles, 8¢ for   Signature of Claimant
next 450 miles and 5¢ for all miles over
600 for any claimant during one month.   _____
                                            Signature of Advisor

*Miscellaneous use of auto @ 8¢ a mile.

FIGURE 5.5

ASSOCIATED STUDENTS

***MEAL ADVANCE**

PLEASE READ BEFORE SIGNING NAME-Received from the Associated Students at State University the amount listed under "Amount of Money Received" for the named meals. Cost of such is certified by your signature.

NO.	NAME (print)	DATE	MEALS (name each meal received)	Amount of Money received		*SIGNATURE

I certify this to be a true signature of the above named individuals and further certify that the amount rendered each, by me, is true and correct.

____

SIGNATURE

FIGURE 5.6

item under consideration, which authorizes the vendor to bill the student body for the amount of the purchase order.

• INSURANCE. Since it is customary for the student body office to arrange for insurance coverage for both the men's and women's competitive sports programs, certain procedures are usually established so that the office has the names of participants on file. In some cases the director is required to turn in the list of participants in each sport prior to the beginning of the competitive season. In other situations, it may be necessary to file a travel report for each off-campus event, listing the names of the students and faculty involved, and the names of the drivers if private cars are to be utilized for transportation (see fig. 5.7). Institutions utilizing the letter method frequently require the Travel Report to be submitted before requests for funds for the trip will be approved. Needless to say, all procedures relating to insurance coverage should be diligently followed by the coach who is responsible for getting the needed information to the director who in turn must submit it in proper time to the student body office.

At the high school level, most schools require permission in writing from parents before a student can participate in the sports program. It is therefore important that a description of the program, including aims, objectives, values derived from participation, nature of practices and competitive events, and requirements for participation, be sent to all parents, all this to be accompanied with a permission affidavit which the parents must sign and return to the school. Form for such an affidavit should be developed with the appropriate school or district administration to ensure legal validity. It should include provisions for insurance coverage as determined by the individual school or school district.

Coordinating with Records Office

With the expansion of girls' and women's competitive sports programs has come also the need to establish eligibility requirements. Verification of participant eligibility is usually the responsibility of the director of the competitive sports program. In most cases, however, such verification is dependent upon access to student records, necessitating cooperation and a close working relationship with personnel in the records office.

In the men's athletic program, responsibility for the verification of academic eligibility usually rests with designated personnel in the records office. It is suggested that the director of the women's

---

ASSOCIATED STUDENTS

TRAVEL REQUEST

A. Name of Individual, Group or Organization traveling:

_____

B. Name of each person traveling (students and college officials):

_____   _____

_____   _____

_____   _____

_____   _____

_____   _____

C. Trip to _____

D. Hour of Departure _____ M., _____ 19 ___

E. Time of Return _____ M., _____ 19 ___

F. Mode of Transportation _____

_____
Signature

_____
College Position

FIGURE 5.7

Competitive Program follow a similar pattern in requesting that the records office verify the eligibility status of women participants. A composite list of criteria for eligibility, including institutional requirements, league or conference requirements, and AIAW requirements (if teams hope to participate in regional or national championships), should be submitted and reviewed for clarity with personnel in the records office. A list of names of all participants could then be submitted to the records office at the beginning of the semester and academic eligibility of participants verified or rejected in accordance with established criteria. Immediate notification to those students found to be ineligible should be made by the appropriate coach.

To facilitate the process of checking eligibility, institutions may wish to develop individual participant record cards. A sample of such a record card is shown in figure 5.8. Such cards should be completed by the individual each semester or quarter, for each sport in which she participates. It is further suggested that the student complete two cards so that one can be retained by the coach and the other can be kept on file in the director's office. The use of individual cards facilitates alphabetizing of cards for development of master lists to submit to the records office and the health service. Following recording of data from these offices, the cards can be regrouped according to sport and eligibility lists established for each sport. By keeping the individual record cards on file in succeeding years, the number of seasons of participation in a sport can be easily verified. In addition, pertinent data is readily available for follow-up studies, such as the comparison of the number of participants each year, the academic majors of the participants, and the average number of years of participation.

Coordinating with Health Service

Coordination with the school nurse or the college health service is vitally important. Procedures need to be developed cooperatively with respect to the required physical examination and the care of students who are injured during participation in the competitive sports program.

• PHYSICAL EXAMINATION. The necessity for certification by a physician of a student's health status prior to participation in athletic practices and events cannot be overemphasized. At the college level, procedures for the physical examination should be developed jointly by the women's physical education department and the college health service. The level of competition, extent of practices and events, and physical demands placed upon the participants in the various sports should be explained so that the health service personnel might have a realistic understanding of the state of physical health needed for participation in the program.

For those situations in which physicians at the health service conduct the physical examinations, arrangements for individual appointments or group physicals need to be formulated. The latter procedure may involve the health service bringing in a team of

Fall or Spring Semester, 19___Instructor_____Sport_____
    (circle one)
                    INTERCOLLEGIATE SPORTS PARTICIPANT RECORD CARD

Leave Blank	Entering Freshman ___ Male ___	Leave Blank
Credit ___	New Transfer ___ Female ___	
Audit ___	Continuing Student ___	GPA_____
Other ___	Re-entering Student ___ Health ___	MED.
	Last Semester of ___ Classification	
	Attendance Year	

_____/_____
LEGAL NAME   (Last)   (First)   (Middle)   Student Number

Class   ___   ____   ___   ___   ____   Unit Load This Semester_____
        Fr. Soph. Jr. Sr. Grad. Units Passed Last Semester_____

Date of Birth_____Year of Birth_____Age_____Major_____

College
Address_____Phone_____
                                    (Zip Code)

Home
Address_____Phone_____
                                    (Zip Code)
Parent or relative to contact in case of an emergency:

Name_____ Amateur Status___   ___
                                                      Yes   No

Address_____
                                    (Zip Code)   (Phone)
Previous number of years of participation on an Intercollegiate
Team in this sport:
    As an undergraduate:_____years   As a graduate:_____years

                RECORD OF PARTICIPATION IN THIS SPORT

College or JC   Year   Extent of Competition
_____
_____
_____
_____
_____
_____

Out-of-School Participation in Sports
_____
_____
_____
_____
_____

FIGURE 5.8

specialists, thereby being able to accommodate many students in a relatively short time period. Such a procedure is frequently utilized for men's intercollegiate athletics, and has also worked well for women's intercollegiate sports. Either procedure necessitates sending a list of competitors to the health service. When the schedule of examinations has been established, it becomes the responsibility of the coach to inform the students on her team of the time of the examination, of the reason for examination, of the type of examination to expect, of the specific procedures to be followed, and of the necessity for completing the examination in order to be eligible to participate. Results of the examinations will then be forwarded by the health services to the director of the competitive sports program, who can record the date and result on the individual's record card, and forward the information to the appropriate coach. Guidance pertinent to the situation should be given to students not approved by the health service, and any follow-up procedures recommended by the health service should be carefully observed.

In situations where the college or high school is not equipped to give the above services, students will need to have a physical examination from their personal physicians. It is highly desirable that a written letter explaining the program be taken by the student to her physician. Depending upon the policies of the institution or school district, the physician may be asked to complete an official physical examination form and/or to sign an affidavit of the student's fitness to participate in the competitive sports program. This form should then be filed with the appropriate administrative personnel (school nurse, health service, women's physical education department, coordinator of sports program, or coach).

• PROVISION FOR EMERGENCY CARE. Each institution differs with respect to ways of providing for emergency care of students, but the most important detail is that procedures be established for accidental injury during practices at the school and during competitive events conducted at the home school or at another institution. Such provisions should be developed cooperatively with the school nurse and/or health service, and be approved by the school administration. It is of utmost importance that all concerned (students, parents, coaches, administrators) have a clear understanding of who is responsible for meeting financial obligations which are incurred as a result of the treatment of accidental injury. If the institution carries an insurance policy to cover the competitive sports program, then the director of the program is usually responsible for completing the necessary information on insurance report forms so that the claim can be processed. If students are required to carry individual insurance, then the responsibility lies with the parents and/or physician involved.

In order to have an accurate record of the injury, it is vitally important for the coach to complete an official accident report as soon as possible. Information requested on the accident report form usually includes name, address, and age of person injured, name and address of parent or guardian, date, time, and location of accident, nature of injury, cause of accident, name of supervisor, name and address of witnesses, and emergency first-aid procedures followed. One copy of the report should be filed with the school nurse or the health service, with a carbon being retained by the director of the program. In cases where insurance coverage is involved, established procedures for the specific institution or school district should be followed.

Following an injury, illness, or surgery, the student should not be allowed to participate in practice sessions or in competitive events until approval is given by the school nurse, health service, or her personal physician. It would enhance the coach's understanding and supervision of the student involved if such approval were received on a referral form which would include follow-up suggestions regarding the care of the student.

Figures 5.9, 5.10, 5.11, and 5.12 are examples of the health procedures which have been developed by a specific women's physical education department in cooperation with the student health service for the women's intercollegiate sports program at that institution.

Coordinating with Other Institutions

• LEAGUE OR CONFERENCE Since competitive sports programs necessarily involve other institutions, an important function in the organization and administration of the program relates to institutional representation in the local league or conference, and membership in each successive level of governing organization. The expansion of such governing groups is a fairly recent phenomenon, especially at the regional and national level. Although many areas of the country have had league or conference governing groups operating for some time, most are still in a state of transition attempting to stay abreast of the rapid growth of competitive sports programs all over the country.

Membership in a league or conference involves attending meetings and having a voice and a vote in determining league philosophy,

```
        Women's Physical Education Department
        Women's and Coed Intercollegiate Sports

              ACCIDENT AND ILLNESS REPORT
```

Policy Number	Policy Period	Name and Location of Agent

Name of School or Organization

Address of School or Organization

Name and Address of Student	Age

Name and Address of Attending Physician

DUE TO ACCIDENT	Date and Time of Accident Place of Accident
	Nature of Injury
	What Caused the Accident?
	Describe Type of Sport or Activity Engaged in at Time of Accident
	Name of Supervisor of the Activity
	Witnesses to Accident (Name and Address)
DUE TO ILLNESS	Nature of Illness
	Date Illness Commenced

Date Submitted_____ Submitted By_____
                                Sport_____

MUST BE RETURNED TO DIRECTOR OF WOMEN'S AND COED INTERCOLLEGIATE
SPORTS ON NEXT SCHOOL DAY FOLLOWING OCCURRENCE OF ACCIDENT OR ILL-
NESS.

FIGURE 5.9

```
                        STATE UNIVERSITY
              Women's Physical Education Department
              Women's and Coed Intercollegiate Sports

                 AUTHORIZATION FOR MEDICAL TREATMENT

                                          Date_____

To_____ Sport_____
             (Hospital and/or Doctor)

This authorization verifies that_____is a stu-
dent athlete in the Women's or Coed Intercollegiate Sports Program
and has been referred to you for medical treatment as the result of
an athletic injury:

    Nature of Injury_____

    Caused by_____

    On (exact date)_____


The athletic insurance coverage provided the student athlete by the
Associated Students, State University, shall be payable only on an
excess basis over and above any benefits or services provided by
the student athlete through his own or his family insurance plan(s),
regardless of any coordination of benefits, non-duplication of bene-
fits, or similar clause contained in such plans. The benefit payable
under the coverage provided by the Associated Students shall be re-
duced to the extent necessary so that the sum of such reduced bene-
fits and all the benefits provided for by any other plan shall not
exceed the total expenses incurred by the person insured herewith.

Payment for any medical service can be greatly expedited if all
bills are sent to:

            Director, Women's and Coed Intercollegiate Sports,
            Women's Physical Education Department,
            State University.

            ATTN: Athletic Insurance.

Should any questions arise, please call the Women's Physical Edu-
cation Department.




                            _____
                            Authorized Agent, SU

cc: White:    Hospital and/or Doctor
    Blue:     Athletic Team Physician
    Yellow:   Women's Physical Education Department.
    Pink:     Copy retained by coach
```

FIGURE 5.10

```
                        STATE UNIVERSITY
                   Student Health Service
                            and
              Women's Physical Education Department


         PARENTAL ENDORSEMENT FOR EMERGENCY CARE OF MINORS

    In case of accident or illness, permission is hereby granted the
    team coach to seek emergency medical treatment for:



    _____, who is_____years old, at an
    appropriate medical facility. Sport_____



    PERSON TO BE NOTIFIED IN CASE OF EMERGENCY:


    NAME _____


    ADDRESS_____
                    (Street)        (City)          State)


    TELEPHONE _____



    PRIVATE PHYSICIAN PREFERENCE:
    _____ M.D.    _____
              (Name)                  (Signature of Mother or legal guard-
                                      ian)

    _____     _____
              (Street)                (Signature of Father or legal guard-
                                      ian)

    _____     _____
         (City)      (State)                       (Street)

    _____     _____
            (Telephone)                          (Telephone)


         TO BE FILLED OUT IN DUPLICATE AND RETURNED TO THE COACH.
```

FIGURE 5.11

STATE UNIVERSITY

Student Health Service
and
Women's Physical Education Department

WOMEN'S AND COED INTERCOLLEGIATE SPORTS MEDICAL POLICIES

I. Purposes of the athletic medical examination and health clearance.

1. The primary purpose of the medical evaluation is to establish the candidate's fitness to participate in a given sport without undue risk to her health and personal safety.

2. To advise the candidate regarding any remedial health problems and recommend specific safety measures as indicated.

3. To establish and record the student's eligibility for insurance coverage as provided by the Associated Students.

4. To establish a doctor-patient relationship which can be used to good advantage should the athlete later become ill or injured.

II. Purposes of the athletic health clearance card.

1. To provide the coach with information concerning any specific problems the athlete may have and give instructions for any indicated therapeutic or preventive measures.

2. Provide a ready source of information which might be of importance should the athlete be injured and require treatment away from the Student Health Service.

3. The smaller portion of the card, which is retained by the athlete, gives evidence of her having a valid health clearance. All coaches will require a student to present her card prior to beginning participation in any intercollegiate sport (an "A" Health Classification Card will be accepted prior to the examination period).

III. Procedures.

1. Dates for the physical examination shall be requested by the Women's Physical Education Department Chairman through the Director of the Student Health Service sometime during the preceding semester. Scheduling the physical examinations during the third and fourth weeks of the semester seems to be the most desirable time.

2. Coaches are responsible for turning in names of all students participating in their sport by the end of the second week of each semester to the Director of Women's and Coed Intercollegiate Sports.

3. The Director of Women's and Coed Intercollegiate Sports formulates a master list of men students and of women students to be examined, submitting these lists to the Health Service at least one week prior to the scheduled examination period.

4. Coaches are responsible for reminding their students of the date and time of the physical examinations. Students who find it absolutely impossible to take the examination at this time must go to the Health Service prior to the day of the scheduled examination, to make an individual appointment. This practice should be discouraged except for hardship cases.

5. Students should present health clearance cards to coach showing that they have received a valid health clearance. The other portion of the card is sent to the Director of Women's and Coed Intercollegiate Sports.

6. No student will be allowed to participate in intercollegiate sports events who does not have a health clearance card on file with the Director of Women's and Coed Intercollegiate Sports.

IV. Insurance Exclusions.

1. Some students have pre-existing injuries or conditions which would not necessarily preclude athletic participation, but could not be covered by the athletic insurance policy.

FIGURE 5.12

IV. Insurance Exclusions (continued)

2. Should such pre-existing injuries or conditions be present, the team physician will notify the Director of Coed and Women's Intercollegiate Sports who will inform the appropriate coach.

3. In such cases where the college declines to accept liability for an uninsurable pre-existing injury and the student is determined to participate, she may be asked to execute a waiver of liability. This procedure should be discouraged and used only in exceptional cases.

4. Every person participating in intercollegiate sports will be given a copy of a statement concerning the policies for athletic insurance coverage. She (and her parents if she is a minor) will be required to sign a statement that she has read and understands the provisions. The signature will be kept with her health record. It is of course, not intended that this constitutes a legal document but is a method of assuring that students are informed of their responsibilities in maintaining athletic insurance coverage.

5. It is the purpose of the provisions of this section to insure as far as possible that a student athlete's insurance eligibility or an appropriate alternative has been clearly established before she is permitted to engage in competitive sports.

V. Medical Coverage.

1. The team physician will be available in the Student Health Service to see athletes without appointments between the hours of 9:00 and 10:00 A.M. and 1:30 and 2:30 P.M. Monday through Friday. He will also be available until 6:00 P.M. for treatment of emergencies during the seasons when men's varsity teams are practicing.

2. As far as it is possible to do so, the team physician will see all athletes for all injuries and medical complaints in order to provide continuity of care and continuance of the student's athletic health clearance.

   a. During the hours that the Student Health Service is open, the team physician will ordinarily be available to see all nonemergent conditions at the specified times or by appointment. He will see emergencies at any time.

   b. During regular working hours if the team physician should not be available and an athlete requires immediate attention she should be seen by any available staff doctor.

      1. If an athlete is seen by another physician, her chart will be routed to the team physician for his information before being returned to the files.

      2. Similarly, in the case of staff specialty consultations whether referred by the team physician or another staff doctor, the chart will be sent to the team physician for information before filing.

   c. Should an athlete need urgent care after regular clinic hours the team coach will contact the team physician for instructions. In the event that the team physician cannot be reached or is not available, the student will be sent to Community Hospital with a request that she be seen by a medical doctor. The coach will be sure to have the proper authorization form accompany the student so that there will be no confusion in billing. The blue copy of the authorization form is to be sent to the Student Health Service to be filed in the athlete's health chart.

   d. If an injury or illness occurs at a game away from home, it is expected that the coach will take the student to the nearest emergency hospital for necessary care. All injuries treated elsewhere should be promptly reported to the team physician on the team's return and the athlete will report to the Student Health Service to make out an accident report.

FIGURE 5.12 (CONTINUED)

policies, and procedures. The importance of decisions made at this level, as well as higher levels, cannot be overemphasized. Decisions concerning eligibility requirements, leadership, conduct of inter-school events, and the handling of protests should be based on a sound philosophy in which the welfare of the participant is of primary concern. Dedicated and sound leadership in such groups is essential if we are to keep our programs focused on providing quality competitive experiences for girls and women through which bene-ficial values are an outcome.

• SCHEDULING   An important phase of coordination with other insti-tutions is that of scheduling competitive events. In some institutions this is done by the director of the program at league or conference meetings. In others, the schedule of games and tournaments is developed at coaches' meetings. Whichever system is utilized, it is imperative that the director of the program be informed of all scheduled events for the teams at her institution. Such schedules should be completed no later than the end of the spring term for the following academic year. As programs become more stabilized it is to be hoped that scheduling can be completed a year in advance, so that annual budget requests will truly reflect actual needs rather than anticipated needs, and so that facilities can be reserved.

With the completion of the master schedule in the spring, every effort should be made to submit the schedule for printing in the annual calendar of events which many institutions publish each year. All events could also be posted on the master calendar of student body activities. In addition monthly or weekly schedules can be reproduced and distributed to personnel involved in the operation of the program, such as department secretaries, equipment room personnel, maintenance staff, security force, department chairperson, and members of the men's and women's physical education depart-ments, as well as to the campus newspaper, activities office, local newspaper, and faculty bulletins.

Coordinating with Boy's and Men's Competitive Athletics

Until recently coordination of men's and women's competitive sports programs has not been a major problem. Men's athletics historically have been an integral part of the total school program both at the secondary and college levels. These programs have been solidly interlocked with school spirit, school unity, prestige, and public relations. There was no question in the minds of anyone that after three o'clock in the afternoon the priority for use of all athletic facilities belonged to the men's program. This program, being a seasonal one, needed the use of certain facilities at specific times in the year. The girls' "GAA" or intramural type program, with an occasional "playday" or "sportsday", of necessity worked around the men's seasonal program. This was easy to do as long as the program remained intramural in nature. The women could simply use what was not being used by the men and it really did not matter a great deal if they played tennis in the early fall and hockey or field sports in the late fall or early spring. Basketball and volleyball were no problem because these sports could be played outside on the blacktop. In some instances schools were fortunate enough to have duplicate facilities, in which case no problem existed. Sport facilities, however, are very expensive and not many schools and colleges have enough facilities to preclude the necessity of some sharing.

With the advent of the "women's liberation" movement and federal legislation preventing discrimination against women and minority groups, the rapid expansion of women's competitive sports program has begun to pose a threat to the traditional priority of athletic facilities. Although no radical changes in this priority are occurring, at least it is being questioned and herein lies the problem. It raises such questions as: Who should have the priority and how should sports facilities be shared between men's and women's programs? Is one program more important than the other? Should the tradition of "all sports facilities rightfully belong to the men's athletic program after three in the afternoon" be continued? These are controversial questions, of course, and could be argued ad infinitum. Solidly entrenched traditions are difficult to displace. There are too many vested interests. Volatile emotions often emerge and real values, such as interdepartmental friendship and cooperation, are at stake.

It would be unrealistic for women's physical education departments to expect a sudden facility priority revision to occur that would give them complete "prime time" equitability. The very seasonal nature of the men's program, which is locked into local, regional and national leagues and conferences, makes this an impossibility.

What then is the solution to the problem? How can facility usage be arranged to enable both programs to function effectively and to the satisfaction of those concerned? One simple approach, and probably a necessary one where facilities must be shared, is for the women to arrange the seasonal nature of their programs to avoid conflict with the men. This of course would not entirely solve the problem because a facility such as the gymnasium may be used for both basketball and wrestling or gymnastics. These activities would restrict the use of the facility for most of the fall and spring semesters. Tennis, on the other hand, would probably work out successfully because normally the courts are not used for any other activity but tennis.

One complicating factor relating this approach to the problem of nonconflicting sports seasons is that of league or conference membership. For this system to operate successfully the women would have to compete with the same schools as the men do in order to have their own schedules coordinate. This would not pose a problem at the secondary level because most high school leagues are based on geographical locations. At the college level, however, this could pose a real problem, considering that the men's programs tend to belong to conferences on the basis of size and strength of athletic programs, while the women tend to affiliate largely on the basis of geographical proximity. As has already been pointed out this latter type of affiliation results in competition among colleges of drastically different sizes which may also make quite a difference in facilities available to each.

Another approach to the problem of facilities might be that of harmonizing practice schedules to avoid conflicts. The thought here is that all activities do not necessarily have to be conducted at the same time, namely from three to five or six o'clock in the afternoon. Practices could be conducted before classes begin in the morning and during the evening hours. This procedure is already being followed by many institutions. The hour from 7–8 A.M. seems to be rather popular for swimming workouts whereas the evening hours seem best suited to such activities as basketball, volleyball, and gymnastics.

The flaws in this approach are obvious, not the least of which might be parental disapproval, insofar as high school girls are concerned. College students are used to taking classes at all hours of the day and evening and would probably find this type of scheduling much less objectionable than would high school students and their parents. It does, however, pose a real problem for those students who must depend on busing for their transportation. A further concern, and a major one with this type of scheduling, has to do with the degree of stress such practice times put upon the students. For many students such a procedure would add hours to their day's schedule. It would require either getting up extremely early, or going to bed much later. Would they still take time to have proper meals? Would there be adequate time in the day for necessary studying? Would they get plenty of rest and sleep? These are all questions that would have to be satisfactorily answered before making the decision to utilize this method of scheduling practices for competitive sports.

One other pertinent question must be asked here. Who would take the "odd hours" practice schedule? Is it just naturally assumed that it would be the women? Would it be rotated by sport, by semester, or year, between the men and the women? The most desirable solution, of course, would be some type of equitable sharing between the two departments.

Many colleges and universities have attempted to solve the problem of facilities by scheduling intercollegiate sports as instructional classes. If this approach is taken the times when such classes are scheduled must be governed by the "master schedule" which is based upon the entire instructional program and the total facilities available to both the men's and women's departments. Problems inherent in this procedure are: harmonizing facility availability with that of the coach, harmonizing scheduling time with the student availability, and coordinating facility and time availability with the men's department. However, if facilities are extremely limited this is one approach that should not be overlooked. A dividend that may accrue from this approach is that the coach can receive teaching load credit for her activities as she does for any other class that she teaches.

This discussion has centered around the problems involved in coordinating the women's competitive sports program with the men's athletic program when facilities must be shared. Perhaps one or another or a combination of these suggestions might be used effectively in enabling a department to develop and conduct a worthwhile competitive sports program. However, each department will ultimately have to arrive at the solutions which seem most appropriate to its unique situation.

One other area of coordination between the men's and women's sports programs is that of the "master schedule" of events. The main factors relate to transportation and would probably be more applicable to the secondary than to the college level. If transportation to competitive events is accomplished by school busing, obviously very close coordination of the schedules of events must occur in order to avoid conflicts and to have buses available for team transportation. The master schedule of competitive sports events must also coordinate with the overall school master schedule of events inasmuch as activities of other departments also often require the services of school buses for transportation.

One must constantly bear in mind that the extent to which coordination between these two important programs occurs will largely depend upon the public relations involved. The women's department must make every effort to gain support for its competitive sports program by demonstrating its worth and value, not only to the men's department but to the students and faculty in general, as well as to the administration and the community.

Coordinating with the Maintenance Department

Coordinating with the maintenance department is a necessary and very important administrative function of the competitive sports program. It should not be assumed that effective relationships "just happen." They are usually the result of careful planning, with resultant policies and procedures which not only promote desirable relationships but help to develop a smooth coordination between the activities of the maintenance department and the needs of the competitive sports program.

Actually effective relationships with maintenance is simply a matter of clear and adequate communications and good public relations. In most instances maintenance departments are interested in sports activities and tend to be cooperative, particularly if they understand what is expected of them, and have ample time in which to accomplish the requested tasks.

Normally the kinds of maintenance tasks required by competitive sports programs relate to such things as field marking, cleaning facilities, setting up bleachers, providing tables and chairs, setting up public address systems, moving heavy equipment, and putting things back in order after competitive events are over. In order to get such things accomplished effectively and efficiently, good communications and public relations are necessary. Under the head of communications the following items are important:

1. Allow ample lead time in making requests for service. (This should be agreed upon by maintenance and the physical education department as policy.)
2. Follow proper channels in making requests. (This may involve approval at higher than department level, depending upon established administrative policy.)

3. Explain in detail what is required in the request. (This means specifying measurements, what materials are to be used, exactly where items are to be placed and when items are to be returned.)

4. Supply detailed drawings, sketches or diagrams for clarification purposes.

5. Explain any new or different procedure that is to be followed.

6. Avoid, insofar as possible, making requests that will necessitate interruption of regular instructional classes. (This avoids conflict between maintenance crews and instructors.)

7. Make all requests in written form. (This provides a record for the department, as well as maintenance, to refer to.)

8. Devise an official maintenance request procedure within the department in order to avoid conflicts. (All requests should be approved at the departmental level by one person, preferably the department chairperson).

9. Coordinate requests with the men's department, if necessary, before processing. (This needs to be done only where facility conflicts may be involved.)

In order to ensure good public relations with the maintenance department the following suggestions are offered:

1. Send notes of appreciation from time to time with a copy to the supervisor of maintenance, for services rendered.

2. Give verbal commendation, as well as written, in casual encounters with maintenance crews.

3. Invite maintenance personnel to competitive events even if their schedule will only permit them to drop by for a few minutes.

4. Treat maintenance personnel as equals, not as subordinates.

5. Avoid being unpleasant if requests cannot be met when desired. (Remember that maintenance services the entire school, not just physical education and athletics.)

6. Avoid getting upset if errors are made by maintenance personnel. (Remember they are human too, and perhaps the error was due to lack of clarity in the request.)

7. Make every effort to solve maintenance problems with their department before going to their supervisors. (The latter only engenders ill will and may destroy what desirable relationships have been developed.)

The smooth functioning of competitive sports activities leans very heavily on the services rendered by the maintenance crew. Indeed it would be most difficult to function effectively without their cooperation. For this reason it is incumbent upon the physical education department to do all it can to establish clear lines of communication and to engender good will between the two departments.

Equipment Issue Policies and Procedures

Issue rooms may range from small, inadequate "cubby holes" to vast complexes containing many rooms with highly specialized functions. Similarly personnel may range from none or students to several full-time equipment issue personnel. The simplicity or complexity of the situation and the size of the competitive sports program will usually determine the policies and procedures to be followed in issuing equipment items for participants.

More often than not ordinary equipment such as balls, rackets, bows, and golf clubs will follow the same issue procedures as do items for regular physical education classes (see fig. 5.13). If certain of such equipment items are set aside for competitive sports only, possibly they may be issued on a different check-out slip. A very specialized item, such as uniforms used exclusively by competitive sports participants, may have a special check-out sheet (see fig. 5.14).

Regardless of the size of the issue room or the number of personnel to service it the primary principle of *security* should be observed. Every coach should be held responsible for the security and care of the equipment used by her sport. This principle should be observed not only by the coaches but also by the students. Students should be taught respect for equipment in regard to its security, care, and maintenance.

The skill level that a player or team achieves is often related to the quality of the equipment used, especially in individual and dual sports. This is not to say that equipment "makes the star performer"; however, most skilled performers would agree that a fine piece of equipment does enhance their skill. This being the case every attempt should be made to equip teams and individuals with the best equipment that the budget can afford. However, unless good security can be maintained by the establishment of issue policies and procedures which are carefully adhered to by all personnel involved, there is little reason or incentive to provide high quality equipment for participants.

Following are suggested procedures which should aid in ensuring security of equipment:

1. Keep a record of all equipment checked out (see sample check-out sheets).

2. If possible indicate a time and/or date by which equipment should be returned.

3. Have all equipment items identified by number, department and institution, i.e. #9, WPE, T.W.U. (This avoids confusion with men's department and also with other schools at competitive events).

```
SU
WPE                    DAILY CHECK-OUT SLIP


REQUEST DATE _____

INSTR. _____ CLASS DATE _____

STUDENT _____ CLASS DAYS _____

CLASS NO. _____ CLASS TIME _____


        All Equipment MUST BE RETURNED IMMEDIATELY
                       AFTER CLASS

Equipment                            Equipment No.

_____          _____

_____          _____

_____          _____

_____          _____

_____          _____

_____          _____

_____          _____

_____          _____


Order filled by _____ Checked in by _____

Remarks _____

_____

_____
```

FIGURE 5.13

4. Equipment check-out sheets should have a place for number of item. (This shows what specific piece or pieces of equipment are issued to a coach, team manager, or participant).

5. When equipment is returned numbers on items should be cross-checked to ensure the same items being returned that were issued.

6. If items are not returned the coach or student responsible for them should be notified.

7. Specialized, high-risk equipment should have a special check-out slip in order to ensure a high level of security.

WARM-UP UNIFORM CHECK-OUT SHEET

SPORT_____   COACH_____

DATE of EVENT_____

TIME of PICK UP_____

DATE of RETURN_____

    Please state number of sizes needed. Turn in at least one day
before uniforms are needed to attendant in the Outdoor Issue.

JACKETS: PANTS:

LL_____ ML_____   8 Regular _____12 Long _____

LM_____ MM_____   10 Regular _____14 Long _____

LS _____ MS_____ 12 Regular _____16 Long _____

                                14 Regular _____18 Long _____

FIGURE 5.14

8. Issue room policies and procedures should appear in faculty and student handbooks and should also be posted near the issue room.

9. Issue policies and procedures should be stressed in orientation sessions for coaches and student team managers.

10. Security problems with equipment should be reported to the director of the competitive sports program and/or the department chairperson.

Regardless of how large or small the issue area is or how simple or complex the issue systems are, suffice it to say that the principle of security of equipment must be provided for by specific policies and procedures which are strictly observed by coaches, team managers, and participants. Ultimate responsibility for the supervision of this function rests with the director of the program and/or the department chairperson.

TENNIS ANYONE?
Photograph by Dr. Richard Lussier
California State University, Long Beach

CHAPTER 6

Public Relations

All too often, especially in competitive sports, the terms public relations and publicity are used synonymously. They are related, of course, in that publicity is an aspect of public relations, but it by no means is the totality of public relations.

Specifically, public relations is concerned with how an individual, organization, business, activity or institution relates to its publics. Obviously it is desirable to have good public relations and it can sometimes be disastrous for such entities mentioned above to have poor public relations. Billions of dollars are spent every year by various organizations and institutions for the purpose of developing public relations programs that will result in constructive and positive attitudes on the part of the public toward them or their activities and products.

The purpose of this chapter is to analyze this important and necessary function as it relates to women's competitive sports and to ascertain the various techniques or procedures available to such programs conducted in schools and colleges.

In analyzing public relations a number of questions immediately arise. Who are the "publics?" What are the goals? Are there immediate as well as long range goals? Are there certain clearly defined procedures that should be followed? Is there sufficient flexibility to allow for innovation? Are there undesirable or unethical procedures that should be avoided? Whose responsibility is the public relations program? How does one evaluate the overall program?

THE PUBLICS

The publics of the women's competitive sports program are many. Of these, the most important are (1) the department of men's physical education and athletics, (2) other school faculty, (3) the students, (4) the associated students' organization, (5) the administration,

(6) the parents and the community, (7) various leagues, conferences, and governing organizations, and (8) other school employees.

Obviously the vested interests of these various groups differ considerably, accordingly different public relations techniques and procedures must be applied appropriately to gain the desired results.

THE GOALS

The goals of public relations are both long-range and short-range. The long-range goals are concerned with gaining support for the program and to "sell it," or to get people to understand that it is worthwhile and has value and merit, not only for the participants but for the school as well.

The short-range or immediate goals are (1) to "inform" people about the program, (2) to "interpret" the program (its aims, objectives, values, policies, and procedures), (3) to stimulate interest in the program, (4) to improve attitudes toward the program and (5) to report the progress and the accomplishments of the program.

PROCEDURES AND TECHNIQUES

A variety of procedures and techniques must be developed in order to successfully accomplish the above goals. Actually if the short-range goals are effectively accomplished the fulfilling of the long-range goals will take place almost automatically.

Informing and Interpreting

Often the public relations of a program are not very effective simply because people don't know very much about the program. Because women's sports programs in the past have been focused, for the most part, merely on the joy of playing and competing in a variety of activities, not much thought had been given to informing others about it. It did not seem important. It was a somewhat self-contained program that really didn't concern itself too much with outside forces. These programs were not especially large, they weren't highly organized, and they might have been termed almost casual in the way they operated. As a result no one except those immediately involved gave too much thought to them. Their needs were not great, they didn't make excessive demands, they adapted to existing programs, and in general their behavior was above reproach.

The picture has changed quite radically however, with women's competitive sports burgeoning into highly organized, very competitive programs, involving many activities, an increased number in participants, and the consequent increase in needs. Three of the most pressing needs relate to budget, facilities, and personnel.

These needs have naturally exerted pressure on women's physical education departments to gain a place of greater importance for their competitive programs. All of a sudden the importance of "informing" others about their programs has become paramount if these programs are to be able to operate successfully. Those who control the program funding, facility usage, and personnel allocation must all be convinced of the worth and value of these programs before they are going to be willing to make realistic commitments to their support. They must be willing not only to change their attitudes toward women and competition, but also to accept the concept of girls and women competing at high levels. They must be convinced that girls and women can compete at such levels without undesirable personality changes.

In order for this support and acceptance to occur much effort must be put forth in developing effective public relations. People must be informed about the program, and answers furnished for the inevitable questions: How is it conducted? By whom is it conducted? What are the qualifications of these people, personally and professionally? What kinds of activities are participated in? How much of the individual's time is spent in participation? What kinds of pressures and demands will the program make on the participants? Is it possible for their health to be adversely affected by such physical stress?

These and many similar questions will be uppermost in the minds of parents, boards of education, administrators and other interested people who have a concern for competitive sports programs for girls and women.

"Interpreting" the program goes hand in hand with informing, and in effect might be thought of as an extension of it. Interpreting connotes explanation. It gives meaning to information. Information or facts taken alone, do not always yield a clear and precise picture of a given situation. Interpretation relates to the aim and objectives of the program. It can explain how the participants benefit. It should reveal the kinds of experiences the students have. It should emphasize the positive values the participants are exposed to. Interpretation should clarify in a positive manner the somewhat disturbing questions of participation in physically vigorous, competitive sports as related to retention of femininity. Interpretation is likewise useful in highlighting the standards of a program as they are projected into policies and procedures which may result in very effective and worthwhile experiences for the participants.

Interpreting, then, is a very important adjunct to informing and indeed enhances that aspect of public relations through explanation and clarification.

Informing and interpreting can be accomplished in a variety of ways. As mentioned in chapter 3, every program should have a policy manual which includes philosophy, aim, objectives, policies and procedures of its program. Such materials should always be placed in the hands of certain key people. In the public schools these people include the board of education, the superintendent, principals, vice-principals and/or deans of girls, and the parent-teacher associations. Others that might benefit by having it are the chairperson of the boys' physical education department, the boys' athletic director (if other than the foregoing), and the board of the student body organization. At the college level such administrative officers as the president, the dean to whom the department is directly responsible, the dean of students, as well as the associated students' board, the chairperson of the men's physical education department, and the director of men's athletics benefit from having such materials. There may be others, depending upon the particular institution.

Other materials, such as articles in professional journals, research reports, the National Association for Girls and Women in Sport (NAGWS) pamphlets, newsletters and reports of meetings — all relating to women's competitive sports — may be shared with the individuals mentioned above, to good advantage. Anything that will help to "inform" or "interpret" should be used by those conducting the program.

Informing and interpreting may also occur on a more personal basis through casual conversation or by previously arranged meetings, depending upon the kind of information one has to impart. At times arranged meetings are necessary, especially when approval for certain actions is necessitated by policy. Meetings with school and college administrators for the express purpose of informing about and interpreting the program can often be very fruitful in gaining better support for one's program.

One should not overlook any opportunity to improve the public relations of the competitive sports program by informing and interpreting through personal contact, whether formal or informal.

Stimulating Interest

For individuals and groups to be supportive of a program they must be interested in it. Although the subjects already discussed will help to stimulate interest two techniques that can be very effective in accomplishing this purpose are "observation" and "involvement." One really needs to see a program *in action* in order to get excited about it. Watching competitive events is not only exciting but also gives one an opportunity to observe how such events are conducted, how players act under the pressure of competition, how the coaches conduct themselves, the fellowship of competitors and teammates, and the overall environment of the situation. Here one has a firsthand opportunity to develop an appreciation of the competitive experience.

Those in charge of the conduct of such programs would be well advised to invite their school administrators, other faculty (including male colleagues), parents and others to view their games and matches. This can involve a certain risk, of course, if desirable and wholesome attitudes are not readily apparent to such spectators. It again points up strongly the necessity of developing high standards of conduct in the planning stages of the program, and careful orientation of coaches and faculty regarding the importance of maintaining such standards at all times.

Involvement is perhaps more difficult to accomplish than observation. Involvement demands energy as well as time. It requires "doing something." Getting people to help some way in one's program is a very effective means of getting them involved. Some of the ways people outside of the women's physical education department can help are:

— Acting as judges at track and swimming meets
— Presenting awards at banquets and assemblies
— Designing covers for programs
— Designing posters for publicity
— Printing programs for events
— Aiding in the chaperoning of teams on trips
— Attending banquets and other such events
— Being guest speakers at special events
— Helping to make special uniforms, if not supplied by the school
— Writing publicity articles for the paper

This is by no means a complete list of how various people could become involved in a competitive sports program. This list of activities could involve such people as teachers, students, parents, administrators, and members of the community at large. When people get involved in a program, even in a small way, and it becomes a satisfying experience, they tend to get involved again and their interest and support for the program develops.

Improving Attitudes

Improved attitudes toward a competitive sports program will usually be accomplished by informing, interpreting, and stimulating interest; this provided, of course, that the program is a worthwhile one. A program has to have something of value to offer if good attitudes about it are to be developed. If negative attitudes have been held by some they can usually be changed to positive ones by the use of the public relations activities discussed here. However, if what people see is an undesirable program with many negative aspects, obviously attitudes will not be improved. Those who are responsible for the conduct of competitive sports programs for girls and women must be constantly sensitive to the attitudes of their "publics." They must be ever alert to those factors that can result in negative and destructive attitudes on the part of individuals, and take immediate steps to correct such undesirable situations even if severe measures are required.

Reporting

Reporting the program has to do with giving information about it. The most common type of reporting is what is ordinarily called "publicity" — publicity about the program in general, publicity about coming events, publicity about accomplishments, and publicity about special events.

Such publicity usually materializes by way of the school newspaper and sometimes the local news media, especially in smaller communities. Traditionally boys' and men's athletics have dominated this type of publicity. However, it is becoming considerably more common now to find stories on the "sports page" about women's competitive events. Even radio and television occasionally cover women's events especially if they have significance for the Olympic Games or other events of such caliber or for professional sports.

Reporting or publicity, although only one aspect of public relations, is important because it calls attention to the program. Some people would not be aware of such programs without this medium of public relations. Those who are aware of the programs are interested in knowing how and what the sports involved in them are doing. Public awareness and interest can be further stimulated by favorable publicity about them. Again it should be pointed out that certain risks are implicit in this kind of public relations. If in a specific instance the publicity is unfavorable it can color attitudes about the program, particularly if the conduct of it or the actions of players and coaches are involved. Thus again it behooves all who are engaged in such programs to conduct themselves at high levels, and at all times to provide favorable and desirable experiences for the participants.

Although the media is more favorably disposed to girl's and women's competitive sports programs, and publicity space is more than it used to be, it must be borne in mind that numerous interest groups in schools and colleges are all competing with each other for space in the institution's newspaper (and in the local news media). It is desirable, therefore, for every program to have some organized plan for publicity. It may involve having a student in the program also become a member of the journalism class. This arrangement works out very nicely because it almost ensures some type of publicity coverage on a regular basis. Admittedly, however, this arrangement is not always feasible. Another possibility would be for all coaches involved in an activity to report pertinent publicity items for their sport to either a specific coach who would be in charge of publicity, or to the director of the program. In some instances individual coaches could report their publicity items directly to the sports editor of the paper or preferably to the sports information director (if there is one).

Obviously, a variety of plans are available for reporting publicity. The important thing is that some plan be in existence for this purpose. Otherwise there may be a dearth of publicity about girls' and women's competitive sports in the paper. The burden for publicity rests with the program rather than with the newspaper, even though there is a gradually increasing interest in coverage of women's sports, as witness the greater number of such articles on the sports page, and the greater amount of space given the individual articles.

INTERPERSONAL PUBLIC RELATIONS

Up to this point the chapter has dealt mainly with an "organized" public relations program for competitive sports for girls and women. One would be remiss, however, to omit in this discussion the importance of interpersonal relationships on a day-to-day basis to the overall public relations program. Everyone involved in the program, from the participants to the director, has a responsibility here. The importance of such relationships between the women's physical education department and such departments as men's physical education and maintenance has already been mentioned in previous chapters, and these cannot be overemphasized. The concern goes deeper than this, however. The question is, "What kind of an image should the women's competitive sports program project?" Most would agree that it should be an image of womanhood at its highest level, functioning in a very vigorous and wholesome manner. If indeed this is the sought-for image, the question to be posed by each participant, coach and director is, "What image do I project?" The question should not be limited to the competitive situation but must indeed cover the total spectrum of human relationships.

How do the participants appear to their peers — in the classroom? in the cafeteria? in casual encounters? at the local coke and hamburger joint? at school social events? How do they appear to their teachers, to school administrators and to other school personnel? Do they fit the desired image or do they fit the heretofore well-known stereotype of the "woman athlete?"

What image is projected by the coach? How does she appear to school administrators and parents? Is her image that of wholesome womanliness? Is it thought to be worthy of emulation? For indeed she will be emulated and her influence may be far reaching!

And what of the one ultimately responsible for the program, the director and/or the department chairperson? Does she likewise project a desirable and positive image? Do her actions, words, and appearance invite the confidence of administrators, parents and colleagues? Is she, who has the final accountability for the women's competitive sports program, worthy of this critical responsibility? Do she and her personnel provide the most desirable experiences possible for the participants in the program — physically, mentally, socially, and morally?

The implications of these questions are indeed serious and have considerable impact on the total, overall public relations of the competitive sports program for girls and women. They cannot and must not be taken lightly for upon them may well rest the successful future of such programs.

Public relations alone do not "make" a good competitive sports program. A program is good or poor depending upon how it is planned and conducted and upon who conducts it. The caliber of any program largely depends upon the caliber of those involved in it. Public relations can, however, "enhance" a good program and enable it to become more effective and successful by gaining support from its various publics through the processes of informing, interpreting, stimulating interest, improving attitudes, and reporting interesting and important information about the program.

TIME MARCHES ON
Photograph courtesy of Diana W. Anderson
formerly Women's Physical Education Department
University of California, Los Angeles

CHAPTER 7

Historical Development of Competitive Sports for Girls and Women

Competitive sports for girls and women have become increasingly important in our culture. In order to better understand the recent development in these flourishing sports programs, it is necessary to become knowledgeable about the forces that have been influential in guiding their growth. It is our purpose at this point to trace the historical sequence of events which have played a significant role in the development of competitive sports programs for girls and women, primarily in the high schools, colleges, and universities in the United States.

EARLY BEGINNINGS

The appearance of women in sports closely parallels the emerging role of women in our culture. During the nineteenth century, the woman's role was that of wife, mother, and homemaker, and "to be genteel, modest, shy, fragile, conventional, and subordinate to the opposite sex were womanly virtues."[1] Fashions of the day dictated the wearing of long, full skirts, many petticoats, and an abundance of underclothes.

Women began participating in sports about the middle of the nineteenth century. Long dresses and the delicate female image limited their participation to such activities as archery, croquet, golf, hiking, and riding. The popularity of bicycling then swept the country, and women, eager to enjoy this activity, had to shorten their skirts. Lawn tennis, introduced in the United States by Mary Outerbridge in 1874–75, also became a popular activity and again the hemline was raised. As aptly expressed by Coffey, "bicycling started the revolution in the rising hemline, and lawn tennis finally revealed the feminine ankle."[2]

Collegiate institutions, during the middle of the century, were offering calisthenics for their women students. These programs were

1. Coffey, "The Sportswoman," p. 38.
2. Ibid.

then expanded to include light gymnastics and later on colleges adopted one of the various systems of gymnastics which were being promoted at the time. Women's colleges took the first step in offering sports, in addition to calisthenics, to their students. Vassar College in 1865 provided instruction in such activities as riding, boating, swimming, and skating. Durant, who founded Wellesley College ten years later, encouraged rowing and ice skating on the campus lake, and introduced tennis.[3]

Whereas in some women's colleges sports were included in the curriculum, at other institutions sport was more recreational in nature. Students organized clubs for such activities as bicycling, croquet, boating, tennis, walking, archery, and bowling.

Spears summarized the important developments during this period of time from 1833 to 1890 as follows:

> First, Vassar and Durant recognized sport as a means of attaining physical vigor which was essential for the success of their women's colleges. Second, the students at private coed institutions, the universities, and the normal schools enjoyed sport as casual recreation. Third, some colleges, for example, Vassar, taught sport and incorporated it into their physical education curriculums.[4]

TEN ORGANIZATIONS DEVELOPED TO GUIDE AND CONTROL COMPETITION

Establishment of Women's Rules Committee

The introduction of competitive sports for girls and women is generally agreed to have occurred at Smith College, where Senda Berenson introduced the game of basketball in 1892.[5] Although Dr. James Naismith originated the game for men, basketball achieved a much higher degree of popularity initially among women students. The original rules seemed unsuitable for women, however, due to the roughness inherent in the men's game. The original rules were also misinterpreted and so each institution began formulating its own basketball rules.

In order to overcome the problems created by the many diverse modifications in the rules, the American Association for the Advancement of Physical Education Council in June, 1899, appointed a commitee of women to develop a standard set of rules for the

---

3. Spears, "Emergence of Sport."
4. Ibid.
5. Division for Girls and Women's Sports, *Philosophy and Standards*, p. 3.

women's game. The first Official Basketball Guide for Women was published as part of the Spalding Athletic Library Series in 1901. Senda Berenson, director for women's physical education at Smith College, served as editor of the Guide for the next sixteen years. She was also appointed as chairman of the first permanent basketball rules committee organized in 1905.[6]

In addition to basketball, collegiate women also began participating, in tennis, baseball (indoor and outdoor), field hockey, track and field athletics, swimming, and rowing (in 1901).[7]

This period is marked by the transition in the colleges from sports clubs and intramural activities to the introduction and growth of interschool competition; primarily in basketball, and to a more limited extent in hockey and track and field athletics. The University of California, Stanford University, and Mills College held intercollegiate basketball games as early as 1900, the same year in which the University of Nebraska started a varsity basketball program.[8] Basketball and field hockey were popular on the East Coast, but competition was predominately interclass rather than interschool.[9]

As intercollegiate competition progressed during this period, many women physical educators became concerned about the evils associated with such competition, and began substituting intramural programs which they considered to be more desirable for women. Blanche Trilling, in 1913, lead the way toward emphasis on intramurals at the University of Wisconsin by organizing the Women's Athletic Association which sponsored a variety of activities and for which a point system for awards was developed.[10]

Four years later, in 1917, Miss Trilling invited representatives of twenty colleges and universities to discuss the role of women's athletic associations as a replacement for intercollegiate athletics. This group subsequently invited the Women's Intercollegiate Athletic Council of New England, established in 1914, to join forces to form the National Athletic Conference of American College Women.[11]

Despite the intramural emphasis during this period, girls' interscholastic basketball thrived in the small towns of the Middle West and South, and high school basketball tournaments received much publicity. The games were played, in the main, outside the auspices

6. Von Borries, *History and Functions*, p. 7.
7. Hackensmith, *History of Physical Education*, p. 403.
8. Rice, Hutchinson and Lee, *A Brief History*, p. 290.
9. Dudley and Kellor, *Athletic Games*, p. 99.
10. Hackensmith, *History*, p. 403.
11. Ibid.

of the educational system, and lack of qualified leadership resulted in exploitation of the girls. Contests were conducted before unruly crowds, and attacks on officials, intentional roughness, and lack of sportsmanship prevailed.[12]

Such conditions brought down condemnation of interscholastic sports from both physicians and physical educators. As early as 1906, George W. Ehler proposed a resolution to the Public School Physical Education Training Society of New York disapproving of interscholastic athletics for girls and proposing the substitution of intramural competition.[13] Following the lead of the colleges, some high schools had organized girls athletic associations by the end of this period, and were offering intramural programs instead of interscholastic athletics. The State of Illinois organized the Illinois League of High School Girls' Athletic Associations for the purpose of controlling girls' athletic association programs in that state.[14]

Appointment of the Women's Athletic Committee

Although the Women's Basketball Committee had been formed in 1899, it was not until 1917 that the Council of the American Physical Education Association authorized its president to appoint a Committee on Women's Athletics. As expressed by Von Borries,

> The need for such a committee was apparent to the Association because of the "insistent and increasing demands coming in from all parts of the country for assistance in solving problems in connection with the athletic activities for girls and women, which demonstrated the need for a set of standards which should be based on the limitations, abilities, and needs of the sex" and different from the established rules and standards for men.[15]

This Committee sponsored its first program at the American Physical Education Association Convention in 1917, with an address on "Standardization of Athletics for Women." Apropos of this committee's function to formulate and publish official rules for women's sports, sports committees were established by 1922 for basketball, hockey, soccer, swimming, and track and field; this was followed by moderate sports in 1924, baseball in 1925, and athletic games in 1927.[16] The custom of rules for women's sports being written and controlled chiefly by women thus has a long history.

12. Dudley and Kellor, *Athletic Games,* p. 71.
13. Hackensmith, *History,* p. 394.
14. *Ibid.,* p. 395.
15. Von Borries, *History and Functions,* p. 8.
16. Ibid.

In addition to the role of establishing rules for women's sports, the Committee also was charged with the task of rendering advisory service to the rapidly developing program of women's athletics. In this capacity, the Committee adopted the following resolutions concerning interschool competition in 1923:

> *Be it therefore resolved,* that no consideration of interinstitutional athletics is warranted unless,
>
> a.   The school or institution has provided opportunity for *every girl* to have a full season's program of all around athletic activities of the type approved by this committee.
>
> b.   *That every girl* in the school or institution (not merely the proposed contestants) actively participates in a full season of such activities and takes part in a series of games within the school or institution.
>
> c.   These activities are conducted under the immediate leadership of properly trained women instructors who have the *educational value* of the game in mind rather than *winning.*
>
> *Resolved,* that in cases where
>
> 1.   The above conditions obtain and proper responsible authorities (preferably women) deem it desirable *educationally* and *socially* to hold inter-institutional competitions the following requirements are observed:
>
> > a.   Medical examination for all participants.
> >
> > b.   No gate money.
> >
> > c.   Admission only by invitation of the various schools or institutions taking part in order that participants may not be exploited.
> >
> > d.   No publicity other than that which stresses only the sport and not the individual or group competitors.
> >
> > e.   Only properly trained women instructors and officials in charge.
>
> Finally the committee does not want it to be inferred from these recommendations that it is advocating or trying to promote a policy of inter-school games.[17]

While intercollegiate sports for women were being curtailed on college campuses in favor of intramurals, basketball tournaments for high school girls were flourishing. And it was during this period that sports for women outside educational institutions began to expand. Industrial groups, business groups, chambers of commerce, sporting goods companies, and department stores organized and promoted

---

17. "Women's Athletic Committee," pp. 289 – 90.

women's teams for the publicity derived for the promoter. The era
of exploitation of girls through athletics had arrived.[18]

Organization of Women's Division of National Amateur Athletic Federation

It was when the Amateur Athletic Union sent a girls' track and field
team to Paris in 1922 that many women rose to protest the commer-
cialization and exploitation of women athletes. That same year the
National Amateur Athletic Federation (NAAF), a federation of
existing organizations, was formed for the purpose of jointly promoting national standards for athletics.[19] A wide variety of organizations
were represented at the first meeting, including the United States
Army, and the United States Navy, Boy Scouts of America, Young
Women's Christian Association, the Physical Education Association,
the National Education Association, National Collegiate Athletic
Association, and many others.

Prior to the first meeting of NAAF, Mrs. Herbert Hoover, was
invited to promote the membership of women and girls within the
organization. However, though she approved of the general idea,
she felt that factors underlying athletics for boys and men were
fundamentally different from those of women and girls. She therefore
supported the idea that there should be a separate division of the
organization for athletics for girls and women.[20]

Following up her convictions, which were enthusiastically received
by professional physical educators from whom she sought guidance,
a Conference on Athletics and Physical Education for Women and
Girls was held in 1923.

> Realizing keenly that for lack of sound knowledge and guidance
> undesirable tendencies had developed in girls' athletics, and con-
> scious of the need to make information and help more easily avail-
> able for all groups in this important field, these leaders organized
> the Women's Division of the National Amateur Athletic Federation:
>
> (1)   To inaugurate and foster a national movement for sane and
> constructive athletics and physical recreation for the girls and
> women of America.
>
> (2)   To make it possible for all groups interested in such activ-
> ities to come together in a central and unified body for better
> understanding and more effective service.

18. Women's Division, *Women and Athletics*, p. 29.
19. Sefton, *Women's Division NAAF*, p. 2.
20. Ibid.

(3) To formulate standards and establish them nationally for the sound conduct and development of girls' athletics.

(4) To assist groups to put these standards into concrete effect in their work.

(5) To make possible for girls and women a wider participation in suitable athletic activities.

(6) To serve as the national research body and clearing house for all problems of athletics and physical recreation for girls and women.[21]

Mrs. Herbert Hoover was elected permanent Chairman. The following platform, based upon resolutions approved at the 1923 Conference, was adopted at the first Annual Meeting of the Women's Division in 1924:

> The Women's Division of the National Amateur Athletic Federation of America believes in the spirit of play for its own sake, and works for the promotion of physical activity for the largest possible proportion of persons in any given group, in forms suitable to individual needs and capacities, under leadership and environmental conditions that foster health, physical efficiency and the development of good citizenship.[22]

The Women's Division, with Lillian Schoedler as Executive Secretary, engaged in a promotional campaign for memberships, which resulted in 250 memberships representing religious groups, camp organizations, clubs, welfare groups, community and state organizations, industrial groups, as well as educational institutions. The Women's Division of the NAAF not only established standards but worked to publicize these standards through conventions, meetings, workshops, printed materials, newspaper and magazine articles, and by radio. In 1928 a system of state committees was initiated to further publicize the work of the Women's Division throughout the country.[23]

The original resolutions in 1923, and the Platform of 1924 were interpreted by some to mean that competition itself was prohibited. In order to clarify its position (which this organization and its successors have repeatedly had to do) a Statement on Competition was made by the Women's Division of the NAAF from which appropriate excerpts appear below:

> The Women's Division does believe wholeheartedly in competition. It believes that competition is the very soul of athletics, of

21. Women's Division, NAAF, *Women and Athletics*, pp. 4 – 5.
22. Ibid., p. 3.
23. Ibid., pp. 6 – 7.

sports and of games, and that without it they could not exist. What it disapproves of is the *highly intense specialized* competition such as exists when we have programs of interschool competition, inter-group open track meets or open swimming meets, with important championships at stake. The evil in connection with these events lies not so much in the competition itself as in the emphasis which is placed upon winning and which makes that the paramount issue. The evil further lies, not alone in the competition at the actual time of the game or meet, but in the whole process which produces the few experts who battle for supremacy. The same evils might exist in an intramural program where too much emphasis was placed upon winning, but is not so likely to be as the stakes are not so large.

The Women's Division Has Two Big Missions:

First to encourage the promotion of sports and games for *all* girls and women.

Second to establish such ideals and principles in connection with sports and games as will make it certain that these sports and games are being wisely chosen, wisely promoted, and wisely supervised.[24]

The Women's Division stressed play days instead of interschool competition, and felt that the emphasis should be placed on partici-pation and not upon winning *per se*. Their motto became, "A Game for Every Girl and Every Girl in a Game."[25]

Organization of Directors of Physical Education for Women in Colleges and Universities

It was in 1910 that Amy Morris Homans of Wellesley College ex-tended an invitation to women directors of physical training from six New England colleges to discuss mutual concerns and the status of physical training itself. It is interesting to note that Miss Homans also invited the presidents of athletic associations, thereby indicating that the discussion topics must have included the subject of athletics for women. Following annual meetings of this group, Miss Homans in 1915 issued another invitation to Eastern college directors to meet for the purpose of forming a permanent organization, which was the origin of the Eastern District Association.[26]

The Middle West Society was formed in 1917 and the Western Society in 1921. Following much correspondence between the three groups relative to the development of a national organization, the

24. Ibid., pp. 39 – 40.
25. Ibid., p. 41.
26. Halsey, *Life and Lights of NAPECW*, p. 4.

Association of Directors of Physical Education for Women in Colleges and Universities was born in Kansas City in 1924.[27] Southern and central district organizations later joined the Association (in 1935 and 1936 respectively). This group is now called the National Association for Physical Education of College Women (NAPECW).

In commenting on the problems which have concerned the Association memberships throughout its history, Halsey indicated that "Health, research, curriculum, and athletic competition have been perennial program and committee subjects."[28] She has also noted that "controversies arose in the old days over membership, over statements of policy on competition, over the curriculum, and even over the wording of the constitution and the proper length of swimming suits! . . . Standards of athletic competition were always important, since the bequest of a sound, noncommercial sports program by such early pioneers as Senda Berenson Abbott, Ethel Perrin, and C. M. K. Applebee."[29]

The proposal that the United States enter a women's track and field team in the 1928 Olympic Games, to be held in Amsterdam, brought forth considerable concern from women physical educators throughout the country. It was felt that the women were being exploited, that competition was too strenuous, and that over-strain and injury could result. And as was predicted, eleven women collapsed during the eight hundred-meter run.[30]

Prior to the Olympics held in Los Angeles in 1932, the Women's Division of the NAAF passed a resolution disapproving of competition for girls and women in the Olympic Games.[31] This was followed by resolutions which were adopted by the National Association of Directors of Physical Education for Women in Colleges and Universities. This latter group expressed its belief "that the plan of entering women representing the United States in the Olympic Games of 1932, is foreign to the best interests of the girls and women of the United States."[32] Similar resolutions were passed by the Eastern Association, the Midwest Society, and by the Executive Committee of the Section on Women's Athletics of the American Physical Education Association. Nevertheless, the United States did enter a women's team in the 1932 Olympics!

27. Ibid.
28. Ibid., p. 5.
29. Ibid., pp. 7 – 8.
30. Coffey. *The Sportswoman*, p. 41.
31. Sefton, *The Women's Division*, p. 82.
32. Women's Division, *Women and Athletics*, p. 92.

Expansion of Women's Athletic Committee to Women's Athletic Section of the American Physical Education Association.

Beginning in 1927 the Women's Athletic Committee applied to the American Physical Education Association (APEA) to have the Committee named as an official Section of the Association. Much debate followed due to the fact that the Women's Athletic Committee differed from APEA in the way election of officers was conducted, and some men were violently opposed to recognizing the committee as a section.[33] Following a complete reorganization of the structure, policies, and procedures of the APEA under the leadership of the first woman president, Mabel Lee, the National Section on Women's Athletics (NSWA) was finally officially organized and recognized in 1932.[34] The Women's Division of the NAAF merged with the NSWA in 1940.[35]

During the transitional period of 1927 and 1932, officials' ratings were established in 1928, and volleyball and winter sports guides were published in 1929 and 1930 respectively. Five sports were added to the growing list of guides in 1933; lacrosse, speedball, archery, golf, and tennis. The first riding guide was published in 1936, and this was followed by a guide for fencing and badminton in 1940.[36]

In 1933 a Committee on Standards was appointed by the NSWA. Its work resulted in the first *Standards in Athletics for Girls and Women* which was published in 1937. The subtitle of this publication, "Guiding Principles in the Organization and Administration of Athletic Programs," indicates that the publication presented a point of view regarding the nature and conduct of athletics for girls and women. It was designed to be used by administrators, teachers, and leaders of informal and athletic programs in schools, communities, commercial, industrial, and recreational groups.

The first *Standards* monograph included sections on the construction and conduct of athletic programs, leadership responsibilities of the administrator and teacher, and proposed values and objectives for, as well as responsibilities of, the participant. The standards expressed were based on the philosophy that "The One Purpose of Athletics for Girls and Women is the Good of Those Who Play."[37]

A standard is defined in the monograph as "an authoritative rule

33. Metheny, *Connotations of Movement*, p. 138.
34. Ibid., p. 140.
35. DGWS, *Philosophy & Standards*, p. 4.
36. Von Borries, *History*, p. 8.
37. National Section, *Standards in Athletics*, p. 7.

or model constructed as a guide to action."[38] Bases for the standards were the most reliable current expert opinion, available scientific findings, and practice of the time. The standards were meant to be general enough to be operable in many situations and specific enough to indicate a course of action in any given situaton. As expressed at that time, "once established . . . standards have the force of authoritative statement which renders them binding upon all persons subscribing to good practice."[39]

Throughout the years women physical educators have consistently adhered to the principle that basic standards should be used to guide competitive play though the standards themselves have changed, as perceived by need. Nevertheless, standards have always been insisted upon.

Establishment of National Section for Girls and Women's Sports

In order to emphasize the breadth and scope of persons being served by NSWA, the name of the organization was changed in 1953 to the National Section for Girls and Women's Sports (NSGWS). The purpose of this Section of the American Association of Health, Physical Education, and Recreation (AAHPER), "to promote a wholesome sports program for all girls and women" was implemented by "the stating of guiding principles and standards for the administrator, leader, official, and player; the publication and interpretation of rules, technique charts, articles, and teaching aids; and the stimulation and evaluation of research in the field of women's sports."[40] The platform of NSWA, just prior to becoming NSGWS, was as follows:

> The NSWA endorses sound, wholesome sports programs for girls and women under trained leadership in schools, colleges and recreational groups. Sports programs for girls and women should be promoted to the extent that the outcomes are in the best interests of the individual and of our American way of life. Thus:
>
> (1)   Girls and women are given opportunity to participate in a wide variety of sports, individual and team, which are based on the needs and interests of the participants.
>
> (2)   The sports program gives opportunity to develop interest and ability in activities which are recreational and have carryover value.
>
> (3)   Sports instruction and participation should be made available equally to the unskilled-player as well as to the skilled player.

38. Ibid., p. 6.
39. Ibid.
40. "AAHPER's Section on Girls and Women's Sports," p 32.

(4) Adequate safeguards are furnished to protect the health and welfare of the players.

(5) The leadership provided maintains standards conducive to social and spiritual growth as well as physical safety and well-being.[41]

By this time, eight guides were being published by the AAHPER and special publications included *Standards in Athletics for Girls and Women, Desirable Practices in Athletics, Special Events in the Physical Education Program, Girls Athletic Association Handbook, Group Games,* and *Sports Techniques Charts and Sports Teaching Aids* (in the form of an audio-visual catalog).

NSGWS held its first national leadership conference at Estes Park, Colorado, during the summer of 1955. The purpose was to have representatives from the various states and other key personnel meet to discuss how to better make NSGWS more functional within the states. Emphasis was placed on the role of state leadership, the kinds of programs state leadership should provide, and the tools state leaders should use to give effective leadership. The topic of competition was discussed, and the summary of this meeting was written as follows:

> There seemed to be general agreement on the types of competition which meet the needs of girls and women; that a good, broad intramural program should be our goal; that the play day and sports day experiences are valuable for all; and that it may be desirable to expand the intramural program into an extramural program with increasing emphasis on the intensity of competition.[42]

At this conference questions were being asked in regard to the highly skilled girl, and what should be done for her.

Two highly significant statements were published in 1954. The first, entitled "Standards for Girls Sports in Secondary Schools" was formulated by a joint committee of representatives from the AAHPER, the National Association of Secondary School Principals, and the National Federation of State High School Athletic Associations. The Guiding Principles were:

1. The sports program should meet individual needs with consideration given to physique, interests, ability, experience, health, and maturity.

2. A medical examination should be given each girl prior to participating in the sports program.

41. Ibid., p. 33.
42. National Section for Girls and Women's Sports, *Story of National Leadership Conference,* p. 19.

3. A healthful, safe, and sanitary environment should be provided for all activities.

4. Every girl should have the opportunity to participate in a variety of activities including both individual and team sports.

5. Competition should be equitable between girls of approximately the same ability and maturity with due consideration given to players ranging from the unskilled to the expert.

6. Lengths of sports seasons should be limited and maximum number of practice periods and games carefully weighed.

7. Games should be played according to girls' rules and the officiating done by qualified officials.

8. Types of competition should be varied. Intramural competition should be stressed and extramural competition be an outgrowth of the intramural program. Extramural competition should be limited to a small geographic area; should be separate from boys' contests when possible; and should include informal social events after the games.

9. The leadership for the program should be of the highest calibre. The instructing, coaching, and officiating should be by qualified leaders and preferably by women whenever possible.[43]

The second statement, "Policy on Competition for College Women." was adopted by the NAPECW in 1954:

1. The authority for approval of physical education activities involving women students shall rest with the department of physical education for women. This includes intramural activities, extramural activities such as varsity-type competition, play days, sports days, demonstration games, telegraphic meets, dance symposiums, and performances and demonstrations by special groups.

2. Women's varsity-type sports should be conducted only as they meet NSGWS standards of health, participation, leadership, and publicity.

3. Sports days, competition conducted on an informal basis, should not be confused with varsity-type competition; and the emphasis should continue to be on this sports day type.

4. College women shall not participate:
   a. As members of men's intercollegiate athletic teams.
   b. In touch football exhibition games, or any other activities of similar type.
   c. Either with or against men in activities not suitable to competition between men and women such as basketball, touch football, speedball, soccer, hockey, and lacrosse.

43. "Standards for Girls Sports," p. 36.

5. We do not subscribe to college sponsorship of women participating in tournaments and meets with agencies organized
   primarily for competition and for the determination of championships at succesively higher levels (local, sectional, national,
   etc.)

6. Recognizing the great contribution of athletic activities to
   optimum development of children and youth as individuals and
   citizens; the inadequacy of pertinent scientific information; the
   lack of understanding and appreciation of desirable programs;
   the concern and study of other professional groups toward the
   solution of the problems involved, the Board of Directors of
   NAPECW recommends that the efforts of colleges and members of NAPECW may most appropriately be directed toward:

   a. Better informed communities through cooperation with
      local professional and lay groups and individuals in de-
      veloping and maintaining desirable athletic programs in
      girls and women's sports activities.

   b. Better informed major students through special training in:

      (1) Understanding and appreciation of the problems in-
          volved in competitive activities and acceptable ways
          of facing them;

      (2) Planning for and working with the highly skilled
          girl as well as the girl who is average in skills;

      (3) Consideration of policies, standards, and practices
          basic to sound athletic programs for elementary
          schools as well as secondary schools.

   c. Better informed students in the service program through
      the promotion of understanding and appreciation of desir-
      able athletic programs.

   d. Research on the contribution of athletic activities to op-
      timum development of children and youth.[44]

NSGWS Becomes a Division of the American Association for Health, Physical Education and Recreation.

In 1956 the National Section for Girls and Women's Sports was
invited by the AAHPER Board of Directors to consider changing
from a section to a division. The NSGWS Legislative Board voted to
accept the invitation to petition for tentative divisional status, and
the petition was approved by AAHPER in May, 1957. On June 1,
1957, the NSGWS officially changed its name and status to the Division for Girls and Women's Sports (DGWS). Permanent Division
status was granted to both DGWS and the Division for Men's
Athletics in 1958.

44. "NAPECW Policy Statement," p. 50.

Changing from a Section to a Division involved a reorganization of the governing body from the NSGWS Legislative Board to a Division Executive Council. In conformance with AAHPER structure the title of the former position of chairman was changed to AAHPER vice president and chairman of DGWS, and the vice president became a member of the AAHPER board of directors. Division status also provided for election of the Vice President-Elect by the Representative Assembly.[45, 46]

With the increasing interest in girls and women's sports programs, many questions were asked concerning the DGWS position on competition. Widespread misunderstanding of earlier NSGWA and NAAF documents had led many to think that DGWS opposed competition. In an effort to again clearly define its position, DGWS published in 1957 a "Statement of Policies and Procedures for Competition in Girls and Women's Sports." An examination of this document together with earlier statements on the "Organization of Competitive Events" appearing in the Standards Monographs of 1937, 1948, and 1953 indicates that the 1957 Competition Statement was based upon the philosophy and beliefs expressed previously, but more specific procedures were added and the various types or levels of competition clarified. The Introduction of this document succinctly describes the philosophy:

> The Division for Girls and Women's Sports of the American Association for Health, Physical Education, and Recreation believes the competitive element in sports activities can be used constructively for achievement of desirable educational and recreational objectives. Competition in and of itself does not automatically result in desirable outcomes, but competitive experiences may be wholesome and beneficial if they occur under favorable conditions and result in desirable conduct and attitudes.
>
> The adoption of the best practices for the attainment of desirable outcomes is the responsibility of all associated with competitive events. Sponsoring agencies, players, coaches, officials, and spectators must share responsibility for valid practices in competitive sports if essential values are to be realized.
>
> DGWS believes participation in sports competition is the privilege of all girls and women. Sports needs, interests, and abilities are best met through sports programs which offer a wide variety of activities and provide for varying degrees of skill. Limiting participation in competitive sports to the few highly skilled deprives others of the many different kinds of desirable experiences which are inherent in well-conducted sports programs. Development of all

45. Mott, "Status of New DGWS Sections, pp. 50 – 51.
46. Locke, "Section Becomes Division," p. 60.

participants toward higher competencies and advanced skills is a major objective in all sports programs.

Where the needs of highly skilled girls and women are recognized and served, broad physical education, intramural and informal extramural programs take precedence over an interscholastic program. The latter may be an outgrowth of such programs but is not a substitute.[47]

Forms of competition were defined in this Statement as follows:

Intramural Competition is defined as sports competition in which all participants are identified with a particular school, community center, club, organization, institution or industry, or are residents of a designated small neighborhood or community. This form of competition stresses the participation of the many. A well-rounded intramural program which offers a variety of activities, including co-recreational activities, at various skill levels should be sufficient to meet the needs and desires of the majority of girls and women. . .

Extramural Competition is defined as the plan of sports competition in which participants from two or more schools, community centers, clubs, organizations, institutions, industries, or neighborhoods compete. As conceived by DGWS, it also seeks to provide a broad-base plan for competitive activities for participants of all levels of skill.

The most desirable forms of extramural competition are Sports Days (school group participates as a unit), Play Days (representatives from each group are selected to play on Play Day teams), Telegraphic Meets (results are compared by wire or mail), other Invitational Events (such as symposium, jamboree, game, or match).

The extramural play also encompasses the supervised Interscholastic or Intercollegiate form of competitive activities for selected groups trained and coached to play a series of scheduled games and tournaments with similar teams from other schools, cities, or institutions within a limited geographic area. It should be offered only when it does not interfere with the intramural and extramural programs.[48]

A further revised "Statement of Policies for Competition in Girls and Women's Sports" was approved by DGWS in May, 1963. The major change involved the deletion of play days and the inclusion of interscholastic and intercollegiate programs as acceptable forms of extramural competition. It was stated in this document that for colleges and universities, "it is desirable that opportunities be provided

---

47. "Statement of Policies and Procedures," p. 57.
48. Ibid.

for the highly skilled beyond the intramural program."[49] It was further recommended that regulations for the conduct of collegiate competition, developed by the National Joint Committee on Extramural Sports for College Women, be followed.

National Joint Committee on Extramural Sports for Women

The National Joint Committee on Extramural Sports for Women (NJCESCW) was an outgrowth of the Tripartite Committee on Golf for College Women appointed in 1956 to evaluate the Women's Collegiate Golf Tournament. The Golf Tournament had been started at Ohio State University in 1941, and was held there for eight years. After 1952 it was conducted by the women's physical education department in four other institutions. The Tripartite Committee, formed of representatives appointed by NAPECW, the Division for Girls and Women's Sports of AAHPER, and the American Recreation Federation of College Women, first met at Purdue University in 1956 and adjudged the tournament to have been an enjoyable experience for college women golfers of all skill levels. This committee subsequently was charged with the responsibility of establishing policies and practices for the organization and administration of the golf tournament.[50]

The following year a Council on Extramural Sports Competition was appointed by the same three organizations to study the larger implications of extramural sports competition for college women. The Council met in 1957 at the University of Illinois in conjunction with the Women's Intercollegiate Golf Tournament. The Council adopted a Statement of Beliefs and Recommendations for Action; identified problem areas; proposed a survey on extramural sports for college women; and proposed approval for sports events organized for a statewide or larger geographic area based upon the development of policies and procedures which met the standards of the three organizations. It was further recommended that there be a National Council on Extramural Sports for College Women, and the recommendation included the proposed structure, functions, and duties of the Council.[51]

NJCESCW was approved in 1958. A statement entitled "Policies and Procedures for the Conduct of Extramural Sports Events for College Women" was developed by NJCESCW in 1959 and approved

49. "Statement of Policies for Competition," p. 32.
50. Porter, "Tripartite Golf Committee," p. 66.
51. Broer, *Biennial Record of NAPECW, 1955–57*, pp. 105 – 16.

by the three parent organizations. The Statement of Belief was as follows:

> Every college woman has the right to expect opportunities for participation in sports which test her skill and knowledge and afford her the satisfaction of equal competition. A sound instructional program and a well organized intramural program are sufficient for many young women. However, for the college woman who is interested in further challenge in competition and skills, a sound, carefully planned and well-directed program of extramural sports is desirable.
>
> It should be the purpose of an extramural event to provide opportunities for college women interested in a sport to participate and compete with women of other institutions who are of comparable skill. Experiences should be provided for women of different skill levels, either within the event or in the over-all extramural program. The events should be so planned and conducted as to extend to participants educational and social benefits beyond those available at the local level. The quality of the program and of the participant's experience will reflect the leadership provided; good leadership is the heart of any sound program.
>
> In the belief that it can assist with the improvement of programs of extramural sports for college women, the Joint Committee has developed policies and procedures for the conduct and administration of such events. The list, based upon the ARFCW Policy Statement on Competitive Sports, the DGWS Standards in Sports for Girls and Women, and the NAPECW Policy on Competition, follows.[52]

Policies and procedures were then listed under the headings of Purpose, Leadership, Administration, and Conduct.

Tripartite sport committees were appointed to develop policies and procedures for the conduct of each sport, and a special committee was established to review applications from schools and organizations desiring the sanction of NJCESCW for their extramural events.

In June, 1964, the NJCESCW recommended to the parent organizations that the Joint Committee be discontinued as of June, 1965, and that its functions be assumed by DGWS. Having established desirable standards for competition for college women, it was felt that the joint committee structure was then inadequate to meet the needs of the increasing scope of college competitive activities.[53]

The 1963 DGWS Statement on Policies for Competition reflected a growing interest in providing more competitive opportunities for

---

52. *Conduct of Intercollegiate and Other Extramural Sports.*
53. Hall, *Biennial Record of NAPECW, 1963–65,* pp. 114 – 16.

girls and women at all levels of skill. With interscholastic and intercollegiate sports programs complementing the instructional and intramural programs in many schools it became apparent that guidelines for this level of competition should be established in order to ensure the achievement of desirable educational objectives for the participants. A Study Conference was sponsored by the DGWS in February of 1965 to determine the problems and to develop the guidelines which would serve the best interests of girls and women desiring competition in this level of sports.[54]

The twenty leaders who attended the Conference, eight men and twelve women, worked mainly in two groups, one developing guidelines for high schools and the other for colleges. The relationship of the intercollegiate and interscholastic to the instructional and intramural programs was clarified in the respective guidelines as follows:

> *High School:* Competitive sports are an important part of the total physical education program for high school girls. A program of intramural and extramural participation should be arranged to augment a sound and inclusive instructional program in physical education. The interscholastic program should not be promoted at the expense of the instructional or the intramural program.[55]

> *College:* An intercollegiate athletic program for women should be an extension of an existing extramural program and in addition to established instructional and intramural offerings. Extended programs should not be attempted without adequate leadership, facilities, and budget in addition to what is needed for the basic programs.[56]

Both groups reiterated in their guidelines the prerequisites for an interscholastic or intercollegiate program appearing in the 1963 Statement on Competition: "For the best welfare of the participants, it is essential that the program be conducted by qualified leaders, be supported by budgeted funds, be representative of approved objectives and standards for girls and women's sports, including acceptable conditions of travel, protective insurance, appropriate facilities, proper equipment and desirable practices in the conduct of events."[57]

Implementation of the high school interscholastic program was delegated to the already existing State High School Athletic Associations but no such organization existed at the college and/or university level to guide and control intercollegiate athletic programs for women. The National Joint Committee had dissolved with the recom-

54. "DGWS Statement on Competition for Girls and Women," p. 34.
55. Ibid., p. 35.
56. Ibid., p. 36.
57. Ibid., p. 34.

mendation that DGWS be charged with its responsibilities. Sensitive to the need for such an organization which could devote itself exclusively to women's intercollegiate athletics, DGWS authorized the formation of the Commission on Intercollegiate Athletics for Women (CIAW). The Commission was approved by the Board of Directors of AAHPER in March, 1966, and began its official operation in September of 1967.[58]

Commission on Intercollegiate Athletics for Women

The purpose of the Commission, as defined in the Operating Code was as follows:

> The purpose of this Commision shall be to encourage and promote philosophically sound, educationally oriented, and physically satisfying intercollegiate athletic contests for college women by:
>
> A.   Developing and publishing guidelines and standards for the conduct of such events.
> B.   Providing assistance in the planning of intercollegiate events.
> C.   Sanctioning of organizational plans for intercollegiate events in which there are participants from five or more schools.
> D.   Providing leadership in the development of DGWS national championships as the need for these becomes apparent.
> E.   Evaluating intercollegiate championships in terms of desired outcomes.
> F.   Encouraging the development of organizational patterns to deal with the conduct of intercollegiate athletic opportunities for college women.[59]

The first edition of Procedures for Women's Intercollegiate Athletic Events was published in 1967.[60] It was designed to serve both as a guide in planning women's intercollegiate events and as a set of procedures which were to be followed by an institution desiring to request sanction for approval of an intercollegiate event by the CIAW. Conditions necessary for sanctioning were described under the categories of facilities, equipment, conduct of events, finances, insurance, medical and first aid services, officials, awards, rules, and eligibility.

At a press conference held on December 7, 1967, Dr. Katherine Ley, Chairman of CIAW, announced that an annual schedule of

58. Scott and Ulrich, "Commission on Intercollegiate Sports," pp. 10, 76.
59. Division for Girls and Women's Sports. "Commission on Intercollegiate Athletics," p. 1.
60. Division for Girls and Women's Sports, *"Procedures for Women's Events."*

national intercollegiate championships in athletics for college women would be initiated in 1969 under the jurisdiction of the Commission. It was further announced that national championships in gymnastics and in track and field were scheduled for 1969, and the following year national championships were to be held in swimming, badminton, and volleyball. In addition, CIAW was to continue sponsorship of the National Golf Tournament, and would continue its cooperation with the U.S. Lawn Tennis Association Championships.[61]

CIAW itself was originally composed of three Commissioners assigned to the individual responsibilities of national championships, sanctioning, and mail tournaments. The Code of Operations adopted by the Commission made provisions for the appointment of commissioners on a three-year basis by the DGWS Vice President. Later a fourth member was added to assume the responsibilities of national championships formerly assigned to the chairman, and regional development was added to the responsibilities of the commissioner in charge of mail tournaments. Three ex-officio members were added as nonvoting members: the DGWS chairman, representative from NAPECW, and the AAHPER consultant for the Division for Girls and Women's Sports.[62]

At the time that CIAW was formed, local, state, and regional groups were at varying stages of organization throughout the country. The establishment of the Commission and the initiation of national championships provided further motivation for these groups to develop under the guidance of the Commission and within the standards and guidelines established by DGWS.

The first National DGWS Conference on Sports Programs for College Women held at Estes Park, Colorado in June, 1969, gave women from all over the country an opportunity to examine the current status and explore future directions of sports programs for college women. Topics explored included ethics and values; programs, problems, and directions; and involvement-interrelationships with other sport organizations and governing bodies including CIAW, NAPECW, and DGWS. The opportunity for interchange and communications resulted in increased knowledge and understanding of the rapid developments that had been taking place in intercollegiate sports.[63]

A similar DGWS National Conference on Girls Sports Programs

61. "DGWS National Intercollegiate Championships," pp. 24 – 27.
62. Division for Girls and Women's Sports, "Commission on Intercollegiate Athletics."
63. Division for Girls and Women's Sports, *Sports Programs.*

for Secondary Schools was held at Estes Park in August, 1971, to examine the current status and future direction of girls' sports in grades 7–12. To accomplish this purpose the program format was designed to: (1) share philosophical concerns with state, city, and school personnel; (2) determine the needs in relation to leadership, understanding, interpretations; (3) examine and explore the implications of cultural, social, and political influences; (4) investigate the relationships among sport clubs, intramurals, extramurals, and interscholastics; (5) examine the nature of competition in relation to the well-being of the participants and the purpose and nature of sports programs; (6) reassess the values of sports programs; (7) explore relationships between school, community and agency-sponsored programs.[64] It was the general concensus of opinion that the trend at the secondary level was to provide more opportunities for girls to participate in intramurals, extramurals, and interscholastic sports.

Fall of 1971 brought still another step forward in women's intercollegiate sports. A joint announcement was made by the chairman of CIAW and the vice president of DGWS, of the formation of a new organization, the Association for Intercollegiate Athletics for Women (AIAW), to provide direction and leadership for women's intercollegiate sports in the United States. The proposed operating code for this organization was developed by CIAW in consultation with representatives from various regional governing groups, to continue and expand the purpose and functions formerly carried out by the Commission.[65] A more complete description of this organization is given in the next chapter.

The reorganization of the American Association for Health, Physical Education and Recreation into the American Alliance of Health, Physical Education and Recreation (AAHPER), approved in 1974, has resulted in yet another change in name, structure, and function for the former DGWS. This organization is now called the National Association for Girls and Women in Sport (NAGWS) and is discussed more fully in the following chapter.

The Women's Board of the United States Olympic Development Committee

Another organization which has been influential in promoting competitive sports programs for girls and women is the Women's Board of the United States Olympic Development Committee. First

---

64. Barron, "Report of First DGWS National Conference," pp. 14 – 17.
65. Magnusson, "What and Why of AIAW," p. 71.

appointed as a Women's Advisory Board in 1961, the Women's Board in 1963 became a functional organization under the auspices of the United States Olympic Development Committee. Its purpose is the same as that of the Olympic Development Committee, that is, "to expand, improve and coordinate programs involving Olympic activities . . . by:

> Working to increase opportunities for girls and women to participate in sports.
>
> Increasing opportunities for the skilled girl to reach her potential in sports.
>
> Providing opportunities for women physical educators, coaches and recreation leaders to become more competent in teaching and coaching girls in specific sports.
>
> Providing opportunities for women to become more competent in officiating and judging Olympic sports.
>
> Providing opportunities for women physical educators and leaders to clarify and to give leadership toward properly organized and administered sports experiences for girls and women.
>
> Interpreting the role of competition in our culture and society both nationally and internationally.[66]

One of the most significant activities of the Women's Board has been the development of National Institutes on Girls' Sports in cooperation with the DGWS of AAHPER. The purpose has been to increase the depth of experience and expand the opportunities for girls and women in sports. The following five institutes have been held:

- Gymnastics and Track and Field, 1963[67]
- Fencing, Diving, Kayaking and Canoeing, Gymnastics, and Track and Field, 1965[68]
- Figure Skating and Skiing, 1966[69]
- Coaching Basketball and Volleyball, 1966[70]
- Basketball Coaching and Officiating, Gymnastics Officiating, and Track and Field, 1968[71]

These institutes have brought teachers from all over the country together to improve their competence in teaching, coaching, and officiating under expert instruction. Follow-up workshops given by

66. Women's Board, "Purpose - History."
67. *Proceedings, First National Institute,* 1965.
68. *Proceedings, Second National Institute,* 1966.
69. *Proceedings, Third National Institute,* 1967.
70. *Proceedings, Fourth National Institute,* 1968.
71. *Proceedings, Fifth National Institute,* 1969.

institute participants have strengthened local programs throughout the country.

SUMMARY

In tracing the somewhat tedious historical development of competitive sports for girls and women, the authors have in this chapter attempted to present an overview of organizations and events which have through the years influenced the development of sports programs for girls and women in educational institutions.

Because these series of events are difficult to follow we have in the next few paragraphs attempted to summarize the most important facts for the reader.

With the appointment of the first committee to develop basketball rules in 1899 by the American Association for the Advancement of Physical Education Council, a pattern was established in which women physical educators, concerned with girls and women's sports programs, united as a group within the national association to promote desirable standards and guidelines for such programs and to provide services necessary for the conduct of such programs. Through each stage of its growth, the organization now known as the National Association for Girls and Women in Sport (NAGWS; formerly DGWS) has expanded its services, and has gained increased recognition as the organization representing the best interests of girls and women who are desirous of participating in educational sports programs.

Inherent in the guidelines and standards currently expressed by NAGWS is much the same philosophy which was originally developed by the Women's Division of the National Amateur Athletic Federation. This group, organized in 1923, promoted sports for all girls and women and worked diligently to oppose the exploitation of girls through athletics. The Women's Division subsequently united with the National Section on Women's Athletics in 1940.

In 1917 the National Athletic Conference of American College Women was organized to promote the development of women's athletic associations to replace intercollegiate athletics in colleges and universities.

A few years later, in 1924, the Organization of Directors of Physical Education for Women in Colleges and Universities was developed. Although this group was concerned with all aspects of physical education for college women, the sports program was frequently discussed and recommendations made.

As competitive sports flourished outside the control of educational institutions during the 1920s and 1930s, these four groups spoke out against the exploitation of girls in athletics and made resolutions condemning the participation of women in the Olympic Games. Emphasis was placed on providing sports programs for all girls, and intercollegiate and interscholastic competition was replaced with intramural programs.

With the increasing interest, during the 1950s, in providing opportunities for competition for more highly skilled girls, the Division for Girls and Women's Sports, the Athletic and Recreation Federation of College Women (formerly the National Athletic Conference of American College Women) and the National Association for Physical Education of College Women (formerly the Organization of Directors of Physical Education for Women in Colleges and Universities) joined forces in developing the National Joint Committee on Extramural Sports for College Women (NJCESCW) as a means of guiding the growth of such programs. When the task of coordination became unwieldy, responsibility for the control of such programs was given by ARFCW and NAPECW to DGWS. Since DGWS was not organized to serve as a governing body for either interscholastic or intercollegiate sports, the Commission for Intercollegiate Athletics for Women (CIAW) was organized to control intercollegiate sports, and the National Federation of State High School Associations was recommended as the organization to control interscholastic sports.

References

"AAHPER's Section on Girls and Women's Sports." JOHPER 24, no. 4 (April 1953): 32–33.

Ainsworth, Dorothy. *History of Physical Education in Colleges for Women.* New York: A.S. Barnes, 1930.

"Athletic and Recreation Federation of College Women." JOHPER 38, no. 1 (January 1967): 34–35, 66.

Barron, Alice A. "Report of the First DGWS National Conference on Girls Sports Programs for the Secondary Schools." JOHPER 42, no. 9 (November-December 1971).

Bishop, Thelma. "DGWS – A Permanent AAHPER Division." JOHPER 28, no. 7 (October 1957): 56–58.

Broer, Marion R., ed. *Biennial Record of the National Association for Physical Education of College Women 1955–57*. Washington, D.C.: National Association for Physical Education of College Women, 1958.

Cheska, Alyce. "Current Developments in Competitive Sports for Girls and Women." JOHPER 41, no. 3 (March 1970): 86–91.

Coffey, Margaret A. "The Sportswoman Then and Now." JOHPER 36, no. 2 (February 1965): 38–41, 50.

Conduct of Intercollegiate and Other Extramural Sports for College Women. National Association for Physical Education of College Women, Athletic and Recreation Federation of College Women, Division for Girls and Women's Sports.

Division for Girls and Women's Sports. *Philosophy and Standards for Girls and Women's Sports*. Washington, D.C.: AAHPER, 1969.

Division for Girls and Women's Sports. *Commission on Intercollegiate Athletics for Women Operating Code*. Washington, D.C.: AAHPER, November 1969.

Division for Girls and Women's Sports. *Procedures for Women's Intercollegiate Athletic Events*. Washington, D.C.: AAHPER, 1967.

Division for Girls and Women's Sports. *Sports Programs for College Women*. Washington, D.C.: AAHPER, 1970.

Division for Girls and Women's Sports. *Standards in Sports for Girls and Women*. Washington, D.C.: AAHPER, 1958.

"DGWS National Intercollegiate Athletic Championships for Women." JOHPER 39, no. 2 (February 1968).

"DGWS Statement on Competition for Girls and Women: Guidelines for High School Programs, Guidelines for College and University Programs." JOHPER 36, no. 7 (September 1965): 34–37.

Dudley, Gertrude, and Kellor, Frances A. *Athletic Games in the Education of Women*. New York: Henry Holt & Co., 1909.

"Extramural Sports for Women." JOHPER 31, no. 9 (December 1960): 63.

"Guidelines for Interscholastic Athletic Programs for Junior High School Girls." JOHPER 37, No. 7 (September 1966): 36–37.

Hackensmith, C.W. *History of Physical Education.* New York: Harper & Row Publishers, 1966.

Hall, Barbara C. ed. *Biennial Record of the National Association for Physical Education of College Women 1963–65,* Washington, D.C.: AAHPER, 1966.

Halsey, Elizabeth. *The Life and Lights of the NAPECW.* National Association for Physical Education of College Women, 1962.

Hillas, Marjorie, and Knighton, Marian. *An Athletic Program for High School and College Women.* New York: A.S. Barnes & Co. 1929.

Lee, Mabel. *The Conduct of Physical Education.* New York: A.S. Barnes & Co. 1937.

Lee, Mabel, and Bennett, Bruce. "This Is Our Heritage." JOHPER 31, no. 4 (April 1960): 25–76.

Ley, Katherine, and Jernigan, Sara Staff. "The Roots and the Tree." JOHPER 33, no. 6 (September 1962) 34–36, 57.

Locke, Mabel. "The Section Becomes a Division." JOHPER 29, no. 4 (April 1958).

Magnusson, Lucille. "The What and Why of AIAW." JOHPER 43, no. 3 (March 1972).

Metheny, Eleanor. *Connotations of Movement in Sport and Dance.* Dubuque, Iowa: Wm. C. Brown Company Publishers, 1965.

Mott, Jane A. "Status of New DGWS Sections and Convention Forecast." JOHPER 28, no. 9 (December 1957).

NAPECW Policy Statement." JOHPER 25, no. 10 (December 1954).

National Section for Girls and Women's Sports. *Standards in Sports for Girls and Women.* Washington, D.C.: AAHPER, 1953.

National Section for Girls and Women's Sports. *The Story of the National Leadership Conference on Girls and Women's Sports.* Washington, D.C.: AAHPER, 1956.

National Section on Women's Athletics. *Standards in Athletics for Girls and Women.* Washington, D.C.: AAHPER, 1937.

Porter, Nancy. "Tripartite Golf Committee." JOHPER 29, no. 1 (January 1958).

Proceedings, First National Institute on Girls Sports. Washington, D.C.: AAHPER, 1965.

Proceedings, Second National Institute on Girls Sports. Washington, D.C.: AAHPER, 1966.

Proceedings, Third National Institute on Girls Sports. Washington, D.C.: AAHPER, 1967.

Proceedings, Fourth National Institute on Girls Sports. Washington, D.C.: AAHPER, 1968.

Proceedings, Fifth National Institute on Girls Sports. Washington, D.C.: AAHPER, 1969.

Remley, Mary Louise. "Twentieth Century Concepts of Sports Competition for Women." Ph.D. dissertation, University of Southern California, 1970.

Rice, Emmett A.; Hutchinson, John; and Lee, Mabel. *A Brief History of Physical Education.* New York: Ronald Press Co., 1958.

Scott, Phebe M., and Ulrich, Celeste. "Commission on Intercollegiate Sports for Women." JOHPER 37, no. 8 (October 1966).

Sefton, Alice A. *The Women's Division National Amateur Athletic Federation.* California: Stanford University Press, 1941.

Soladay, Doris. "Functions and Purposes of NSGWS." JOHPER 27, no. 7 (October 1956): 51, 53.

Somers, Florence. *Principles of Women's Athletics.* New York: A.S. Barnes & Co., 1930.

Spears, Betty. "The Emergence of Sport in Physical Education." Paper presented at the AAHPER National Convention, April 13–17 1973, Minneapolis.

"Sports Competition for College Women." JOHPER 28, no. 8 (November 1957): 64.

"Standards for Girls Sports in Secondary Schools." JOHPER 25, no. 8 (October 1954).

"Statement of Policies and Procedures for Competition in Girls and Women's Sports." JOHPER 28, no. 6 (September 1957).

"Statement of Policies for Competition in Girls and Women's Sports." JOHPER 34, no. 7 (September 1963).

United States Olympic Development Committee. *Proceedings National Conference on Olympic Development.* Washington, D.C.: AAHPER, 1966.

Von Borries, Eline. *History and Functions of the National Section on Women's Athletics.* Washington, D.C.: AAHPER, 1941.

Van Dalen, Deobold B.; Mitchell, Elmer D.; and Bennett, Bruce L. *A World History of Physical Education.* Englewood Cliffs, N.J.: Prentice-Hall, 1953.

Wayman, Agnes R. *Education Through Physical Education.* Philadelphia: Lea and Febiger, 1928.

"Women's Athletic Committee." *American Physical Education Review* 23, (1923).

Women's Board of the United States Olympic Development Committee. "Purpose — History — Accomplishments — Needs."

"Women in Athletics." JOHPER 24, no. 3 (March 1953): 50–51.

Women's Division, National Amateur Athletic Federation. *Women and Athletics.* New York: A.S. Barnes & Co., 1930.

FORE!
Photograph by Gary Moats
California State University, Long Beach

CHAPTER 8

Current Organizational Structure of Competitive Sports Programs

The purpose of this chapter is to assist the reader in becoming more familiar with the leadership and functions of *current* organizations which serve in an advisory or regulatory role in governing interscholastic and intercollegiate sports programs at the national, state, and local levels: the National Association for Girls and Women in Sport; the Association for Intercollegiate Athletics for Women; the College Women in Sport; and the National Federation of State High School Associations. The chapter begins with a summary describing the functions of each and then concludes with details about each.

DGWS (now NAGWS) is an advisory group which through the years has been influential in promoting desirable sports programs by recommending guidelines and standards for the conduct of such programs. Although never a regulatory organization, its service through the publication and interpretation of rules, through the training and rating of officials, and through its many other publications, has been of primary importance in the development of sound competitive sports programs for secondary schools, colleges, and community recreation agencies. In addition, DGWS has provided consultant service for student organizations which have been concerned with sports.

Realizing the need for the development of regulatory bodies for the rapidly expanding intercollegiate sports programs, the DGWS organized the Commission for Intercollegiate Athletics for Women (CIAW), an organization which subsequently and presently is organized as the Association for Intercollegiate Athletics for Women. As AIAW, it has become the regulatory body at the national level for women's intercollegiate sports, and although its policies and procedures are geared basically for national championships, member institutions and local and regional governing groups operate under its jurisdiction.

At the high school level, the National Federation of State High School Associations (NFSHSA), which is responsible for controlling boys' interscholastic athletics, was deemed to be in the best position to assume control of the girls' interscholastic sports program. As has been pointed out, state high school associations, with the assistance of women advisory committees, are now the governing authority for interscholastic sports programs for girls within their respective states.

NATIONAL ASSOCIATION FOR GIRLS AND WOMEN IN SPORT

The American Association for Health, Physical Education and Recreation was reorganized in 1974 and became the American Alliance for Health, Physical Education and Recreation (AAHPER). Among the seven associations functioning under the Alliance is the National Association for Girls and Women in Sport (NAGWS). Formerly known as the Division for Girls and Women's Sports (DGWS), this group has assumed leadership throughout the years and has served as the spokesman for women physical educators on desirable sports programs for girls and women. The historical development of the DGWS, from the appointment of the first Women's Basketball Committee in 1899 to its status as a Division in AAHPER was presented in chapter 7. It is the intent of this section to explain the purpose and function of this Association, and to bring into focus the currently revised structure for carrying out these functions.

The stated purpose of the NAGWS is to foster the "development of sports programs for the enrichment of the life of the participant."[1] As a foundation for its leadership in reaching toward this goal, the former Division (DGWS) developed a Statement of Beliefs which appear in chapter 1.

The Division for Girls and Women's Sports promotes desirable sports programs through:

1. Formulating and publicizing guiding principles and standards for the administrator, leader, official, and player.
2. Publishing and interpreting rules governing sports for girls and women.
3. Providing the means for training, evaluating, and rating officials.
4. Disseminating information on the conduct of girls and women's sports.
5. Stimulating, evaluating, and disseminating research in the field of girls and women's sports.

1. Division for Girls and Women's Sports, *Philosophy and Standards*, p. 5.

6. Cooperating with allied groups interested in girls and women's sports in order to formulate policies and rules that affect the conduct of women's sports.

7. Providing opportunities for the development of leadership among girls and women for the conduct of their sports programs.[2]

As preparation for becoming an Association for Girls and Women in Sport under the new Alliance, the structure of the former Division was reorganized to provide for better services to members, to give members more voice in decision making, and to improve the lines of communication.

The board of directors of NAGWS is made up of twelve voting members. The president, president-elect, past president and a member-at-large are elected by a mail vote of the total NAGWS membership. The remaining eight voting members are chosen by autonomous groups which assume responsibility for a particular phase of girls' and women's sports programs. These groups or categories which elect a member to represent them on the board of directors are:

1. Organization of GWS State Chairpersons
2. Affiliated boards of officials
3. National Coaches Council
4. Organizations with club sports, intramural or sports interest focus
5. Organization for sports promotion at the secondary level
6. Association for Intercollegiate Athletics for Women
7. Organization of Students for Girls and Women in Sport
8. Public representative.

Nonvoting members on the board of directors include representatives selected from school-affiliated organizations with a sport focus and non-school-affiliated organizations with a sport focus.

Standing committees to carry out the functions of NAGWS include: Bylaws; Fiscal; Nominating; Recognition Award; Publications; Liaison; Rules; Research; Officiating Standards; Examinations and Techniques; Membership; Guides.

The Officiating Standards, Examinations and Techniques Committee (1) determines the mechanics used by referees, umpires, and judges in officiating games, meets or matches; (2) prepares, revises, and analyzes the officiating theoretical examinations; and (3) pro-

2. Ibid., p. 6.

vides materials for the training and rating of officials and sets standards for officiating ratings.

The actual training and rating of officials is carried out by local boards of officials. Officiating ratings are established for badminton, basketball, gymnastics, softball, swimming, synchronized swimming, tennis, track and field, and volleyball. Criteria have been established with respect to the formation of local officiating boards, and certain qualifications must be met in order to be able to give ratings in each sport. A list of all officiating boards with the sports in which ratings are given appears in the Basketball Guide published each year. In addition, the guide for each sport contains the list of officiating boards which give ratings in that particular sport.

A section on "standards for officiating ratings" is included in each guide. Qualifications for types of ratings in each sport are described. Also included is information on the amateur standing of officials for the various sports, steps indicating how to become a rated official, pertinent information for affiliated and provisional boards and the procedures to be followed in establishing a board of officials.

The Sports Guides and Official Rules Committee revises and interprets rules, and edits and publishes numerous Guides: Aquatics, Archery-Golf, Basketball, Bowling-Fencing, Field Hockey-Lacrosse, Gymnastics, Outing Activities and Winter Sports, Soccer-Speedball-Flag Football, Softball, Tennis-Badminton-Squash, Track and Field, and Volleyball.

In addition to the Guides mentioned above, the NAGWS publishes a number of other publications. A list of these is included in each guide, and can be ordered from the American Alliance for Health, Physical Education and Recreation, 1201 Sixteenth Street, N.W., Washington, D.C. 20036.

The Liaison Committee maintains relationships with allied national sports and educational groups through representatives to: Amateur Athletic Union and the United States Olympic Committees for basketball, diving, gymnastics, swimming, synchronized swimming, and track and field; Council for National Cooperation in Aquatics; Women's Collegiate Advisory Committee of the United States Lawn Tennis Association; United States Federation for Basketball, Gymnastics, Track and Field; United States Volleyball and United States Olympic Committee for Volleyball; Women's National Aquatics Forum; National Association for Physical Education of College Women; and the National Federation of State High School Athletic Associations.

The functions of NAGWS at the state level are carried out by a

NAGWS state chairman and committee who serve the needs and interests of administrators, teachers, leaders, coaches, and participants of sports programs for girls and women in schools, colleges, recreation agencies, community centers, industrial plants, military services, and so on. Although there is no set pattern for the organization of state committees, many include a chairman for each sport, officiating board chairmen, representatives from local units of the state Health, Physical Education and Recreation (HPER) Association, and special representatives from allied organizations. State services include conducting clinics, workshops, and master lessons in specific sports, providing information on rating examinations and rule interpretation clinics for officials, working with the State High School Athletic Federation and other allied organizations in establishing desirable sports programs for girls and women, keeping state HPER executive committee and members informed of standards and guidelines adopted at the national level, as well as aware of national publications, trends, and decisions.

ASSOCIATION FOR INTERCOLLEGIATE ATHLETICS FOR WOMEN

The Association for Intercollegiate Athletics for Women (AIAW) became operative on July 1, 1972. The significance of its initiation is best described by the communication sent to all two- and four-year institutions of higher education by CIAW Chairman, Lucille Magnusson, and DGWS Vice President, Jo Anne Thorpe, dated September 15, 1971:

> It is with anticipation and a sense of history in the making that the Commission on Intercollegiate Athletics for Women extends to your institution an invitation to charter membership in a new organization. The Association for Intercollegiate Athletics will provide direction and leadership for women's intercollegiate programs in the United States of America.[3]

Purposes of this organization, as outlined in the *AIAW Handbook* are:

> 1. To foster broad programs of women's intercollegiate athletics which are consistent with the educational aims and objectives of the member schools and in accordance with the philosophy and standards of the NAGWS.

3. Commission on Intercollegiate Athletics, Letter from Lucille Magnusson.

2. To assist member schools in extending and enriching their programs of intercollegiate athletics for women based upon the needs, interests, and capacities of the individual student.

3. To stimulate the development of quality leadership for women's intercollegiate athletic programs.

4. To foster programs which will encourage excellence in performance of participants in women's intercollegiate athletics.

5. To maintain the spirit of play within competitive sport events so that the concomitant educational values of such an experience are emphasized.

6. To increase public understanding and appreciation of the importance and value of sports and athletics as they contribute to the enrichment of the life of the woman.

7. To encouarge and facilitate research on the effects of intercollegiate athletic competition on women and to disseminate the findings.

8. To further the continual evaluation of standards and policies for participants and programs.

9. To produce and distribute such materials as will be of assistance to persons in the development and improvement of intercollegiate programs.

10. To hold national championships and to sponsor conferences, institutes, and meetings which will meet the needs of individuals in member schools.

11. To cooperate with other professional groups of similar interests for the ultimate development of sports programs and opportunities for women.

12. To provide direction and maintain a relationship with AIAW regional organizations.

13. To conduct such other activities as shall be approved by the governing body of the Association.[4]

Active charter memberships were available in 1971–72 to colleges and universities meeting membership criteria. Requirements include being an accredited college or university of higher education in the United States or its territories, providing an intercollegiate athletic program for women, and being willing to abide by the policies stated in the *AIAW Handbook*. In addition, an institution applying for membership must belong to the official governing organization in its region.

The payment of active membership fees entitles the institution to one vote in the Association; copies of the *Handbook*, *Directory*, newsletters, and informational materials; opportunity for participa-

4. Association for Intercollegiate Athletics, *AIAW Handbook,* p. 8.

tion at AIAW national championships; and attendance at coaches' and athletic directors' meetings.

An associate membership is available for institutions subscribing to the policies, and such membership entitles the institution to a copy of the *Handbook, Directory,* newsletters, and informational materials; a voice but no vote in the Association; and attendance at coaches' and athletic directors' meetings at AIAW national intercollegiate championships upon payment of a registration fee. An affiliate membership is available for organizations not eligible for active or associate membership, but who are interested in supporting AIAW, and such membership entitles the organization to a copy of the *Handbook, Directory,* and Newsletters.

AIAW is administered by an executive board which is responsible for general policy implementation and the overall operation of the organization. The members of the executive board include officers elected by the total membership: President, President-Elect, Past-President, Treasurer, Commissioner of National Championships, Commission of Junior/Community College National Championships, Ethics and Eligibility Chairperson; nine regional representatives elected by the AIAW member schools within each region; one junior college representative elected by junior/community college AIAW member schools; and the NAGWS president.

The First Delegate Assembly of the AIAW, convened in November, 1973, was made up of the appointed voting representatives from each active member institution. The AIAW constitution was approved by the Assembly, and the constitution and bylaws were later ratified by a mail ballot of the official voting delegates of each institution.

Basic to the structure of AIAW is the regional organization, for which the United States was divided into nine geographic regions, taking into account natural competitive boundaries and retaining already established governing groups wherever possible. One person from each region, elected by the member schools within that region, serves as representative on the executive board. Each region is responsible for holding qualifying events where specified by AIAW. Regional organizations existing at the present time are as follows:

Region 1   Eastern (EAIAW)

A. Northeast — Connecticut, Maine, Massachusetts, New Hampshire, Rhode Island, Vermont

B. Mid-Atlantic — Delaware, District of Columbia, Maryland, New Jersey, Pennsylvania, New York

Region 2   Southern — Kentucky, North Carolina, South Carolina, Tennessee

Region 3   Southeastern — Alabama, Florida, Georgia, Mississippi

Region 4   Southwest — Arkansas, Louisiana, Oklahoma, Texas

Region 5   Midwest (MAIAW) — Illinois, Indiana, Michigan, Ohio, West Virginia, Wisconsin

Region 6   "Region 6" AIAW — Iowa, Kansas, Minnesota, Missouri, Nebraska, North Dakota, South Dakota

Region 7   Intermountain — Arizona, Colorado, New Mexico, Utah, Wyoming

Region 8   Western (WAIAW) — California, Hawaii, Nevada

Region 9   Northwest College Women's Sports Association — Alaska, Idaho, Montana, Oregon, Washington

COLLEGE WOMEN IN SPORT

The Athletic Conference of American College Women was established in 1917 as a student organization for college women interested in sports. By 1933 the name had been changed to the Athletic Federation of College Women and, by 1936, a platform had been developed, seven national conferences had been held, and standards for conducting playdays and sports days had been established. Geographical sections were developed, were replaced by districts, and state associations grew. Regional associations came into being in 1955. The name of the organization was changed in 1957 to the Athletic and Recreation Federation of College Women (ARFCW).[5]

In 1962 ARFCW associated with the Division for Girls and Women's Sports and since that time has been served by a consultant for student services on the national headquarters staff for AAHPER.

The purpose of this student organization was to promote interest in sports and athletics for girls and women, and to improve the quality of intramural and extramural sports activities. Membership was open to any junior college, college, or university having an association which provided opportunities for participation and student leadership in athletic and recreational activities for women, and which was a qualified student organization on the local campus.

Member schools received *Sportlight,* a magazine for college sportswomen, published three times a year, as well as a packet of materials containing ideas for the improvement of sports programs.

5. Flinchum, "DGWS Involvement," pp. 79–80.

ARFCW held national conferences biennially in the odd-numbered years, with regional conferences being held in the even-numbered years. These conferences, including annual state conferences, provided an opportunity for the participants to discuss various topics of interest pertinent to college women taking part in sports and recreational programs.

At the 23rd ARFCW Conference held at the University of California, Berkeley, in the spring of 1971, the delegates voted to adopt a new name, College Women in Sport (CWS), to eliminate the existing constitution, and to approve new guidelines for operation. Sport, as used in the title, was defined as "any sport and/or dance activity used for recreational, performance, and/or competitive purposes."[6] The purpose of College Women in Sport was stated as follows: "To bring college women together in a biennial conference, which would encourage leadership, promote an exchange of ideas, and further nationwide interest in sport for college women."[7] College Women in Sport thus became an organization functioning solely to sponsor a biennial conference, with the Chairperson School, elected at each conference, responsible for hostessing and presiding over the next conference.

NATIONAL FEDERATION OF STATE HIGH SCHOOL ASSOCIATIONS

The National Federation of State High School Associations (NFSHSA) is made up of the fifty individual state high school athletic and/or activities associations and the association of the District of Columbia. Its function is best described in its Statement of Philosophy:

> Interscholastic athletics shall be an integral part of the total secondary school educational program that has as its purpose to provide educational experiences not otherwise provided in the curriculum, which will develop learning outcomes in the areas of knowledge, skills and emotional patterns and will contribute to the development of better citizens. Emphasis shall be upon teaching "through" athletics in addition to teaching the "skills" of athletics.
>
> Interschool athletics shall be primarily for the benefit of the high school students who participate directly and vicariously in them. The interscholastic athletic program shall exist mainly for the value which it has for students and not for the benefit of the sponsoring institutions. The activities and contests involved shall be psycholog-

6. Athletic and Recreation Federation, "ARFCW Becomes CWS," p. 19.
7. Ibid.

ically sound by being tailored to the physical, mental, and emotional maturity levels of the youth participating in them.

Any district and/or state athletic meet competition to determine a so-called champion shall provide opportunities for schools to demonstrate and to evaluate the best taught in their programs with the best taught in other schools and in other areas of the state.

Participation in interscholastic activities is a privilege to be granted to those students who meet the minimum standards of eligibility adopted cooperatively by the schools through their state associations and those additional standards established by each school for its own students.

The state high school associations and the National Federation shall be concerned with the development of those standards, policies, and regulations essential to assist their member schools in the implementation of their philosophy of interscholastic athletics. Interschool activities shall be kept in proper perspective and must supplement the academic program of the schools.

Nonschool activities sponsored primarily for the benefit of the participants in accordance with a philosophy compatible with the school philosophy of interscholastics may have values for youth. When they do not interfere with the academic and interscholastic programs and do not result in exploitation of youth, they shall be considered as a worthwhile supplement to interschool activities.[8]

The Federation is administered by an executive committee of eight members elected by the National Council, one from each geographical section. The National Council consists of one representative elected from each member association and is the legislative body of the Federation. Bylaws of the Federation include articles on the eligibility of players for interstate contests, provisions governing interstate contests, and playing rules. It is important to note that the third article states "The Executive Committee shall be authorized to set up machinery for the formulation, publication, and distribution of playing rules for those sports in which high school students participate. At their discretion, they may negotiate with the National Collegiate Athletic Association, the Y.M.C.A., and similar organizations with a view to securing adequate active representation for the National Federation on joint committees where such committees seem to be desirable."[9] The Federation also publishes recommended minimum eligibility requirements which were discussed in chapter 2.

Most state high school associations supervise all activities for both boys and girls. The increased interest in providing interscholastic

---

8. National Federation of State High School Associations, 1974–1975, *NFSHSA Handbook,* p. 8.
9.   Ibid., p. 15.

athletics for girls was studied by the NFSHSAA Competition Committee at its meeting in 1964. The following resolution was approved and adopted by the National Federation:

> WHEREAS, it is the responsibility of the Board of Education and its duly appointed principals and superintendents to administer the educational program of the school, and
>
> WHEREAS, interscholastic athletics are a part of the educational program of the school, and
>
> WHEREAS, it is the duty, obligation and responsibility of each school to determine its program, and
>
> WHEREAS, the administrators of the schools of the several states and provinces have caused to be created the high school athletic or activities association for the purpose of controlling, organizing, and supervising such interscholastic programs as may be deemed by them necessary and desirable to serve the interscholastic needs of boys and girls and
>
> WHEREAS, there is an increasing interest in the development of interscholastic programs for girls;
>
> THEREFORE be it resolved that the National Federation of State High School Athletic Associations assembled in Jackson Lake, Wyoming on this day, July 1, 1964, hereby recommends and urges that all control and supervision of girls' interscholastic athletics be administered through existing state and provincial athletic or activities associations.[10]

The rationale behind this resolution follows:

> The purpose of this resolution was to urge state associations to recognize the feasibility and advisability of conducting a girls' interscholastic program in athletics which would probably differ considerably from that conducted for the boys. However, it was felt necessary that these programs conducted for the girls should be administered by those associations which are controlled by the member high schools. If athletics for girls or boys are to contribute to the general well-being of high school students, then it follows that these programs must necessarily be administered by professional educators who are familiar with the needs of the school and the developmental progress of youth. Moreover, it is highly important that those who administer these programs be responsible to the local taxpayers and patrons of the district for insuring that interscholastic athletic activities are to serve the best interest of girls, it is important that these interests be formally outlined and that the program follow the dictates of school administrators. The girls' program as well as the boys' program must be protected from exploitation by non-school groups.

10. National Federation of State High School Athletic Associations, *1970–71 NFSHSAA Handbook*, p. 63.

The purpose of founding the state association was to eliminate this type of overzealousness on the part of any interested group in conducting the interscholastic program. There is a vehicle through which schools can operate and be assured that the program does meet certain standards and serves the best interests of education. This is the state athletic or activities association in existence. There is no need for any additional organization to try to subject its standards (and presumably its authority) on a developing program which can actually be handled with the machinery now at hand.[11]

At the DGWS Study Conference on Competition for Girls and Women held in February, 1965, the following principles were formulated and later endorsed by the DGWS Board:

Competitive sports are an important part of the total physical education program for high school girls. A program of intramural and extramural participation should be arranged to augment a sound and inclusive instructional program in physical education. The interscholastic program should not be promoted at the expense of the instructional or the intramural programs.

As the interscholastic program is expanded, the State High School Athletic Association will be the regulatory body for its member schools. For schools that are not members a regulatory body may need to be formed. The state Department of Education should be involved.

1. Existing legislative and administrative bodies for interscholastic programs will retain ultimate control of the total program for girls within the state. However, a women's advisory board composed mainly of women high school physical educators will be formed to propose policies to these administrative and legislative groups and to review policies approved by them.

2. Total responsibility for the administration and supervision of the local interscholastic athletic program is vested in the local school administration and the appropriate persons designated by the administration.

3. The responsibility for leadership of the local girls' interscholastic program should be delegated to the women physical education teachers. The school administration should delegate to them the major responsibility for planning, organizing, coaching, and supervising the program with the understanding that the ultimate authority remains in the hands of the administration.

. . .

7. DGWS approved standards should be used in all sports. It is strongly recommended that DGWS rules be used in those sports in which DGWS publishes rules.[12]

11. Ibid.
12. Division for Girls and Women's Sports, *Philosophy and Standards*, p. 43.

A major problem developed between DGWS and NFSHSAA in 1969 when it was learned that NFSHSAA was considering the publishing of girls rules. Discussions between the two groups followed, with NFSHSAA officers expressing the point of view that only regulatory bodies should make policies, and DGWS officers pointing out that policies and guidelines recommended by DGWS become regulations only when adopted by a regulatory organization. Despite the concern expressed by DGWS, the Federation decided, in February, 1970, to publish basketball rules for secondary school girls. Although the NFSHSAA is not insisting that their state federations use these rules, nevertheless it is obvious that each state association will be forced to make a decision between the adoption of NFSHSAA or DGWS rules. To express the concern of DGWS that women have a voice, through a DGWS advisory committee working with the state high school association, in determining their own programs and the policies that regulate them, the following resolution was passed by the DGWS Executive Council in 1971:

> WHEREAS, the State High School Associations are committed to providing educationally sound sports programs and are the bodies legally constituted and responsible for the direction and conduct of all interschool programs, and
>
> WHEREAS, the Division for Girls and Women's Sports of AAHPER shares in the educational goals of the state associations and has a professional interest in maintaining high standards in sports programs for girls,
>
> THEREFORE, be it resolved that the DGWS urge the high school women in every state to participate in the development of the state associations, encouraging the use of DGWS rules and standards. Whenever the state high school association chooses to use their rules, women should pursue all opportunities to participate in the development of such rules.[13]

References

Association for Intercollegiate Athletics for Women. *AIAW Handbook of Policies and Operating Procedures 1974–75.* Washington, D.C.: AAHPER, 1974.

Athletic and Recreation Federation of College Women. "ARFCW Becomes CWS." *Sportlight,* AAHPER, no. 3 (Spring 1971).

13. *Division for Girls and Women's Sports Newsletter,* May 5, 1971.

Commission on Intercollegiate Athletics for Women. Letter from Lucille Magnusson and Jo Anne Thorpe, AAHPER, September 15, 1971.

Division for Girls and Women's Sports Newsletter, May 5, 1971, Washington, D.C.: AAHPER.

Division for Girls and Women's Sports. *Philosophy and Standards for Girls and Women's Sports.* Washington, D.C.; AAHPER, 1973.

Flinchum, Betty. "DGWS Involvement in Student Sports Organizations," JOHPER, September 1971.

National Federation of State High School Athletic Associations. *1970–71 NFSHSAA Handbook.* Chicago: NFSHSAA

National Federation of State High School Associations, *1974–1975, NFSHSA Handbook.* Elgin, Ill.: NFSHSA.

BEAUTY IN SPACE
Photograph by Dr. Richard Lussier
California State University, Long Beach

CHAPTER 9

A New Era

Twenty or thirty years from now those who make a study of such things as the history of competitive sports for women may well label the period which we are now entering a "new era." The reason for this is a piece of federal legislation which is commonly referred to as "Title IX." This innocuous-sounding designation will have far-reaching implications for both men's and women's competitive sports programs.

Title IX is part of the Education Amendments Act of 1972 and relates to discrimination on the basis of sex in education programs receiving federal financial assistance. It provides that "no person in the United States shall on the basis of sex, be excluded from participating in, be denied the benefits of, or be subjected to discrimination under any education program or activity receiving federal financial assistance."[1]

The responsibility for developing guidelines to effectuate Title IX was assigned to the Department of Health, Education, and Welfare (HEW). In the Federal Register of June 24, 1974, under the title *Education Programs And Activities Receiving Or Benefiting From Federal Financial Assistance,* HEW proposed rules to implement Title IX. *Section 86.35 (d)* provided for separate financial assistance for members of each sex as part of separate athletic teams of each sex.[2] *Section 86.38 Athletics* dealt with participation on teams, determination of student interest, informing students as to opportunity for athletic participation equal to those available to members of the other sex, providing support and training activities for members of a sex for which athletic opportunities have been limited, equalization of opportunities for athletic participation of both sexes, provision for necessary equipment and supplies without discrimination on the

---

1. Department of Health, Education, and Welfare, "Education Programs and Activities Receiving or Benefiting From Federal Financial Assistance," Federal Register, vol. 120, pt. II, June 20, 1974, Washington, D.C., pp. 22228–40.
2. Ibid., p. 22236.

basis of sex in the case of separate teams for members of each sex, and equal aggregate expenditures for athletics for members of each sex.[3]

Discrimination against girls' and women's competitive sports programs has been a glaring reality historically and traditionally. Among the more obvious aspects of discrimination have been those related to:

1. Allocation of funds
2. Use of facilities
3. Remuneration for coaching
4. Allocation of coaching personnel
5. Financial aid to participants
6. Provision of equipment and supplies
7. Publicity
8. Medical and training facilities and services.

The sections mentioned above in the proposals zeroed in directly on the areas of discrimination listed in the previous paragraph. These proposals were widely circulated among those institutions upon which the legislation would have a major impact. Because one of the critical areas of concern was elimination of discrimination in athletics, on the basis of sex, it was to be expected that a great hue and cry would be heard, especially from those who conceivably might have limitations placed on their programs as a result of the legislation. Naturally, the proposals gave rise to much discussion, pro and con. Some felt that the proposals had gone too far, some that they had not gone far enough, and some were relatively happy with them.

Much fear and considerable anxiety was engendered by the proposals because many saw them as a threat to the hallowed traditions of their own programs. One individual from a prominent athletic conference went so far as to express the fear that such proposals, if actuated, would cause the complete ruin of men's intercollegiate athletic programs. As was to be expected, the question of funding caused the greatest concern among the male athletic directors because it seemed that the only answer to financial equitability of the two programs meant "take" from one and "give" to the other.

Unfortunately, because the proposals were rather general in nature, there were a number of different interpretations put upon them. Some were indeed "misinterpretations." As a result of this, and of precipitous overreaction on the part of some institutions, program reorganization was hurried into and in some instances completed before the actual proposals were revised and finalized. Such hurried

3. Ibid., p. 22236.

and haphazard actions could ultimately lead to considerable regret on the part of such institutions.

HEW obviously circulated the guidelines for the express purpose of getting reactions, ostensibly to ascertain if they were being realistic in their proposals, to test the intensity of the feelings of those in the profession who would be the most affected, and to find out if the proposals were something that could be lived with.

The reactions, both verbal and written, came hot and heavy. Meetings were held, suggestions for changes were received, interpretations were requested and so on. As a matter of fact HEW received over 9700 comments which were taken into consideration before the final rules and regulations were adopted and submitted for approval in June, 1975 to the President and the Congress of the United States. The Federal Register of June 4, 1975 contains these rules and regulations which were approved and are now law.

In order to clarify the impact that the Title IX rules and regulations will have on competitive sports throughout the country those sections which apply are quoted here followed by a discussion of those general and specific effects they will/may have on men's and women's athletic programs.

Section 36.37 (c) *Athletic Scholarships* states the following:

(1) To the extent that a recipient awards athletic scholarships or grants-in-aid, it must provide reasonable opportunities for such awards for members of each sex in proportion to the number of students of each sex participating in interscholastic or intercollegiate athletics.

(2) Separate athletic scholarships or grants-in-aid for members of each sex may be provided as part of separate athletic teams for members of each sex to the extent consistent with this paragraph and 86.41 of this part.[4]

Section 86.41 *Athletics* states the following:

(a) General. No person shall, on the basis of sex, be excluded from participation in, be denied the benefits of, be treated differently from another person or otherwise be discriminated against in any interscholastic, intercollegiate, club or intramural athletics offered by recipient, and no recipient shall provide any such athletics separately on such basis.

(b) Separate teams. Notwithstanding the requirements of paragraph (a) of this section, a recipient may operate or sponsor

4. Department of Health, Education, and Welfare, "Nondiscrimination on Basis of Sex," Education Programs and Activities Receiving or Benefiting from Federal Financial Assistance. Federal Register, vol. 40, pt. II, June 4, 1975, Washington, D.C., p. 24142.

separate teams for members of each sex where selection for
such teams is based upon competitive skill or the activity is a
contact sport. However, where a recipient operates or sponsors a team in a particular sport for members of one sex but
operates or sponsors no such team for members of the other
sex, and athletic opportunities for members of that sex have
previously been limited, members of the excluded sex must
be allowed to try out for the team offered unless the sport
involved is a contact sport. For the purpose of this part,
contact sports include boxing, wrestling, rugby, ice hockey,
football, basketball and other sports the purpose of major
activity of which involves bodily contact.

(c)   Equal Opportunity. A recipient which operates or sponsors
interscholastic, intercollegiate, club or intramural athletics
shall provide equal athletic opportunity for members of both
sexes. In determining whether equal opportunities are available the Director will consider, among other factors:

(I)   Whether the selection of sports and levels of competition effectively accommodate the interests and abilities
of members of both sexes;

(II)   The provision of equipment and supplies;

(III)   Scheduling of games and practice time;

(IV)   Travel and per diem allowance;

(V)   Opportunity to receive coaching and academic tutoring;

(VI)   Assignment and compensation of coaches and tutors;

(VII)   Provision of locker rooms, practice and competitive
facilities;

(VIII)   Provision of medical and training facilities and services;

(IX)   Provision of housing and dining facilities and services;

(X)   Publicity.

Unequal aggregate expenditures for members of each sex or unequal
expenditures for male and female teams if a recipient operates or
sponsors separate teams will not constitute noncompliance with this
section, but the Director may consider the failure to provide necessary funds for teams for one sex in assessing equality of opportunity for members of each sex.

(d)   Adjustment Period . . . A recipient which operates or sponsors
interscholastic, intercollegiate, club or intramural athletics at
the secondary or post-secondary school level shall comply
fully with this section as expeditiously as possible but in no
event later than three years from the effective date of this
regulation.[5]

For purposes of clarification the term *recipient* refers to any education program or activity receiving federal funds. Generally speaking

5. Ibid., pp. 24142–43.

secondary schools, colleges, and universities are the recipients referred to in the following discussion.

Although the sections quoted seem to be fairly specific, at first glance, they are, nevertheless, general enough in some instances to cause considerable confusion, and there is need for more specificity (in certain situations) on the part of those who drew up the regulations. Questions continue to be addressed to the regulations from institutions regarding situations which either exist or are being proposed in their athletic programs. It should be borne in mind, therefore, that any commentary concerning the interpretation of the regulations must be partially speculative.

It seems clear that scholarships for women will certainly be increased, where institutions award athletic scholarships or grants-in-aid. However, the term "reasonable opportunities" can certainly lend itself to a variety of interpretations. The *number* of students of each sex participating in competitive athletics at an institution will be an important factor in determining the number of scholarships to be given to members of each sex. The thing to be remembered here is that the legislation does not state "equal" number, and one should therefore not expect the women to get twenty scholarships if the men get twenty scholarships.

It appears that separate scholarship programs for each sex may be provided when separate athletic teams exist, as long as the balance in keeping with the regulations relative to total scholarships is maintained.

These scholarship rules are now, and probably will continue to be, of major concern to both men's and women's athletic programs. Some questions are obvious: (1) where will the money be procured?; (2) will the number of scholarships for men have to be reduced?; (3) will the women have to develop booster clubs, or (4) will the men's booster clubs now have to provide for the women's programs? These are only a few of the more obvious questions that will arise relative to this facet of the legislation.

A problem which may or may not be so obvious to some is a philosophical one. Strange as it may seem, many women physical educators and/or coaches do not favor scholarships for women athletes. The results of the granting of scholarships in the men's programs have been all too obvious to the women over the years, and many of them have no desire to get involved in these same problems. Where scholarships come into the program, recruitment soon follows, and the men themselves are the first to admit to the evils of this practice. It is interesting to note that legislation which is designed to abolish sex discrimination in athletics can result in forcing a profound philosophical change on the part of many in the conduct of their programs.

Some of the greatest implications for change in the women's programs are found in Section 86.41 *Athletics*. The first paragraph of this section is a very strong statement against any kind of discrimination in athletic programs on the basis of sex. The remainder of the section more or less attempts to clarify and undergird the meaning of this statement.

Considerable confusion arises from the statement on "separate teams." It seems clear that an institution may have separate teams for members of each sex if certain conditions exist — as, for example if the sport is a contact sport, or where selection for membership on the team is based on competitive skill. However, if there is a tennis team for men, for example, and none for women, then women must be allowed to tryout for the men's tennis team, or vice versa. The confusing part is the statement "and athletic opportunities for members of that sex have previously been limited." Does this means that athletic opportunities *in tennis* (for example) have previously been limited? Or does it mean that opportunities in *all* athletics have been limited? Also, *how* limited? If one has played tennis in high school competition but has not had that opportunity in college, is that limited? Or if one played intramural tennis in college but did not have the opportunity to play intercollegiate tennis, is that limited? These questions and others like them are bound to occur, and legitimately so, in the face of such a nonspecific statement in the rules and regulations.

The section on *equal opportunity* clearly states that a recipient which conducts interscholastic, intercollegiate, club, or intramural athletics *shall* provide equal athletic opportunity for both sexes. This section also states the factors that will be taken into consideration in determining whether equal opportunities are available. As is to be expected, these factors are concerned with facilities, scheduling, equipment and supplies, travel and per diem allowance, medical and training facilities, publicity, and the like.

The section includes a concept which will not only be controversial but can also be manipulated by unethical administrative practices to cause considerable discrimination. The concept is expressed in the statement

> unequal aggregate expenditure for members of each sex or unequal
> expenditures for male and female teams if a recipient operates or
> sponsors separate teams will not constitute noncompliance with this
> section, but the Director may consider the failure to provide nec-
> essary funds for teams for one sex in assessing equality of opportu-
> nity for members of each sex.[6]

6. Ibid., p. 24143

It would seem that this statement clearly negates the first state-ment of this section. It appears to be one of those all-too-prevalent "loopholes" commonly found in governmental legislation. Actually most people did not expect a matching dollar for dollar expenditure to occur in men's and women's athletic programs. This is obviously not a realistic concept nor is it needed at this stage in the develop-ment of women's programs. What was needed was, first, a realization of the *gross* discrimination against women in athletics, and secondly, the necessity of bringing the women's program into a more equitable relationship to the men's by taking women out of the "second class citizen" category and providing for their needs in a fair and impartial manner, especially in relation to the ten factors mentioned in the section on "Equal Opportunity." Unless Title IX results in this kind of upgrading of girls' and women's athletic programs it will have definitely failed in its mission. How the phrase "unequal aggregate expenditures will not constitute noncompliance" will be interpreted, and how or if it will be used to manipulate, will have tremendous implications for women's athletic programs.

It is interesting to note that Title IX does not mandate any specific administrative structure for either men's or women's athletic pro-grams. This fact would lead one to conclude that a variety of administrative structures might emerge as long as the program struc-tures comply with the rules and regulations. There are, however, those who read into Title IX, even into what is not mandated, that the administrative design of programs must follow a certain specific structure. So confusion looms even about what is not said. This confusion, however, may arise from the bias or vested interests of those who make such claims. This is simply one more point that will have to be clarified by the designers of the legislation.

Secondary and postsecondary schools must comply with Title IX rules and regulations no later than three years from their effective date. However, such institutions are urged to comply as soon as possible. This gives institutions a reasonable amount of time in which to carefully evaluate present programs in light of the rules and regulations and to correct any discriminatory practices found to be present.

As was indicated previously in this chapter, some institutions were very precipitous in their actions and hastily began reorganizing their programs on the basis of the "proposals" rather than waiting for the finalized rules and regulations. Because the reorganization of athletic programs to comply with the rules and regulations of Title IX will be so complex, especially for already highly developed, large programs, considerable thought should go into the procedure. Following is a suggested procedure which could be termed a "framework" as a guide to action, which would result in necessary and desirable reorganizational changes:

1. Appointment, by an appropriate individual or group, of an objective study committee composed of:

   a. Administrator responsible for overseeing all athletic programs.

   b. Two student body representatives: one male and one female. (Perhaps the treasurer and one other)

   c. Four faculty from disciplines other than health, physical education, and recreation: two male and two female.

   d. In the case of a secondary school there should be one or two district representatives.
   (If the reorganizational plan applies to a school district, the composition of the study committee should be broadened to include representation from all appropriate schools in the district, adequate student representation, and appropriate administrative personnel; and the principle of equal representation of both sexes should be observed.)

   e. Representatives from the departments of athletics or physical education, as the case may be, should act as consultants to the committee.

2. Development of a plan of action by the study committee which would include all of its operational procedures.

3. Careful study of the "charge" to the committee for the purpose of clarification and understanding. (This should include the limits of the charge and the time factors involved.)

4. Steps to be taken after 1, 2, 3 above:

   a. Definitive study of Title IX rules and regulations concerning athletic programs.

   b. Evaluation of present athletic programs in relation to mandates of Title IX, especially relative to the ten factors in section 86.41c.

   c. Pinpoint areas of discrimination in the athletic programs under consideration.

   d. Ascertain present and future needs of each athletic program.

   e. Identify support sources available for each athletic program.

   f. Study the philosophy, aims, and objectives of both athletic programs.

   g. Carefully review any proposals submitted by those directing each athletic program.

h. Sift through and logically organize all pertinent data gathered.

i. On the basis of all data gathered, including interviews with all appropriate people, develop one or more possible proposals for consideration.

j. Submit proposal(s) to appropriate individuals for their consideration and evaluation.

Point "j" may conclude the "charge" of the study committee. Whether or not a proposal is acceptable, with agreed-upon changes, to all concerned, would undoubtedly demand considerable negotiation between those who will administer the programs at the "grass roots" level and the person(s) in the institution to whom those individuals will be responsible. Before final approval the proposal should be thoroughly checked for compliance with Title IX rules and regulations.

The structure of the study committee would naturally vary depending upon the organization of the institution involved. A university composed of various schools might desire to have a representative from each school, with representation divided equally between men and women — rather than the four-faculty-member representation suggested. And as has already been mentioned, a school district committee would necessarily vary in composition from that of an individual institution. One caution should be noted and that is that the committee should not be so large as to be cumbersome, nor should it be so small as to not be representative of the total entity involved.

There are undoubtedly other approaches that could be taken to reorganize the athletic programs. This one was suggested because it attempts to (1) represent the entire entity (institution or district); (2) be objective, to provide for evaluation of the present programs as well as for future proposals; (3) to identify and eliminate areas of discrimination in keeping with Title IX rules and regulations; (4) to provide for consultation and discussion among all appropriate personnel for necessary input; and (5) hopefully to submit a proposal that is impartial, in compliance with Title IX, and as acceptable as possible to all concerned.

Obviously such program reorganization will be a traumatic experience for those directly involved in the administration and conduct of men's and women's athletic programs. It is to be hoped that through it all the integrity of neither program will be destroyed. Since the purpose of the legislation is to eliminate discrimination on the basis of sex, it would be just too bad if, after all, programs were so organized as to have one absorbed into the other, thus resulting in more rather than less discrimination. Good faith on the part of all personnel involved will have to be exhibited if discrimination is to be eliminated and if the students are to be well served. Any program wherein the best interests of the students are not the prime concern does not deserve to exist. Vested interests will have to be cast aside and philosophies will have to be reevaluated and perhaps reformulated. The focal point should once again be the entire student body and what is best for each of its members — away from ego trips and institutional prestige. It is to be hoped that from all of this some of those ideals upon which competitive sports were once based will resurface, and coaches and participants alike may be the better for it.

Examples

A. Constitution of Local Women's Intercollegiate Athletic Conference

B. Rules and Regulations Governing Girls' Interscholastic Athletics Activities

C. High School Student Athletic Coordinator Handbook

D. University Women's Intercollegiate Budget Request to Associated Students

E. University Women's Intercollegiate Sports Departmental Budget Request

APPENDIX

Example A

Revised Spring, 1973

CONSTITUTION OF THE SOUTHERN CALIFORNIA WOMEN'S INTERCOLLEGIATE ATHLETIC CONFERENCE*

ARTICLE I
Name

The name of this organization shall be the Southern California Women's Intercollegiate Athletic Conference, hereafter referred to as S.C.W.I.A.C.

ARTICLE II
Purpose

The purpose of this organization shall be:

A. To promote, provide and coordinate intercollegiate athletic experiences for college women including co-educational activities.

B. To introduce and maintain desirable standards for these intercollegiate experiences through:

   1. The formation and maintenance of policies governing all women's and co-ed intercollegiate athletic events.

   2. The establishment of a governing committee through which standards and policies are recommended and maintained.

   3. The sanctioning of intercollegiate athletic events.

C. To further the opportunities for greater understanding and to increase acquaintance among the students of the Southern California Colleges.

---

*Permission to use granted by the Southern California Women's Intercollegiate Athletic Conference.

ARTICLE III
Membership

Section 1

A regular member shall be:

> Any four (4) year college or university from and including Fresno and San Luis Obispo, south to and including San Diego, provided that that institution has administrative sanction for an intercollegiate program.

Section 2

An associate member may be:

> Any four (4) year college or university outside the geographical limits of the organization that is otherwise eligible for membership.

ARTICLE IV
Administration

Section 1

The council of S.C.W.I.A.C. shall consist of the following:

A. Voting members:

1. The director of the Women's and Co-ed Intercollegiate Sports Program from each member institution, or her appointed representative.

B. Non-voting members shall be the following:

1. Ex-officio members: A.A.H.P.E.R. Southwest District G.W.S. Chairman, C.A.H.P.E.R. Vice President for G.W.S., California South G.W.S. (A.A.H.P.E.R.) Committee Chairman, and W.A.I.A.W. President.
2. Student representatives from member institutions.
3. The Chairman of the Sport Councils as ex-officio members of S.C.W.I.A.C.
4. The members of the Governing Committee as ex-officio members of S.C.W.I.A.C.

Section 2

The officers of S.C.W.I.A.C. shall be faculty members and shall be:

A. President

B. President-elect

C. Secretary-treasurer

Section 3

The Governing Committee shall be elected and shall consist of the following nine voting members:

A. One faculty member to represent each of the five (5) geographically defined areas.

B. One faculty member to represent institutions with a student population of 5,000 or less.

C. One faculty member to represent institutions with a student population of more than 5,000.

D. One faculty member at large shall be elected to represent the entire membership of the Council on the Governing Committee.

E. The President of S.C.W.I.A.C.

F. Any members(s) of this committee shall relinquish her/their voting privileges upon her/their involvement in any cases before the committee.

Section 4

The Executive Committee be composed of:

A. President

B. President-elect

C. Secretary-treasurer

D. Representative elected by Governing Committee from its membership.

E. Past President

ARTICLE V
Quorum

Section 1

In order to convene an official business meeting, a majority of the individual voting members shall be present at roll call of the first session; after which, business shall be conducted by the individual voting members present.

Section 2

General business shall be transacted with a majority of the votes cast.

Section 3

Amendments to the constitution shall be passed with ⅔ of the votes cast.

ARTICLE VI
Meetings

Section 1

The Council shall meet semi-annually in the Fall and Spring, and special meetings may be called when deemed necessary.

Section 2

The semi-annual meetings shall be composed of two (2) sessions:

    A. Session I — meetings with interest groups:

        1. Women's Intercollegiate Sports Coordinators from each institution.

        2. Sports Council chairman.

        3. Students.

        4. Other.

    B. Session II — council meetings:

        1. Open meetings with voting and ex-officio members seated in designated areas.

        2. Following council meeting, newly elected officers and Governing Committee members meet with their respective committees to receive information, notebooks and to determine meeting times.

Section 3

Business at the meeting shall be conducted as specified by Article V Quorum, Section 2 and 3.

Section 4

The Governing Committee shall meet annually and as deemed necessary.

Section 5

The Executive Committee shall meet annually and as deemed necessary.

ARTICLE VII
Amendments

All Amendments to the Constitution shall be:

    A.   Submitted by mail to regular member schools or by presentation on the floor at the Council meeting.

    B.   Voted upon at the Council meeting if a quorum is present.

    C.   Adopted according to Article V Section 3.

BY-LAWS

ARTICLE I
Administrative Duties

Section 1

The Council shall:

    A.   Meet semi-annually in the Fall and Spring.

    B.   Approve the annual budget.

    C.   Coordinate the activities of the member schools.

    D.   Establish a schedule of events.

    E.   Review S.C.W.I.A.C. Policy Statement once a year.

    F.   Approve the financial report.

Section 2

The executive committee:

    A.   The President:

        1.   Hold office for one year.

2. Convenes and presides over all Council meetings.

3. Convenes and presides over all Executive Committee meetings.

4. Represents S.C.W.I.A.C. to other sports governing bodies.

5. Maintains communication with sports organizations outside S.C.W.I.A.C. and forwards all pertinent information to proper officer or total membership.

6. Collect and keep file reports from all committees and officers of the organization.

7. Appoint special committees as deemed necessary.

8. Appoint a parliamentarian.

9. Be responsible for seeing that elections of the Governing Committee are held.

10. Serve as ex-officio member of the Governing Committee.

11. Be responsible for coordinating meetings and activities with the Southwestern College Women in Sports.

B. The President-elect:

1. Hold office for one year.

2. Presents Executive Committee report and recommendations to Council.

3. Editor of the Newsletter.

4. Maintains master calendar of championship tournaments, invitational tournaments and other events of interest to S.C.W.I.A.C. members.

5. Attend all Council meetings and assist the President when necessary.

C. The Secretary-Treasurer:

1. Keep records of Council and Executive Committee meetings.

2. Conduct membership drive and maintain a mailing list of all regular and associate member institutions.

3. Submit financial report at each Council meeting.

4. Assist with Newsletter.

5. Disperse money budgeted by the Council. Allocate funds for non-budgeted items under $10.00.

6. Submit a written report to the Council at the Spring meeting to include a record of the income/expenditures for the current year.

7. Submit a projected budget for the following year, to be approved by the Council.

8. Purchase a ledger book to become a permanent record of the S.C.W.I.A.C. financial status.

9. Close books July 1 as concluding the fiscal year, and the Executive Committee will audit the same.

D. The Past President:

1. Hold office for one year.

2. Serve as chairman of the Nominating Committee.

3. Submit a report to the President, which shall include the responsibilities and activities of the office.

E. Governing Committee Representative:

1. Liaison with Executive Committee.

Section 3

The Governing Committee:

A. Structure and function of:

1. The term of office for Governing Committee members shall be for two (2) consecutive years.

2. Hold at least one (1) annual meeting and others when deemed necessary.

3. Develop and maintain an Operating Code for this Committee to be approved by a quorum of the Council.

4. Continually review the Policy Statement and where necessary make recommendations to the Council for revision.

5. Act as a referral body to review problems involving participating members.

6. Approve original policies and procedures recommended by Sports Councils. Continually review policies and procedures recommended by Sports Councils.

7. Sanction S.C.W.I.A.C. events. A sanctioned event is defined as one co-sponsored by a member institution and the S.C.W.I.A.C.

8. Oversee and evaluates S.C.W.I.A.C. sanctioned events.

9. Adhere to only those duties as outlined in the S.C.W.I.A.C. Constitution.

B. Governing Committee elections:

1. The outgoing representative shall be responsible for conducting an election for a new representative from that area.

2. A general election shall be held to elect the member-at-large of the Governing Committee.

C. Governing Committee Chairman shall:

1. Be elected from the committee membership and hold office for one year.

2. Call annual Governing Committee meetings and others as deemed necessary.

3. Preside over Governing Committee meetings.

4. Submit recommended changes in the Operating Code to the Council for approval.

5. Submit a report of the Governing Committee meetings to the President.

Section 4

The Executive Committee shall:

A. Communicate with other sport governing bodies locally, regionally and nationally through the S.C.W.I.A.C. President.

B. Distribute information of interest to member schools.

C. Handle business of the Council between meetings of S.C.W.I.A.C.

D. Establish agenda for S.C.W.I.A.C. Council meeting.

E. Recommend S.C.W.I.A.C. Constitution and By-Laws revisions.

F. Submit an annual budget for approval at the Spring Council meeting for the succeeding year.

G. Approve all expenditures which exceed budgeted items by $10.00.

Section 5

The Sports Council shall:

A. Be composed of one (1) faculty representative from each member institution participating in that sport.

B. Be composed of one (1) student representative from each member institution participating in that sport.

C. Submit to the Governing Committee, for their approval, any changes in their policies.

ARTICLE II
Dues

Section 1

Annual dues shall be $20.00 per regular and associate member institutions.

Section 2

Dues shall be collected prior to the Fall Council meeting for the ensuing year.

ARTICLE III
Membership

Section 1

A regular member is a member of the Council.

A. Privileges:
1. May hold office.
2. May have the opportunity of serving as a representative of the Governing Committee.
3. The institution that that member represents may have the opportunity to participate in all open events.
4. Have voting privileges.

B. Requirements of each member institution:
1. Shall pay dues.

2. Shall abide by all standards of the Council and directives to the Governing Committee.

Section 2

An associate member is a non-voting, non-office holding member of the Council.

A. Privileges:
   1. May attend Council meetings.
   2. May participate in all open S.C.W.I.A.C. events.
B. Requirements of each associate member institution:
   1. Shall pay dues.
   2. Shall abide by all standards of the Council and directives of the Governing Committee.

ARTICLE IV
Nominations and Elections

Section 1

S.C.W.I.A.C. President:

A. Nominations may be made by a regular member by mail at least four (4) weeks prior to the Spring Council meeting and on the floor of that meeting.
B. Elections shall take place at the spring meeting of the Council.
C. One ballot may be cast from each member institution.

Section 2

Governing Committee:

A. The members in each of the five (5) geographically defined areas shall elect representatives to this committee.
   1. Three (3) members, who shall serve as representatives from the North, South and Los Angeles-East, shall be elected in the odd-numbered years.
   2. Two (2) members, who shall serve as representatives from the Los Angeles-West and the Inland, shall be elected in the even-numbered years.

B. The member institutions with a student population of 5,000 or less shall elect one (1) representative to this committee and the member institutions with a student population of more than 5,000 shall elect one (1) representative to this committee.

   1. The member representing institutions with a student population of 5,000 or less shall be elected in the odd-numbered years.

   2. The member representing institutions with a student population of more than 5,000 shall be elected in the even-numbered years.

C. The member-at-large shall be elected by the general membership in the even-numbered years.

D. Should a member be unable to complete her term of office, the Governing Committee shall appoint a representative to be a replacement for the remainder of that term.

E. The chairman of the Governing Committee shall be nominated and elected by the members of the Governing Committee.

ARTICLE V
Geographical Areas

Section 1

The geographical areas are North, Los Angeles-West, Los Angeles-East, Inland and South.

A. North shall include Fresno, San Luis Obispo and Santa Barbara Counties.

B. Los Angeles-West shall include all of Ventura County and San Fernando Valley State College, University of California at Los Angeles, Mt. St. Mary's College, Immaculate Heart College and Occidental College within Los Angeles County.

C. Los Angeles-East shall include California State University at Long Beach, California State College at Los Angeles. University of Southern California, Pepperdine College,

Pasadena College of the Nazarene, Marymount College, and Whittier College within the eastern section of Los Angeles.

D. Inland shall include all of Riverside and San Bernardino Counties and including the Claremont and Pomona Colleges.

E. South shall include all of San Diego and Orange Counties.

ARTICLE VI
Amendments

Section 1

All amendments shall be:

A. Submitted by mail to regular member schools or by presentation on the floor at the Council meeting.

B. Be voted upon at the Council meeting, if a quorum is present.

C. Adopted according to Article V Section 3 of the Constitution.

ARTICLE VII
Parliamentary Authority

The rules contained in *Robert's Rules of Order Revised* shall govern S.C.W.I.A.C. in all cases which they are applicable and in which they are not inconsistent with this Constitution or these By-Laws.

APPENDIX

Example B

RULES AND REGULATIONS GOVERNING

GIRLS'

INTERSCHOLASTIC ATHLETICS ACTIVITIES*

SENIOR HIGH SCHOOL

LOS ANGELES CITY UNIFIED SCHOOL DISTRICT

*Permission has been granted by the Los Angeles City Unified School District to use the following excerpts from *Rules and Regulations Governing Girls' Interscholastic Athletic Activities — Senior High Schools*. Certain portions of the Rules and Regulations not considered to be pertinent to this book have not been included.

CONTENTS

*Portion not included

APPENDICES°

°Portion not included

FOREWORD

Every girl enrolled in high school should have the opportunity to receive instruction and participate in a varied sports program. A major objective of this program should be to encourage the participation of many girls through the offering of a variety of activities, including individual, dual, and team sports, that will meet and challenge the competitive needs of girls of varying abilities. Intramural competition should be stressed, and extramural competition should be an outgrowth of the intramural program. This program should meet the student's needs, interests, and abilities; should contribute to the development of young womanhood; should contribute to the total educational program; should have value in after-school community life; and should be conducted under the direction and supervision of a woman professionally trained in physical education.

Adopted by
Senior High School Principals' Association
Girls' Vice-Principals' Association
Girls' Interscholastic Athletics Committee

1972–73

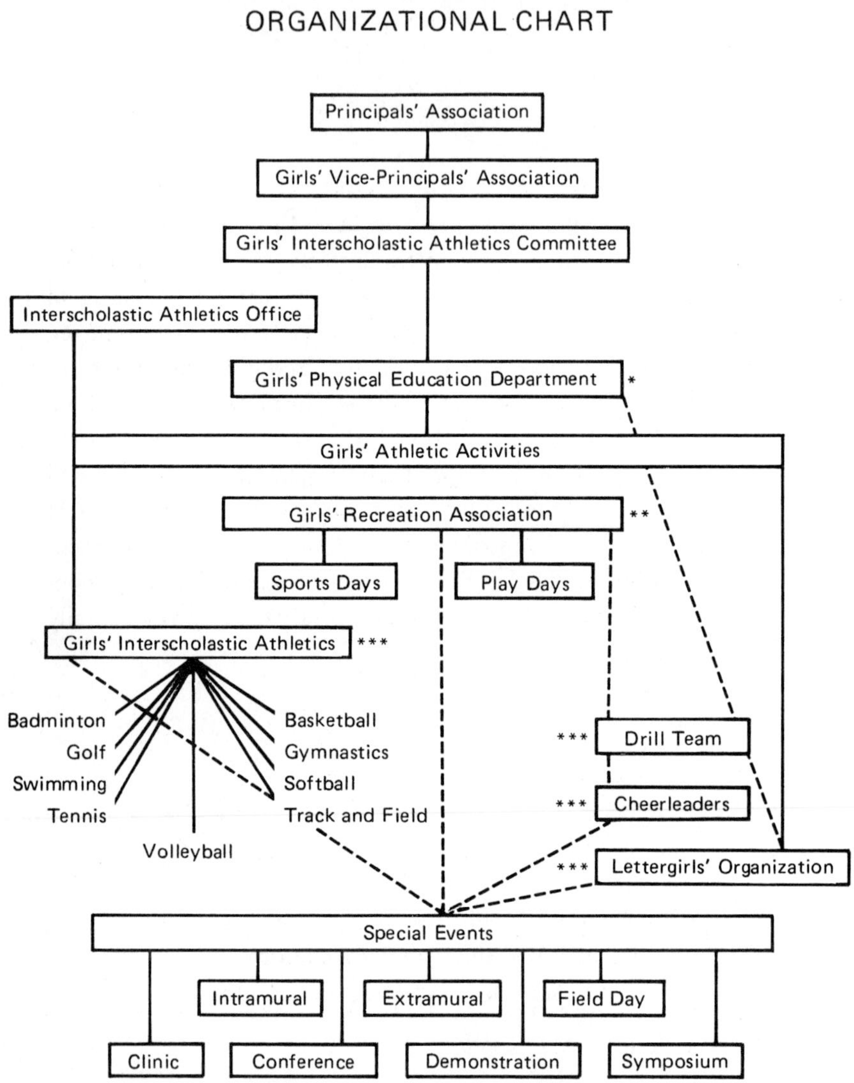
ORGANIZATIONAL CHART
Principals' Association
Girls' Vice-Principals' Association
Girls' Interscholastic Athletics Committee
Interscholastic Athletics Office
Girls' Physical Education Department *
Girls' Athletic Activities
Girls' Recreation Association **
Sports Days
Play Days
Girls' Interscholastic Athletics ***
Badminton
Golf
Swimming
Tennis
Volleyball
Basketball
Gymnastics
Softball
Track and Field
*** Drill Team
*** Cheerleaders
*** Lettergirls' Organization
Special Events
Intramural
Extramural
Field Day
Clinic
Conference
Demonstration
Symposium

*The *Girls' Physical Education Department* is directly responsible for all athletic activities conducted by the Girls' Recreation Association, Girls' Interscholastic Athletics, Lettergirls' Organization, Drill Team, and Special Events; and may be responsible, at the discretion of the Girls' Vice-Principals' Association, for Cheerleaders.

**The *Girls' Recreation Association* may sponsor Sports Days, Play Days, Special Events, Drill Team, and Cheerleaders.

***The Drill Team, Lettergirls' Organization, Girls' Interscholastic Athletics Teams, and Cheerleaders may sponsor Special Events.

GENERAL POLICIES FOR
GIRLS' ATHLETIC ACTIVITIES

1.   The following are approved activities:

Archery	Gymnastics	*Skiing
Badminton	Handball	Soccer
Basketball	*Hiking	Speed-A-Way
*Bicycling	Hockey (Field)	Speedball
Bowling	Officiating	Swimming
Cheerleading	Paddle Tennis	Table Tennis
Conditioning & Fitness	Rhythms	Tennis
Dancing	*Riding	Touchdown
Drill Team	*Riflery	Track & Field
Fencing	**Scuba Diving	Volleyball
Flag Football	Self Defense	
Golf	Skating	

---

* These activities require the exercise of extra safety precautions.

** This activity must have prior approval of the Girls' Inter-
scholastic Athletics Committee.

Any other activity which is part of the curriculum or recreational program of the individual school may be included
in the program if authorized by the principal. Those sports
approved specifically for interscholastic athletics are listed
in the Interscholastic Athletics Section.

2.   The sponsor must have on file a signed parent approval form
for each girl participating in an athletic activity away from
school. (See Appendix G.)

   a.   Only one parent approval form need be completed for the
   school year if the dates of all trips to be conducted are
   listed. Otherwise, a signed approval form must be obtained
   and placed on file for each trip that was not included.

   b.   Copies of the form are available at the school.

   c.   The sponsor should distribute the copies sufficiently in advance of an event to assure that they can be returned and
   checked prior to the date of the activity.

    d.   Each signed parent approval form must be kept on file for one year following the last date of travel.

3.   The sponsor must arrange for appropriate transportation. (See Appendix K.)

    a.   Transportation shall be by bus or other recognized public carrier when 20 or more students are involved.

    b.   The request for use of a bus should be made to the Transportation Branch at least one month in advance of the scheduled activity.

    c.   The sponsor should consult with the principal or his or her designated representative regarding transportation procedures.

    d.   One or more District certificated employees shall ride on each bus to supervise the students being transported.

    e.   With approval of the principal, the sponsor can arrange for transportation of students by means other than by bus. Alternatives may include use of private cars or private carriers. If feasible, girls may walk to the destination.

    f.   It is strongly recommended that adult drivers be used when students are transported by private cars. If this is impossible, the sponsor must obtain prior approval of the principal and place on file a driver approval form. (See Appendix H.) It must be stated on the signed parent approval form that the driver is under 21 years of age.

4.   The sponsor must arrange for each student to be covered by proper health insurance. For procedures, the sponsor should check the current insurance bulletin that is on file at the school.

5.   The sponsor must arrange for each student to be covered by proper health clearance. Each year, current regulations should be checked.

6.   It is recommended that the girls' vice-principal attend girls' athletic activities when possible.

7.   The head sponsor of the Girls' Recreation Association must submit to the girls' vice-principal or her delegated representative an activity assignment list.

8.   Dates for intramural events must be cleared with the head sponsor of the Girls' Recreation Association and with the chairman of the Girls' Physical Education Department. To inform

the principal and girls' vice-principal regarding the program, the head sponsor, with the approval of the department chairman, should provide each with a completed copy of the report form for girls' athletic activities. (See Appendix I.) The sponsor must clear all other proposed girls' athletic activities with the head sponsor, department chairman, girls' vice-principal, and principal through submittal and circulation of an activity request form. (See Appendix J.)

9.   The budget for all girls' athletic activities should be submitted each year by the chairman of the Girls' Physical Education Department to the student body finance committee. Proposed expenditures for sport days, play days, all special events, girls' interscholastic activities, and purchase of Girls' Recreation Association equipment and awards should be included in the budget.

10.   A healthful, safe, and sanitary environment must be provided for all activities.

11.   Girls must wear gym suits, uniforms, or other appropriate clothing during each activity.

   a.   The only organization clothing that a girl may wear during girls' athletic activities is the approved Girls' Recreation Association and/or Lettergirls' Organization attire.

   b.   Jewelry that might be hazardous to the participant must not be worn.

   c.   Girls should not take valuables to another school.

12.   Competition should be scheduled during the appropriate season for each sport and must be preceded by practice sessions.

13.   Various types of tournaments should be conducted to provide competition appropriate to the activity and girls' involved.

   a.   Arrangements should be made in advance for the use and distribution of equipment.

   b.   Tournaments should be publicized, and schedules, regulations, and results should be posted.

   c.   Inexpensive awards may be presented to the winners.

14.   It is the responsibility of the sponsor to emphasize the quality of performance in the game played and to develop within each player the ability to accept defeat or victory in a gracious manner.

15.   Official rules published by the Division of Girls' and Women's Sports of the American Association for Health, Physical Education, and Recreation shall govern the playing of all games. Speed-A-Way rules copyrighted by Marjorie Larson and published by Burgess Publishing Company shall govern the playing of Speed-A-Way. Touchdown rules published by the District shall govern the playing of Touchdown.

    a.   Girls should know the official game rules before competing.

    b.   Decisions of the officials should be accepted as final by all competitors.

16.   Consistency and quality should be considered in the selection of officials. College, junior college, or high school girls who have been taught how to officiate may be used as officials.

17.   An evaluation should be conducted following each activity.

GIRLS' INTERSCHOLASTIC ATHLETICS PROGRAM
PHILOSOPHY

The purpose of the Interscholastic Athletics Program conducted in district senior high schools is to provide sports competition for highly skilled senior high school girls. To assure the success of the program, it is essential that it be conducted by qualified women leaders and be consistent with approved objectives and standards for girls' sports activities. Policies pertaining to administrative approval, insurance coverage, yearly health examinations, approved transportation, eligibility standards, and financial support must be observed. In addition, the program should contribute to the development of pride, sportsmanship and ethical behavior, commensurate with the physical, mental, emotional and social maturity of all participants.

Policies and standards have been formulated to maintain consistency of direction and control in interscholastic activities. The Girls' Interscholastic Program is under the jurisdiction of the Girls' Interscholastic Athletics Committee.

CONSTITUTION OF
THE GIRLS' INTERSCHOLASTIC
ATHLETICS COMMITTEE

ARTICLE I
Name

This organization shall be known as the Girls' Interscholastic Athletics Committee of the Los Angeles Unified School District.

ARTICLE II
Jurisdiction and Purposes

A. Jurisdiction

1. The Girls' Interscholastic Athletics Committee, established through authorization of the Los Angeles Senior High School Principals' Association, is concerned with the policies for girls' athletics activities other than those included in the girls' physical education program. The committee is directly responsible to the Senior High School Principals' Association.

2. Although the principal at each senior high school is responsible for implementation of the overall policy and philosophy, he or she may delegate to the girls' vice-principal the responsibility for school planning and administrative guidance of the girls' interscholastic athletics activities.

B. Purposes

The Girls' Interscholastic Athletics Committee shall be responsible for:

1. Unifying and coordinating city-wide policies related to girls' interscholastic athletics activities.

2. Formulating rules and regulations on matters of policy governing girls' interscholastic athletics activities.

3. Hearing appeals on all matters concerning girls' interscholastic athletic activities that are brought to the committee's attention.

4. Making decisions on any and all matters within its authority that have been brought to the committee's attention by:

    a. Individual schools (See Article VI.)
    b. The Senior High Girls' Vice-Principals' Association
    c. The Senior High Principals' Association
    d. The District Athletics Office

ARTICLE III

Membership

A. Voting Members

The voting membership of this committee shall consist of a chairman and four principals appointed by the Senior High School Principals' Association, four girls' vice-principals appointed by the Senior Girls Vice-Principals' Association, a representative elected from each of the girls' athletic leagues, and the Consultant for Girls' Athletics.

B. Ex-Officio Members

Ex-officio members shall consist of the Associate Deputy Superintendent (or his delegated representative), the Area Superintendent in Charge of Athletics, the Director of Interscholastic Athletics, a Representative of the Women's Athletics Board, the Supervisor of Senior High School Youth Services, a Representative from the

Student Activities Branch, and other designated representatives (as deemed necessary by the chairman). Ex-officio members and observers shall not vote.

ARTICLE IV

Officers; Terms of Office

A. Officers

The officers of the Girls' Interscholastic Athletics Committee shall be appointed by each organization for staggered terms to maintain continuity of membership. The chairman shall be a principal appointed by the Senior High School Principals' Association. The vice-chairman shall be a Senior High School Girls' Vice-Principal. The Secretary shall be the Consultant for Girls' Interscholastic Athletics.

B. Terms of Office

The term of office for members of the Girls' Interscholastic Athletics Committee shall be two years. One new member from each organization is to be appointed each school year. If appointments have not been made, incumbents shall continue to serve in offices until vacancies are filled.

ARTICLE V

Meetings

As soon as possible after the opening of the fall semester, there shall be a general meeting of the Committee to plan activities for the coming year. Additional meetings shall be scheduled by the chairman or upon the petition of two or more members of the committee.

ARTICLE VI

Referrals

All matters concerning grievances that involve the Girls' Interscholastic Athletics Program shall be referred in writing to the chairman of the Girls' Interscholastic Athletics Committee. The grievances shall be reported by the principal. Copies of the grievances shall be sent to the chairman of the Girls' Interscholastic Athletics Committee, to the principal of each school concerned, to the Senior High School Girls' Vice-Principals' Association, and to the Girls' Interscholastic Athletics Office.

ARTICLE VII
Suspension of or Exceptions to Rules

Rules governing policies for girls' interscholastic athletics activities in the Los Angeles city senior high schools may not be changed or suspended except upon recommendation of the Girls' Interscholastic Athletics Committee. This committee has the authority to make decisions in all cases covered by these policies, subject to the approval of the Senior High School Principals' Association.

ARTICLE VIII
Quorum

A quorum shall consist of a majority of the voting members of the committee.

ARTICLE IX
Amendments

This constitution may be amended by:

A.   A two-thirds vote of the committee and

B.   A majority vote of the Senior High School Girls' Vice-Principals' Association, subject to

C.   A majority vote of the Senior High School Principals' Association

SECTION I: GENERAL RULES

101.   *Questions and Interpretations*

   101–1.   Communications or questions pertaining to girls' interscholastic athletics contests shall be referred to the Girls' Interscholastic Athletics Committee.

   101–2.   Communications addressed to the Girls' Interscholastic Athletics Committee shall be prepared in duplicate, the original to be forwarded to the chairman and the copy to be sent to the Director of Interscholastic Athletics.

   101–3.   Grievances that involve the girls' interscholastic athletics program shall be referred in writing to the chairman of the Girls' Interscholastic Athletics Committee. The statement of grievance shall be reported by the principal, who will also send copies to the principal of each school concerned, to the Senior High School Girls' Vice-Principals' Association, and to the Girls' Interscholastic Athletics Office.

102. **Suspensions of/or Exceptions to Rules**

    102–1.   Rules governing the conduct of the districts' girls' interscholastic athletics program may not be changed nor suspended except on recommendation of the Girls' Interscholastic Athletics Committee.

    102–2.   The Girls' Interscholastic Athletics Committee has the authority to render decisions in all cases referred to it, including those matters which are not fully covered by these rules.

    102–3.   The Girls' Interscholastic Athletics Committee may delegate limited authority to individual committee members in the event of emergencies.

103. **Length of Season**

The *season for a given sport* is that period of time between the date of the *first* scheduled practice and the date of the *final* league contest.

104. **Length of Practice Schedule**

For rules applicable to the length of the practice game schedule refer to the section relating to the sport concerned.

105. **Length of Practice Period**

    105–1.   A practice period is one in which active participation in a sport is limited to a maximum of two hours per day in addition to a physical education period.

    105–2.   A maximum of five weeks is allowed for the duration of the practice period, which must conclude prior to the first league contest.

106. **Limitation on Practice and League Contests**

There shall be no directed and organized practice or league contest held on Saturdays, Sundays, holidays, or during any vacation period, except as regularly scheduled. Requests for exceptions to this rule must be submitted in writing to the Consultant for Girls' Interscholastic Athletics Program, stating the place, time, and that the proposal has received administrative approval.

107. *Limitation on Number of Games*

107–1. Interschool competition for any team is not to exceed two games per week. This rule applies to either practice or league games, or any combinations thereof, but it does not apply to playoffs.

107–2. The same team may not engage in two contests on consecutive dates. Request for exceptions must be directed to the Area League Director and to the Consultant for the Girls' Interscholastic Athletic Program.

108. *Officials*

108–1. Requests for rated officials for practice games will not be sanctioned nor controlled by the Area League Director.

108–2. Assignments of officials for league competitions will be arranged by the Area League Director.

108–3. When at all possible, a rated official shall be used to officiate at a league game. However, a league game must be conducted as scheduled if a rated official does not appear.

108–4. Problems that involve officiating should be referred to the Area League Director.

108–5. When a rated official is not available for a league game, the following procedures shall be applicable:

a. If time permits, the home school shall obtain a qualified trainee to officiate.

b. If time does not permit, the home school may obtain (with the consent of the coach of the opposing team) a qualified physical education teacher to serve in this capacity.

c. Mutual consent of the coaches of both teams must be recorded on the reverse side of the official scoresheet.

d. If mutual consent cannot be reached, the dissenting coach shall be responsible for rescheduling the game, assigning officials, and notifying the Area League Director.

109. **Reporting Results**

109–1. The GAA Coordinator for the home school shall be responsible for reporting game results to the Area League Director. This report should be made by phone on the day following the competition.

109–2. The official scoresheet, completely filled out and including the full names of the players, and the official's signature, must be forwarded to the Area League Director within 24 hours following the competition.

110. **Uniforms and Appearance**

110–1. Contestants in all league competitions must be fully and properly attired, including shoes. All aspects of feminine appearance should be of primary concern in the selection of the approved uniform.

110–2. It is the responsibility of each school to assure that its participants are properly groomed in compliance with the standards of that particular school.

110–3. Instructions relative to the uniforms and appearance of participants in specific sports appear in the sections dealing with these sports.

111. **Outside Competition**

The Girls' Interscholastic Athletics Committee has the authority to sanction the participation of a school team during the season of the sport in competition not sponsored by the Los Angeles Unified School District, provided that written request is received from the principal of the school concerned.

112. **Insurance Coverage**

All girls participating in the interscholastic athletics program must be protected by travel and medical insurance that meets the standards required by the California Education Code.

113. *Health Appraisal*

Each girl must be cleared by the school nurse prior to the girl's participation in the interscholastic athletics program. This clearance must be noted on the girl's school health record. In addition, the Girls' Interscholastic Athletics Committee recommends that every girl who plans to engage in competition be examined and cleared by a private physician.

114. *Coaches*

114-1.   Each participating coach must be a woman. She must possess a valid California Teaching Credential and be assigned to a teaching position in a district secondary school.

114-2.   A student teacher may assist in coaching activities at the school to which she is regularly assigned for practice teaching in accordance with the provisions of the California Education Code. The student teacher must be supervised by a regular coach.

115. *Faculty Representative*

The coach or a teacher from the Girls' Physical Education Department must accompany and be responsible for the conduct of the members of teams. The coach or teacher must remain with the team until the contest is over and all girls from her school have left the grounds of the school where the competition was held.

116. *Tie-Breaker Rule for Seeding*

116-1.   Policies governing the tie-breaker rule for entering a city championship playoff will be determined by the individual league.

116-2.   Recommendations regarding use of the tie-breaker rule appear in the section for each sport concerned.

SECTION II: ELIGIBILITY RULES

201. *Administrator in Charge*

The Girls' Vice-Principal, or her representative, shall be responsible for verifying the eligibility of girls seeking to participate in the girls' interscholastic athletics program in accordance with the rules set forth in this section. The vice-principal shall certify to this eligibility in writing.

202. *Eligibility Certification*

    202–1. Prior to the first league event, schools must submit to the Girls' Athletic Office a certification of eligibility in which are listed the names of all girls participating in the sport concerned. Supplemental certifications should be forwarded to the Girls' Athletics Office as girls are added to teams during league play. (See Appendix O.)

    202–2. The certification of eligibility shall include each participant's legal address, birthdate, number of semesters in attendance in secondary schools (including the current semester), the name of the school last attended (junior or senior high), and a statement verifying compliance with district policies relating to cooperation, health, insurance, and parent consent requirements as recorded on the Girls' Interscholastic Record Card (blue card) on file at the school.

203. *Amateur Standing*

    203–1. Only girls who are amateurs may participate in athletic contests held under the jurisdiction of the Los Angeles City Schools.

        An amateur is defined as a person who:

        a. Engages in a sport for its physical, mental, and social benefits and/or for its recreational value.

        b. Has never used and is not now using her knowledge or athletic skill for monetary gain or to earn a personal prize or award of more than $10.00 in value. (Refer to 203–2.)

        c. Has not played on any team on which there were paid players.

        d. Has not signed a contract to play with a professional team.

        e. Has not participated in a public tryout for or with a professional team.

203–2.   Officiating, recreational, playground, or camp employment of a public or semi-public nature is not construed as a violation.

203–3.   A girl who has violated the rules pertaining to amateur standing shall automatically be disqualified from further competition during the remainder of the season.

204.   *Age Limitation*

Any girl who has reached her nineteenth birthday prior to September shall not be eligible to compete in the girls' interscholastic athletics program.

205.   *Birthdate*

The birthdate recorded on the cumulative record or given by the student when she enrolls in high school shall be treated as her official date of birth during her attendance. This date may be changed only by evidence submitted in the form of a birth certificate or other document deemed as satisfactory to the Girls' Vice-Principal concerned and to the Girls' Interscholastic Athletic Committee. In the event of a question or discrepancy, the earliest date of birth recorded on a school document shall be treated as official when a birth certificate is not available.

206.   *Scholastic Standing*

206–1.   To be eligible to compete in girls' interscholastic athletics contests, a girl must have earned passing marks and at least 20 semester credits in new work leading to completion of the high school program during the preceding semester.
Five of these semester credits *must* have been earned in the field of physical education or in a subject officially scheduled in lieu of physical education. The marks to be counted must have been earned during ten or more weeks of actual class attendance.

206–2.   An incomplete mark given on the final day of the semester that school is in session may not be counted as part of the twenty semester credits of work required for eligibility, inasmuch as marks must be received during the semester in which they are earned. For this purpose, the semester is considered to have closed on the last day of classes.

207. *Scholastic Eligibility*

For those girls who are declared eligible, continued scholastic eligibility (subject marks and citizenship) shall be determined by the marks earned at the end of the marking period nearest to the time of competition and by such other reports of academic progress and citizenship as are made during the season in which this competition is conducted.

208. *Duration of Eligibility*

A student who is ineligible scholastically to compete on the first day of a semester is ineligible for the entire semester.

209. *Subject Marks*

209–1. A girl is eligible to compete in any current semester if she has earned marks and passing at least twenty semester credits (as prescribed in the California State Board of Education 5 Cal. Adm. 101.1) in new work during the semester immediately preceding that of the competition.

209–2. Five of these semester credits must have been earned in physical education or in a subject officially scheduled in lieu of physical education (as prescribed in the California Education Code, Sec. 8557 and Sec. 10060, and in Instructional Program Support Bulletin #3, dated August 25, 1972, II. A. la.).

209–3. Marks or credits earned in summer session courses shall not be utilized in determining eligibility.

209–4. Girls who are participating in an accelerated academic program that includes one or more advanced (either high school or college) courses approved by the principal may use one or more of these in totaling the required number of semester credits.

210. *Citizenship*

Participation in athletics is regarded as a privilege, not as a right. A girl meets citizenship requirement if she (a) maintains high standards of citizenship within the school and community and (b) has no more than one unsatisfactory mark in cooperation. Citizenship eligibility shall be determined at the same time as scholastic eligibility.

211. **End of Semester**

    211–1. For computing total credits, the semester is considered to close on the last day that school is in session.

    211–2. For participation in athletic events, the semester is not considered to close until the next semester begins.

212. **Residence**

    212–1. If a girl is legally enrolled, she is considered to be eligible to represent the school in interscholastic competition *provided* that she meets all other eligibility requirements.

    212–2. A girl who is regarded in her school as ineligible to compete because of poor citizenship and who is given an opportunity to transfer to another school shall be ineligible to compete in her new school for a period no longer than the balance of the current semester plus the duration of the ensuing semester. The decision as to eligibility on the basis of citizenship shall be made by the sending school.

213. **Continuation School Enrollment (Necessary Small High School)**

    213–1. While enrolled in a continuation school (see 5 Cal. Adm. Code 115), a girl is ineligible to represent her home school.

    213–2. A girl who transfers from a continuation school (see 5 Cal. Adm. Code 115) to her regular school is eligible immediately, providing that:

        a. She was currently passing in at least 20 semester credits, or in a maximum continuation school program; and

b. She was eligible under all rules at the time she was transferred from her regular school to the continuation school.

c. Semesters of attendance at a continuation school are to be counted in determining a girl's eligibility.

   Exception: If a girl spends a full semester or more in a continuation school and passes all required subjects that are considered to represent a full program, she is eligible immediately upon transfer to a regular school.

214. *Junior High School Enrollment*

Junior high school girls may not participate or practice with a senior high school team, unless the girls are *legally* enrolled in Grade 9 in that school.

215. *Maximum Number of Semesters*

A girl may participate in interscholastic athletics for a maximum of eight semesters at a four-year high school following her completion of Grade 8, or for a maximum of six semesters following her completion of Grade 9.

216. *Limited Participation*

A girl may participate concurrently as a member of one team and as an individual performer in another sport in the event that the seasons overlap. A girl may compete in any number of sports as long as the league play does *not* overlap.

217. *Practice Period*

217–1. A practice period is one in which active participation is limited to a physical education period (if scheduled) in addition to a maximum of two hours per day.

217–2. A maximum of five weeks may be used as a practice period prior to the first league contest.

217–3. Each girl must have a minimum of eight hours of organized practice prior to her participation in the first league competition.

217–4.   The number of practice games allowed is specified in the sections of this publication concerning each sport.

218.   **Attendance on Day of Event**

To be eligible for participation in any athletic event, a girl must attend at least three-fourths of her regular classes the day of the contest. Exceptions may be made by the principal in the event of deaths in families, court orders, or other extreme emergencies.

219.   **Outside Competition**

During the season of a sport, the Girls' Interscholastic Athletics Committee has the authority to sanction a school team's participation in an event not sponsored by the Los Angeles Unified School District, provided that a written request is received from the principal of the school concerned.

220.   **Falsifying Information**

Any student who knowingly fails to provide complete and accurate information regarding her eligibility to participate in athletics shall be declared ineligible to represent her school in any sport for one year following the date of the discovery of the offense. The girl may be reinstated only by action of the Girl's Interscholastic Athletics Committee.

221.   **Ineligible Player**

221–1.   If a school permits a girl who is ineligible to participate in competition involving team play, either knowingly or unknowingly, the contest must be forfeited.

221–2.   If a girl who is ineligible represents her high school in an individual sport, only the points she earned shall be forfeited.

222.   **Reports of Ineligibility**

When it is noted by an individual that eligibility rules are being violated, that person is obligated to report the violation IMMEDIATELY to an administrator at her school. This administrator is then obligated to report the violation IMME-DIATELY IN WRITING to an administrator at the school which the ineligible participant represents.

SECTION XII: FINANCES

1201. *Girls' Interscholastic Athletics Committee Trust Fund*

   1201–1. This fund shall consist of all monies, accruing to the Girls' Interscholastic Athletics Committee from play-off games, all-city finals, and other similar events held during the year.

   1201–2. This fund is currently supported by a contribution from the Boys' Interscholastic Athletics Committee for purchase of equipment, awards, payment of officials, and other necessary expenditures for all-city finals.

1202. *Admission to Play-Offs and Finals*

   1202–1. Admission to all athletic contests must be by ticket only, however, personnel presenting credentials validated by the Director of Interscholastic Athletics will be admitted.

   1202–2. Student tickets shall be sold only to bona fide secondary or elementary students and to Board of Education employees and their families.

   1202–3. General admission tickets shall be sold to the public. Alumni shall be classed as general public.

   1202–4. Students of non-competing high schools shall be classed as general public.

1203. *Receipts and Expenses (Play-offs and Finals)*

   1203–1. Receipts accruing to the Girls' Interscholastic Athletics Committee Trust Fund:

   a. Advance sale of tickets

   b. Sale of all tickets at the time of the event

   c. Profit from program sales at game

1203–2. All expenses connected with the event must be approved by Girls' Interscholastic Athletics Committee and disbursements made through the Student Activities Branch.

1204. *Concessions (Play-offs and Finals)*

Prior approval for the operation of a concession shall be obtained from the Student Activities Branch (Form 34. EHJ–8).

SECTION XIII: AWARDS

1301. *League Championship Patches*

1301–1. League championship patches may be purchased for awarding to members of championship teams, for individuals, as well as, team sports in both "A" and "B" Divisions.

1301–2. Each school must purchase these patches through their student body funds.

1301–3. Requests for purchase must be sent in writing to the Chairman of the Girls' Interscholastic Athletics Committee Awards Committee.

1302. *All-City Play-Off Ribbons*

1302–1. Each all-city play-off finals shall conclude with the presenting of special ribbons designed for that specific event.

1302–2. Each member of the following teams, including the coach and manager, shall receive these ribbons:

Basketball, Softball, Volleyball
"A" Division: Places First — Fourth
"B" Division: Places First and Second

Tennis: Places First and Second

Badminton
Teams: Places First — Fourth
   Individual: Singles, First and Second
                Doubles, First, Second, and Third

Gymnastics: This activity shall also receive pins symbolic of each of the five events (balance beam, free exercise, unevens, vaulting, and tumbling) in each classification.

1303. *Championship Perpetual Trophies*

> 1303–1. Perpetual sports trophies have been donated by the Area Superintendents and/or Area Administrative Office of the championship schools beginning with the school year 1972–73.

> 1303–2. The championship team shall retain the trophy from the time of presentation until the finals for that event are held the following year.

> 1303–3. The trophy becomes the complete responsibility of that school. Any loss or damage to the trophy must be reported immediately to the Interscholastic Athletics Office.

> 1303–4. Beginning with the school year 1973–74, the engraving cost for the championship plate will be the responsibility of the winning school.

> 1303–5. It will be the responsibility of the championship school of each preceding year to deliver the trophy (in good condition) to the Athletics Office two days prior to the championship play-off date.

1304. *Honor Awards*

> 1304–1. Perpetual Citizen-Savings (Helms) Athletic Foundation honor plaques are awarded each June to all first place champions in each approved interscholastic sport.

> 1304–2. A plaque shall be presented to *each* champion, each coach, and each administrator of the first place team.

> 1304–3. These awards are presented at a special awards brunch sponsored by the Citizen-Savings Athletic Foundation. The time, place, and date are established jointly by the Citizen-Savings Athletic Foundation and the Girls' Interscholastic Athletics Office.

1305.   *League Trophy or Plaque*

    1305–1. An individual league may purchase a perpetual trophy or plaque to be awarded to the winner of the championship in any given sport. If desired, this trophy or plaque may become the property of the school which wins it three times. The cost of such a trophy or plaque should be prorated among the member schools of the league. The trophy shall not exceed 18½ inches in height. The plaque shall not exceed 10 inches by 14 inches.

    1305–2. An individual league may purchase an annual trophy or plaque to be awarded to the winner of the championship team in any given sport. This trophy or plaque shall be retained by the winning school. The cost of such a trophy or plaque should be pro-rated among the member schools of the league. The trophy shall not exceed 14½ inches in height. The plaque shall not exceed 9 inches by 12 inches.

    1305–3. At the onset of each school year, a representative of each sport from each league shall meet to review award structure and report their recommendations to the Awards Committee.

SECTION XIV: BUS TRANSPORTATION

1401.   *Purposes*

    1401–1. To provide the maximum number of buses for athletic purposes with a minimum of interruptions to school schedules, it is necessary to regulate the travel of teams as set forth below.

    1401–2. These regulations are intended to assist the Transportation Branch in providing buses to leave the schools on athletic trips as late as possible consistent with school-to-home transportation requirements.

1402.   *Basic Policy*

    1402–1. One bus will be furnished to transport visiting athletic teams on each date athletic contests are scheduled.

1402–2. Any school who does not elect to use the bus transportation scheduled must notify the Girls' Athletics Office in writing.

1402–3. The above decision should be made by the principal of that school.

1403. *Change in Schedule*

When a change in schedule is made (Appendix Q), the proper application should be made to the Transportation Branch at least one week in advance of the contest in order to insure the availability of a bus.

1404. *Type of Team(s) Specified*

On every application for an athletic trip, the Transportation Branch must know the kinds of teams to be transported; example, basketball ("A" and "B" Divisions) and Tennis.

1405. *Participants Must Ride Buses*

1405–1. When a bus is furnished to transport athletic teams to contests, only those participants traveling by bus will be eligible to compete. Girls assigned to bus travel must return by bus. Return by private car is not permitted unless specifically approved for a student by the principal of her school.

1405–2. This rule may be waived during City Play-offs, if the need for private transportation is the result of involvement in college entrance tests. IN EMERGENCIES A PRINCIPAL MAY GIVE SPECIAL PERMISSION TO TRAVEL BY CAR.

1406. *Supervision on Athletic Trips*

When one or more athletes representing a given school team rides a school bus to an athletic contest, the Coach normally responsible must accompany such athletes, unless due to illness or extraordinary emergency, the Principal of the school concerned assigns a substitute for her.

1407. *Practice Buses*

Presently, consideration for practice buses *cannot* be provided. Requests for special situations regarding the transporting to distant off-campus practice grounds may be submitted to the Athletics Office.

GIRLS' INTERSCHOLASTIC ATHLETICS COMMITTEES

(1) *CALENDAR AND SCHEDULING*
  - Evaluate league structure and propose changes
  - Draft and present calendar for upcoming year
  - Consider changes in calendar

(2) *RULES AND REGULATIONS*
  - Interpret rules
  - Evaluate amendments
  - Propose changes to GIAC

(3) *GAMES*
  - Confer on playoffs
  - Consider new sports
  - Sanctions to events, etc.

(4) *ETHICS AND STANDARDS*
  - Confer and coordinate with Coaches' Ethic group
  - Handle problems dealing directly with officials
  - Consider all problems related to coaches, players, administrators and other working personnel related to program.

(5) *FINANCE*
  - Study problems of needy schools
  - Propose budget for each year
  - Evaluate requests for special purchases
  - Establish means of increasing GIA Trust Fund

(6) *AWARDS*
  - Study types of Awards
  - Review awards recommendations and existing system
  - Responsible for league-patch awards (funding, type, method of distribution, etc.)
  - Propose changes, additions, etc. to program

APPENDIX

Example C

EL CAMINO REAL HIGH SCHOOL

GIRL'S INTERSCHOLASTIC ATHLETICS

Responsibilities

of the

STUDENT ATHLETIC COORDINATOR

TABLE OF CONTENTS

I. GENERAL DUTIES OF STUDENT ATHLETIC COORDINATOR

1. Assist GIA Coordinator

2. Responsible for obtaining competitive packets from all girls participating in the interscholastic athletic program. Packets shall include:

    a) Health card
    b) Parent consent form
    c) GIA Record Card
    d) Insurance waiver form
    e) CIFPF Insurance form
    f) Competitive contract

3. Obtain health clearance for all competitive players through school nurse.

4. Submit eligibility commitment rosters for all sports in the current season. Submit roster deletions or additions during the season.

5. Check grade eligibility every 10 weeks.

6. Keep competitive files neat and up to date.

7. Keep blue GIA record cards accurate and up to date.

8. Issue and collect warm up suits and competitive socks.

9. Request payment for officials, entry fees, and other GIA expenses. Keep accurate and current record of GAA Account.

10. Serve as an active member of GAA Board.

II. THE COMPETITIVE PACKET

The competitive packet should be distributed as soon as possible at the beginning of each season. Keep an accurate account of who has and who has not turned in their completed forms. Inform the sports managers of the players in their sports who have not submitted forms and hold the managers responsible for getting them returned as soon as possible.

The packet distributed to each student participating in the Girls' Interscholastic Athletic Program contains the following:

(1) *Green Health Form*

After these have been collected, compile a list of the names in alphabetical order and submit the list and the cards to the school nurse. When list of names is returned, check off the health clearances on the blue record card. Make sure the parent signatures are on this form.

(2) *Insurance information*

A. Insurance Waiver
B. CIF Protection fund green information sheet
C. C.I.F.P.F. Purchase form

Note: Students must either purchase C.I.F.P.F. Insurance or submit a waiver stating their coverage by another policy. Some may desire both coverages.

When all money has been collected for C.I.F.P.F. Insurance, type the names in alphabetical order on the CIF form and submit the form with the money to the Student Store. You will receive a receipt.

(3) *Blue GIA Record Card*

All girls attending ECR who have and/or are presently participating in the Interscholastic athletic program should have a blue GIA record card on file. Record cards need only be distributed to those girls who do not currently have one on file. Check for parents' signatures on the returned record cards. Cards should be filed under the sport in which the girl is currently participating. If the girl is not participating during the current season, her card should be put in the inactive file.

Record cards must be kept up to date with the following information:

(a) Health clearance
(b) Insurance
(c) Parent consent forms
(d) Credit awarded
(e) Scholarship check

(4) *Player Information Slip*

This is primarily for the use of the Student Athletic Coordinator in filling out eligibility commitment rosters. It is helpful to have each girl's age, name, sport, etc. recorded on one sheet.

(5) *Parent Consent Form*

This is for Games and meets to be played AWAY from ECR.

These should be filled out before distribution with the following information:

a) Names of schools where away games will be played
b) Time of leaving and return
c) Name of supervisor (coach).

(6) *Competitive Contract*

The contract is to be filled out by each player for each sport. Check for student and parent signatures. Players should retain the contract and just return the tear-off. If they turn in the contract with the tear-off, give it back!

III. ELIGIBILITY COMMITMENT ROSTERS

An eligibility roster for each sport is to be prepared in triplicate no later than the Monday prior to the first league game. All competitive packets must therefore be returned by this time. Names should be typed in alphabetical order. After obtaining signatures of the coach and Girls' Vice Principal, send two copies to the Girls Athletics Office downtown and retain the third copy in the competitive file. If names are to be added or deleted in the course of the season, complete a roster addition/deletion form in the same manner, sending two copies downtown and retaining one for the files.

IV. GRADE ELIGIBILITY

All participants in interscholastic or extramural athletic activities must present a ten and twenty week report card with passing marks in 20 credits, no more than 2 U's in work habits, no more than 1 U in cooperation, and a C or better in P.E. with no U's. It is the responsibility of the Student Athletic Coordinator to review the progress reports of all current participants to determine their eligibility status, and to record the grade check on the blue record cards. If a participant does not meet these grade requirements she will be ineligible to compete in league play until she can verify that her grades meet the eligibility standards.

V. WARM-UP SUITS AND COMPETITIVE SOCKS

Warm-up suits are to be issued at the beginning of each sports season for the rental fee of $1.00. The Student Athletic Coordinator should maintain a file with an index card for each warm-up suit, indicating the suit number, size, to whom it is issued, date issued, date returned, and the condition of the suit when returned. Warm-up suits should be issued by the numerical order of each size, if possible.

Participants cannot be issued a warm-up suit until paying the rental fee of $1.00. Students renting warm-up suits must sign a class receipt sheet, available from the student store, after they have paid the fee and received their suit. After all suits have been issued, turn money and receipt sheet into the student store.

Every suit must be turned in at the close of each season, even if girls may be continuing their participation the following season. Suits should be laundered and neatly folded when returned. Record the condition of each suit on the file card.

Competitive socks are to be issued for basketball, volleyball, softball, and badminton. Issue and collect socks with the warm-up suits.

VI. PAYMENT OF OFFICIALS

The sports managers shall provide an official verification slip to the Student Athletic Coordinator after each game or meet specifying the name, address, rank, and fee of the official as well as the date and school played. As soon as possible, fill out a request for a check to pay the official, obtain the GIA Coordinators and Vice Principals' signatures, and turn in to the student store. They will send a check to the official and return a copy of the request for the GIA records. Keep a list of all games and meets scheduled for the season to make sure all payments have been made.

Although the above is the procedure followed in most cases, some schools may pay the full official fee at ECR away games and bill El Camino for half the amount. This transaction is handled through the student store, and the GIA Coordinator will be notifed.

VII. GAA ACCOUNT

It is of extreme importance to maintain an accurate and current record of the GAA account. This will mainly involve expenditures for officials, equipment, tournament entry fees, play-off fees, etc. Record any expenditures only after receiving the yellow copy of the Request for Purchase Order or Check form. It is a good idea to record the # of the check or purchase order issued, so that it can be checked against records of the student store and Vice Principal. It is advisable to periodically request a statement from the student store, compare it to the GIA record, and clear up any discrepancies.

VIII. GAA BOARD

Generally, the Student Athletic Coordinator's responsibility of the GAA Board is to represent the interests of the interscholastic athletic program along with the sports managers.

Specifically, the Student Athletic Coordinator should coordinate activities and duties of the managers, making sure they maintain a contact between GAA Board and the respective team. The Student Athletic Coordinator may also propose legislation to the GAA Board regarding the interscholastic program. For instance — a proposal for the standardization of the rate for reimbursing drivers for gas to and from away games could be worked out by the SAC and presented for approval to the GAA Board. Other areas may include changes in the competitive contract, GIA fundraising activities, methods of promoting games and meets, problems with spectators, or any other areas affecting the interscholastic athletic program as a whole.

GENERAL DUTIES OF SPORTS MANAGERS

1. Assist coach in any way possible.
2. Confirm games with other schools.
3. Arrange for team transportation for away games.
4. Responsible for equipment.
5. Submit review sheets to public relations manager following each game or meet.
6. Greet officials at games or meets and make sure official verification forms are properly completed.
7. Make sure arrangements have been made for refreshments for home games.
8. Take attendance at practices.
9. Represent team on GAA Board.
10. Be responsible for the return of competitive forms by team members.

LOS ANGELES UNIFIED SCHOOL DISTRICT

ATHLETIC INSURANCE CERTIFICATE

Student's Last Name   First   Initial

I certify that this student is covered by insurance carried with _____

(Name of Insurance Carrier)

which provides at least $1,500 insurance protection for *medical and hospital expenses* resulting from accidental bodily injuries incurred while participating in, practicing for, and traveling to and from interschool athletic contests.

I will maintain the above coverage during the current school year or will immediately notify the school if the coverage terminates or does not meet the above requirements.

_____

Signature of Parent or Guardian

_____

Date

NOTE TO PARENT

Education Code Sections 31751-52 require the following in connection with student athlete insurance:

(1) At least $1,500 insurance protection for *medical and hospital expenses* resulting from accidental bodily injuries incurred while participating in, practicing for, and traveling to and from interschool athletic contests.

(2) Payment of *medical and hospital benefits* in amounts equal to or exceeding the minimum fee schedule in use by the Industrial Accident Commission for purposes of medical and hospital benefits under Division 4 of the Labor Code using a 3.50 conversion factor.

(3) Insurance issued by an admitted insurer, or through a benefit and relief association described in subparagraph (1) of subdivision (c) of Section 10493 of the Insurance Code.

If the medical and hospital insurance you have does not meet the above requirements it does not comply with the law. A form of insurance meeting all of these requirements is available through the student body organization of the school of attendance upon payment of following fee:

Football Only	$16.50
All Other Sports	4.50
GAA	1.50

The School District provides, by means of a blanket policy, $1,500 *accidental death insurance* for the *death* of members of athletic teams occurring while such members are engaged in, preparing for, or being transported to or from an athletic event promoted under the sponsorship or arrangements of the educational institution or student body organization.

EL CAMINO REAL HIGH SCHOOL
GIRLS' PHYSICAL EDUCATION DEPARTMENT

COMPETITIVE SPORTS CONTRACT

As a participant in extramural or interscholastic athletic activities at El Camino Real High School you are expected to uphold certain specific standards and meet the requirements for your sport.

You MUST:

1. Have all the items listed below turned in two weeks prior to the first practice week:
    - A. A current insurance waiver on file or evidence of purchase of CIF Insurance ($1.50)
    - B. Parent approval forms on file for all away games or events
    - C. An annual health form (green) on file in health office; or a doctor's note verifying health clearance for the current year
    - D. Driver form on file, if driving
    - E. Blue athletic credit card
    - F. Emergency card
    - G. Signed contract

2. Have current membership in GAA

3. Wear regulation uniform — shorts, blouse, socks, shoes, sweatshirt, leotard, swimsuit, etc.
    - A. Make sure clothes are clean, in good condition, fit properly and wear a bra
    - B. Pull back hair and secure to the head in some fashion
    - C. Numbers in sports where needed —
        1. 4" x ¾" in front   Do not use 1 or 2 alone
        2. 6" x ¾" in back   Do not use a # larger than 5 (BB)

4. Rent an ECR warm-up suit for $1.00 for *EACH* sport season
    - A. Responsibility of renter:
        1. Utilize proper laundry methods
        2. Pay for the replacement of suit if damaged
        3. Wear *only* during the sport practice at school and during the actual game/meet

5. Present a 10 and 20 week report card with:
   A. Passing marks in 20 credits
   B. No more than 2 U's in work habits
   C. No more than 1 U in cooperation
   D. C or better in P.E. and no U's

STANDARD OF CONDUCT

You are expected to demonstrate conduct becoming of a female athlete. The standards are:

1. **SPORTSMANSHIP**
   Courtesy to teammates, officials, opponents and coaches; a spirit of enthusiasm whether or not you play, participate, win or lose; no rowdy or boisterous behavior; no behavior unbecoming an athlete; play fair.

2. **ATTENDANCE AT PRACTICES AND GAMES**
   Your teammates and coach are depending on you. Commit yourself to your sport so you do not let your teammates down. You must attend the practice prior to each game/meet; the coach reserves the right to make an exception. You must attend school ¾ of the day of the game/meet. No cutting classes!

3. **SPIRIT** • Pride in school • Pride in team
   Put forth an all-out effort (110%)
   "Be willing to sacrifice personal interests or glory for the welfare of all." (Wooden)

4. **MAINTAIN GOOD HEALTH** • Mental, moral, physical
   Daily conditioning and rest. Proper diet
   NO smoking, NO drinking, NO drugs, NO foul language or degrading comments on school campus or at any school related function

5. **CONFIDENCE** • Respect yourself, teammates, and coaches
   Have faith in yourself knowing you are prepared.

6. **INTERPERSONAL RELATIONS**
   Learn to work with your teammates. Your behavior affects others.

REMEMBER — You are expected to work hard • think • concentrate • strive • for best skills possible.

If you do not uphold these responsibilities you not only let your team and coach down — you deny yourself an opportunity to acquire a unique experience that provides you with many qualities of life leading to a more fully developed character.

If, in the opinion of the coaches, a gross infraction of the standards of conduct and requirements occurs, this will result in *one* of the following actions:

1. *Total Suspension* from all present and future competitive activities while at ECR.
2. *Suspension* from the team for the remainder of the season.
3. *Probationary Status* for the current year. You may participate but, if an infraction occurs while on probation, total suspension will result.

COACHES' CREED

As coaches we will provide our athletes with a learning environment conducive to the high standard of skill, moral, and ethical development that characterizes the ideal female athlete.

The Women's Coaching Staff
El Camino Real High School
Girls' Physical Education Department

APPROVED: Patricia Ann Walsh
Assistant Principal

Please sign and return the tear-off below with your packet.

- - - - - - - - - - - - - - - TEAR OFF - - - - - - - - - - - - - - - -

I have read the contract and am aware of my responsibilities and will fulfill them to the best of my ability.

Date _____ Grade _____   _____
                                Signature of Student

Sport _____   _____
                                Address

                                _____
                                Phone

I too have read the contract and am aware of and in agreement with the responsibilities my daughter is expected to fulfill.

                                _____
                                Signature of Parent

APPENDIX

Example D

```
                    STATE UNIVERSITY
                  ASSOCIATED STUDENTS
                 1974-1975 Fiscal Year
                    BUDGET REQUEST


     Activity: Women's and Coed Intercollegiate Sports
               Budget Account No.: 8903
```

INCOME	1973-1974 Allocation	1974-1975 Request	Recommendations Treasurer's	B.O.C.	Senate
Ticket Sales					
Revenue from other sources					
1. Participation Fees (other schools)	750.00	750.00			
A.S. Fees	30,788.00*	69,964.48			
Total Income	31,538.00	70,714.48			
EXPENDITURES					
Payroll	100.00	9,000.00			
Travel Local-Regional	7,846.00	24,624.48			
National	17,180.00	20,000.00			
Publicity	100.00	1,300.00			
Administration	295.00	1,350.00			
Repair	200.00	250.00			
Uniforms and Equipment	**	7,235.00			
Other	4,567.00	5,705.00			
Insurance	1,250.00	1,250.00			
Total Expenditures	31,538.00	70,714.48			

```
*Includes original allocation of 21,358.00 plus additional alloca-
tions of 9,180.00 for National travel and 250.00 for Insurance.
**Listed under OTHER in 1973-74 request; total 888.00.
```

STATE UNIVERSITY

ASSOCIATED STUDENTS
1974-1975 Fiscal Year
BUDGET REQUEST

Activity: Women's and Coed Intercollegiate Sports
Budget Account No.: 8903

Line Item Detail

Payroll					9,000.00
1/2 Secretary	4,800.00				
Equipment moving	250.00				
Gymnastics					
Accompanist	800.00				
Maintenance	150.00				
Student Assistants					
Publicity	1,000.00				
Student Assistant					
Trainer	2,000.00				

Travel					44,624.48
Local and Regional	Trans.	Meals	Lodging		
Archery-Coed (8)	374.00	1,275.00	390.00		
Badminton-Coed (16)	376.00	1,283.50	175.00		
Basketball-W (32)	753.78	1,932.00	720.00		
Fencing-Coed (20)	1,341.85	891.50	455.00		
Golf-W (8)	200.10	251.00	105.00		
Gymnastics-W (40)	3,418.40	1,864.50	950.00		
Swimming/Diving-W (25)	891.00	881.50	620.00		
Tennis-W (15)	341.40	644.00	300.00		
Track/Field-W (12)	187.50	299.00			
Volleyball-W (60)	1,164.90	2,153.50	385.00		
	9,048.93	11,475.55	4,100.00		
				24,624.48	

National Championships		20,000.00	

Publicity			1,300.00
Supplies	250.00		
Photography	250.00		
Press Book	500.00		
Publicist's Travel	100.00		
Postage Releases	100.00		
Telephone	100.00		

Administration			1,350.00
Dues		200.00	
AIAW	125.00		
WAIAW	35.00		
SCWIAC	25.00		
Other fees	15.00		
Meetings		650.00	
AIAW	425.00		
WAIAW	100.00		
SCWIAC	25.00		
Other	100.00		

Contingency Fund	500.00	

Repair		250.00
Electrical weapon repair	150.00	
Uniform repair	100.00	

```
Uniforms and Equipment                                              7,235.00
  Game Uniforms and Small Equipment        2,535.00
    Archery                    80.00
    Badminton                 240.00
    Basketball                240.00
    Fencing                   515.00
    Golf                       80.00
    Gymnastics                400.00
    Swimming                  250.00
    Tennis                    150.00
    Track/Field               180.00
    Volleyball                400.00

  Warm-up Uniforms                          4,100.00
    Basketball                600.00
    Fencing                   500.00
    Gymnastics              1,000.00
    Swimming                  625.00
    Tennis                    375.00
    Volleyball              1,000.00

Fencing Weapons                              600.00

Other                                                               5,705.00
  Entry fees-Tournament and League
  Local and Regional                        1,873.00
    Archery                   370.00
    Badminton                 176.00
    Basketball                340.00
    Fencing                   179.00
    Golf                       35.00
    Gymnastics                120.00
    Swimming/Diving           145.00
    Tennis                     87.00
    Track/Field                96.00
    Volleyball                325.00

  National Championships                      800.00

Officials                                                           1,384.00
  Basketball                  466.00
  Fencing                      28.00
  Gymnastics                  160.00
  Swimming                    100.00
  Volleyball                  630.00

Golf Green Fees                              315.00
Golf Cart Rental                              83.50
Awards                                       500.00
Tournament Supplies                          450.00*
Tournament Awards                            300.00*

Insurance                                                           1,250.00
```

*Covered by Entry fees listed as revenue.

STATE UNIVERSITY

ASSOCIATED STUDENTS
1974-1975 Fiscal Year
BUDGET REQUEST

Activity: Women's and Coed Intercollegiate Sports
Budget Account No.: 8903

INCOME AND EXPENDITURE JUSTIFICATION

INCOME JUSTIFICATION:

Participant Fees   750.00
    Revenue from entry fees from other schools to
    pay for supplies and awards for tournaments
    hosted by SU.

A.S. Fees   69,964.48
    Amount needed to run a quality program at local,
    regional, and national level without placing
    financial hardship or excessive time demand on
    students.

EXPENDITURE JUSTIFICATION:

PAYROLL   9,000.00

    1/2 Secretary   4,800.00
        Secretarial help is urgently needed to aid the
        Director and the coaches with clerical work in
        a large scale program.

    Equipment Moving   250.00
        Due to conflicts in scheduling events in the
        Men's Gym (adjacent to Gymnastics Room) all
        women's gymnastics meets will be held in the
        Women's Gym in 1974-1975. This requires ex-
        tensive moving of the heavy equipment and mats
        from the Gymnastics Room for competition.

    Gymnastics Accompanist   800.00
        Gymnastics events are done to specialized music.
        This requires services of a professional
        pianist in order to develop the music and per-
        form for taping. Each gymnast requires her own
        music, with several selections available.

    Student Assistant-Publicist   1,000.00
        Publicity for the Women's and Coeducational
        Intercollegiate program has virtually been non-
        existent, except that which can be generated by
        the individual coaches and the Director, who do
        not have time to do an adequate job. A publicist
        is extremely necessary to establish communication
        for one of the University's most successful but
        least known programs.

    Student Assistant-Trainer   2,000.00
        Athletes in the various sports are gravely in
        need of assistance from qualified trainers.

The prevention of injuries and rehabilitation
from injury is a basic need in any athletic
program, especially one in which the athletes
are under the physical stress experienced in
gymnastics, basketball, track and field, and
volleyball.

TRAVEL   44,624.48

Local-Regional   24,624.48
Needed to provide transportation, meals, and
lodging for the teams in ten intercollegiate
sports to meet their league schedule commitments, and to allow them to compete in regional
qualification meets and tournaments for national championships. The increase noted over
last year's request is a result of the following: (1) Meals are requested at a rate of 2.50
for breakfast, 3.00 for lunch, and 5.50 for
dinner; last year's request was based on a
rate of 5.75 per day for meals, which was to-
tally inadequate. (2) Funds were requested for
meals at all away events for which a student
would miss a meal at home or in the dormitories.
(3) Mileage was based on 10¢ a mile rather than
the previous 7c. (4) The gymnastics team "A"
class team is scheduled for three intersectional
competitions in addition to the local schedule
previously requested; this is justified since
the quality of the team's performers is not
challenged in local competition since several
performers are of national and potential Olympic caliber.

National   20,000.00
During 1972-73 women's teams from SU won the
AIAW National Volleyball Championship, placed
8th in the AIAW National Gymnastics Championships, placed 9th in the Women's U.S. Intercollegiate Archery Championships, and qualified
as one of 16 teams for the AIAW National Basketball Championship. In addition, a SU diver placed
2nd in the 3 meter diving at the AIAW National
Swimming and Diving Championships, 2 gymnasts
were selected as All-Americans at the AIAW Na-
tionals, and 5 volleyball players were selected
to try out for the 1973 World University games,
with 3 selected to the team which represented the
U.S. in Moscow.

As of March 1, 1974, the SU women's volleyball
and basketball teams have won the AIAW National
Championships in their respective sports. The
support of the A.S. for our fine teams to national competition is gratefully acknowledged.
The amount requested is an estimate of the funds
needed to adequately provide for the travel of
those teams and individuals who may qualify to
attend national championships in 1974-1975.

PUBLICITY   1,300.00
    Funds needed to publicize the Women's and Coed
    Intercollegiate program in terms of press re-
    leases, posters, brochures, etc.

ADMINISTRATION   1,350.00

    Dues   200.00
        Memberships are held in the (1) Association
        for Intercollegiate Athletics for Women (AIAW),
        (2) Western Association of Intercollegiate
        Athletics for Women (WAIAW), and (3) Southern
        California Women's Intercollegiate Athletic
        Conference. Money is needed to provide for
        these memberships.

    Meetings   650.00
        Funds are needed for the Director and coaches
        to travel to mandatory meetings to establish
        policies and schedules and represent the Uni-
        versity.

    Contingency Fund   500.00
        Funds needed to cover unexpected expenses in
        a growing program.

REPAIR   250.00
Funds to cover the repair of normal wear of fencing equipment and uniforms.

UNIFORMS AND EQUIPMENT   7,235.00

    Games Uniforms and Equipment   2,535.00
        This is a new item in the Women's and Coed
        Intercollegiate budget request. Up to this
        time teams have been outfitted in game uni-
        forms with the expense being carried by the
        players and coaches. This has resulted in a
        tremendous burden to both. In addition, in
        attempts to keep costs down the quality of
        products was often poor. Also, since purchases
        were made by individuals rather than by an
        institution, institutional discounts were not
        available. This item appears to be clearly
        justified, in as much as the participants'
        appearance during competition is important.
        It is, actually, the key factor in relating
        team members with SU. This item also budgets
        for special small equipment needed on an in-
        dividual basis, such as fencing gloves, golf
        gloves, etc.

    Warm-up Uniforms   4,100.00
        Over the past five years the A.S. has periodi-
        cally funded our budget for warm-up uniforms.
        The warm-ups purchased were a standard style
        and checked out by each team prior to each con-
        test and returned after the contest. This
        method--having a central pool of a basic warm-
        up--is very inadequate. It is inefficient, in view
        of the number of participants in the program.
        Also, each sport has special needs in terms of

style, color, and warmth. The warm-up uniforms
on hand will be allocated to the track team,
the badminton team, and the C volleyball and
basketball teams. The 500.00 allocation for
1973-74 has been assigned to the golf and archery teams for purchase of specialized jackets
and sweaters. This request reflects the amount
to adequately outfit the remainder of our teams
for 1974-75.

FENCING WEAPONS   600.00
   Replacement of blades needed for sabre and elec-
trical foil and epée equipment. Not provided by the
WPE Department because this equipment is used only
in competitive programs.

OTHER   5,705.00

   Entry Fees   2,673.00
      Local and Regional--Amount needed to enter
      teams in league meets, culminating tournaments,
      and regional qualification events.

   Officials   1,384.00
      Cost of officials for practice and league games
      and meets.

   Golf Green Fees   315.00
      Necessary to provide cost of golf course fees
      for both practice and matches.

   Golf Cart Rental   83.50
      Needed for away competition at .50 per golfer,
      since players' own carts will not fit in trunk
      of auto with five players in a car. Also pro-
      vides for electric cart rental for coach at
      home matches to expedite supervision of play
      on the course.

   Awards   500.00
      Funds needed to provide base for an award pro-
      gram being developed for SU's women's and coed
      program in 1974-75 to recognize outstanding
      performers.

   Tournament Supplies and Awards   750.00
      Covered by participant entry fees. Supplies
      and awards for archery, gymnastics, badmin-
      ton, and track and field invitationals to be
      held at CSULB.

INSURANCE   1,250.00
   Needed for medical coverage while practicing,
competing, and traveling to and from program
events.

WOMEN'S INTERCOLLEGIATE SWIMMING AND DIVING

BUDGET REQUEST FOR 1974-75

October

   Swimming relays _____ 2 teams from ____
     Entry fee: 20.00   20.00
     Trans.: 5 cars @ 9.00 ea   45.00
     Meals: 25 lunches @ 3.00 ea   75.00

   SU vs _____ and ____ @ ____
     Trans.: 5 cars @ 21.00   105.00
     Meals: 25 Breakfasts @ 2.50 ea   62.50
           25 lunches @ 3.00 ea   75.00
     Officials: 15.00   15.00

        _____ @ SU
     Officials: 15.00   15.00
     Refreshments: 7.50   7.50

   SU @ _____
     Trans.: 5 cars @ 7.00 ea   35.00
     Officials: 15.00   15.00

November

       _____ @ SU
     Officials: 15.00   15.00
     Refreshments: 7.50   7.50

   SU vs _____ and ____ @ ____
     Trans.: 5 cars @ 23.40 ea   117.00
     Meals: 25 Breakfasts @ 2.50 ea   62.50
           25 lunches @ 3.00 ea   75.00
     Officials: 15.00   15.00

   SU @ _____
     Trans.: 5 cars @ 7.00 ea   35.00

December

      _____ Invitational
  Trans.: 4 cars @ 23.40 ea   93.60
    Meals: 15 Breakfasts @ 2.50 ea   37.50
          15 lunches @ 3.00 ea   45.00
          15 dinners @ 5.50 ea   82.50
    Lodging:
         7 doubles @ 20.00 ea   140.00
         1 single @ 15.00   15.00
    Entry fee: 25.00   25.00

   Championships @ _____ 2 days
     Trans.: 5 cars @ 9.00 ea x 2   90.00
     Meals: 25 lunches @ 3.00 ea   75.00
     Entry fee: 50.00   50.00

February

      _____ Invitational (4 days and 3 nights)
Trans.: 4 cars @ 83.60 ea   344.40
Meals: Breakfast for 15 @ 2.50 ea   37.50
   (2) Lunches for 15 @ 3.00 ea   90.00
   (2) Dinners for 15 @ 5.50 ea   165.00
Lodging:
   7 doubles @ 20.00 ea for 3 nights   465.00
   1 single @ 15.00 for 3 nights   45.00
Entry fee: 25.00   25.00

      _____ Invitational
Trans.: 3 cars @ 7.00 ea   21.00
Entry fee: 25.00   25.00

SUMMARY

Transportation	886.00
Meals	881.50
Lodging	620.00
Officials	75.00
Entry fees:	145.00
Refreshments	15.00
	2,622.50

```
                    WOMEN'S INTERCOLLEGIATE GOLF

                    BUDGET REQUEST FOR 1974-75


October, 1974

        _____ Invitational Tournament (2 days)
        Entry fee: 2 golfers @ 8.00 ea                   16.00
        Trans.: 1 car @ 117.10                          117.10
        Lodging: 1 double @ 20.00 ea for 3 nights        60.00
                 1 single @ 15.00 for 3 nights           45.00
        Meals: (3) Breakfasts for 3 @ 2.50 ea            22.50
               (4) Lunches for 3 @ 3.00 ea               36.00
               (4) Dinners for 3 @ 5.50 ea               66.00
        Practice balls                                    2.00
        Pull carts                                        2.00


February, 1975

        _____ Women's Golf League Entry fee          1.00

        ____ @ ____ or
        4 practice balls                                  2.00
        4 pull carts                                      2.00
        Trans.: 1 car @ 9.00                              9.00
        Meals: 5 lunches @ 3.00 ea                       15.00

CSULA @ ____ Country Club
        4 practice balls                                  2.00
        4 pull carts                                      2.00
        Trans.: 1 car @ 6.50                              6.50
        Meals: 5 lunches @ 3.00 ea                       15.00

        ____ @ ____
        4 practice balls                                  2.00
        4 pull carts                                      2.00
        Trans.: 1 car @ 4.00                              4.00
        Meals: 5 lunches @ 3.00 ea                       15.00

        ____ at ____
        4 practice balls                                  2.00
        4 pull carts                                      2.00
        Trans.: 1 car @ 17.60                            17.60
        Meals: 5 lunches @ 3.00 ea                       15.00

        ____ @ ____
        4 practice balls                                  2.00
        4 pull carts                                      2.00
        Trans.: 1 car @ 26.40                            26.40
        Meals: 5 lunches @ 3.00 ea                       15.00
               5 dinners @ 5.50 ea                       27.50

CA Collegiate Tournament @ ____ (1 practice day and 2 tournament
days)
        9 practice balls                                  4.50
        9 pull carts                                      4.50
        Trans.: 1 car @ 6.50 for 3 days                  19.50
        Meals: (2)lunches for 4 @ 3.00 ea                24.00
        Entry fee: 3 golfers @ 6.00 ea                   18.00
```

```
_____ @ _____
4 practice balls                                      2.00
Greens fees for 10 golfers                           30.00
Refreshments for 10 golfers                           3.00
Cart for coaches                                      7.00


_____ @ _____
4 practice balls                                      2.00
Greens fees for 10 golfers                           30.00
Refreshments for 10 golfers                           3.00
Cart for coaches                                      7.00


_____ @ _____
4 practice balls                                      2.00
Greens fees for 10 golfers                           30.00
Refreshments for 10 golfers                           3.00
Cart for coaches                                      7.00


_____ @ _____
4 practice balls                                      2.00
Greens fees for 10 golfers                           30.00
Refreshments for 10 golfers                           3.00
Cart for coaches                                      7.00


_____ @ _____
4 practice balls                                      2.00
Greens fees for 10 golfers                           30.00
Refreshments for 10 golfers                           3.00
Cart for coaches                                      7.00

Practice match @ _____
4 practice balls                                      2.00
Greens fees for 5 golfers                            15.00
Cart for coaches (shared)                             3.50

Practice greens fees
50 practice rounds                                  150.00

SUMMARY
                          Entry fees          35.00
                          Transportation     200.10
                          Lodging            105.00
                          Meals              251.00
                          Practice balls      33.00
                          Pull carts          12.00
                          Refreshments        15.00
                          Carts for coaches   38.50
                          Greens fees        315.00
                                           1,004.60
```

Notes: Carts for coaches are needed
  (1) for safety reasons in the event that one of our golfers becomes ill or is injured on the course.
  (2) to travel quickly to the site for making rulings during play.

If only one golfer is taken to the Stanford Invitational, the total budget would be reduced by 65.00. It's only a guess that two golfers would be eligible.

The increase in greens fees has added 52.50 to the budget.

```
              WOMEN'S INTERCOLLEGIATE TRACK AND FIELD

                      BUDGET REQUEST FOR 1974-75


  League Meets

      @ _____
         Trans.: 3 cars @ 7.50 ea                         22.50
         Meals: 13 lunches @ 3.00 ea                      39.00
         Entry fees: 12 women @ 50¢ ea                     6.00
                     2 relays @ 1.00 ea                    2.00


      @ _____
         Trans.: 3 cars @ 7.50 ea                         22.50
         Meals: 13 lunches @ 3.00 ea                      39.00
         Entry fees: 12 women @ 50¢ ea                     6.00
                     2 relays @ 1.00 ea                    2.00


      @ _____
         Trans.: 3 cars @ 5.00 ea                         15.00
         Meals: 13 lunches @ 3.00 ea                      39.00
         Entry fees: 12 women @ 50¢ ea                     6.00
                     2 relays @ 1.00 ea                    2.00


      @ _____
         Trans.: 3 cars @ 21.00 ea                        63.00
         Meals: 13 lunches @ 3.00 ea                      39.00
                13 dinners @ 5.50 ea                       71.50
         Entry fees: 12 women @ 50¢ ea                     6.00
                     2 relays @ 1.00 ea                    2.00


      @ _____
         Trans.: 3 cars @ 7.00 ea                         21.00
         Meals: 13 lunches @ 3.00 ea                      39.00
         Entry fees: 12 women @ 50¢ ea                     6.00
                     2 relays @ 1.00 ea                    2.00


      @ _____
         Trans.: 3 cars @ 7.50 ea                         22.50
         Meals: 13 lunches @ 3.00 ea                      39.00
         Entry fees: 12 women @ 50¢ ea                     6.00
                     2 relays @ 1.00 ea                    2.00

  Track and Field League Championships @ _____
         Trans.: 3 cars @ 7.00 ea                         21.00
         Meals: 13 dinners @ 5.50 ea                       71.50
         Entry fees: 12 women @ 1.00 ea                    12.00
                     2 relays @ 2.00 ea                     4.00


  Intercollegiate Track and Field League Dues               10.00

         _____ Relays @ SU _____
         Entry fees: 12 women @ 1.00 ea                    12.00
                     2 relays @ 5.00 ea                    10.00


  SUMMARY                           Entry fees             86.00
                                    Transportation        187.50
                                    Meals                 299.00
                                    League Dues            10.00
                                                          _____
                                                          582.50
```

```
                  WOMEN'S INTERCOLLEGIATE TENNIS

                   BUDGET REQUEST FOR 1974-75


____ Tournament @ _____
  Entry fees: 4 singles @ 4.00 ea                      16.00
              2 doubles @ 5.00 ea                      10.00
  Trans.: 1 car @ 103.00                              103.00
  Meals: (3) Breakfasts for 5 @ 2.50 ea                37.50
         (3) Lunches for 5 @ 3.00 ea                   45.00
         (3) Dinners for 5 @ 5.50 ea                   82.00
  Lodging:
         2 doubles @ 20.00 ea for 3 nights            120.00
         1 single @ 15.00 for 3 nights                 45.00

SU @ _____
  Trans.: 2 cars @ 21.00 ea                            42.00
  Meals: 7 Dinners @ 5.50 ea                           38.50


         @ SU
  Refreshments: 4.00                                    4.00


SU @ _____
  Trans.: 2 cars @ 9.00 ea                             18.00
  Meals: 7 Dinners @ 5.50 ea                           38.50


  _____ @ SU
  Refreshments: 4.00                                    4.00


SU @ _____
  Trans.: 2 cars @ 7.00 ea                             14.00
  Meals: 7 Dinners @ 5.50 ea                           38.50


         @ SU
  Refreshments: 4.00                                    4.00


SU @ _____
  Trans.: 2 cars @ 7.50 ea                             15.00
  Meals: 7 Dinners @ 5.50 ea                           38.50


  _____ @ SU
  Refreshments: 4.00                                    4.00


SU @ _____
  Trans.: 2 cars @ 7.50 ea                             15.00
  Meals: 7 Dinners @ 5.50 ea                           38.50


  _____ @ SU
  Refreshments: 4.00                                    4.00


SU @ _____
  Trans.: 2 cars @ 14.00 ea                            28.00
  Meals: 7 Dinners @ 5.50 ea                           38.50


         _____ @ SU
  Refreshments: 4.00                                    4.00


         _____ Valley Invitational Tennis Tournament
  Entry fees: 1 singles @ 4.00                          4.00
              1 doubles team @ 8.00                     8.00
```

```
Trans.: 1 car @ 25.40                               25.40
Meals: (3) Breakfasts for 4 @ 2.50 ea               30.00
       (3) Lunches for 4 @ 3.00 ea                  36.00
       (3) Dinners for 4 @ 5.50 ea                  66.00
Lodging:
       3 nights for 3 players @ 10.00               90.00
       1 single @ 15.00 for 3 nights                45.00
Tournament Desk Clerk                                2.00


_____ Women's Intercollegiate Tennis League Tournament
Entry fees: "Open Division"
            6 singles @ 3.00 ea                     18.00
            3 doubles @ 5.00 ea                     15.00

            "B Division"
            2 singles @ 3.00 ea                      6.00
            2 doubles @ 5.00 ea                     10.00
Trans.: 3 cars @ 9.00 ea x 3 days                   81.00
Meals: (3) Lunches for 13 @ 3.00 ea                117.00
```

SUMMARY

Entry Fees	87.00
Transportation	341.40
Meals	644.00
Lodging	300.00
Refreshments	24.00
	1,396.40

WOMEN'S INTERCOLLEGIATE VOLLEYBALL

BUDGET REQUEST FOR 1974-75

(2 "A" teams, 2 "B" teams and a "C" team)

```
League fees: 3 teams @ 20.00 ea                              60.00

SU @ _____ (3 teams)
   Trans.: 8 cars @ 4.50 ea                                  36.00

SU @ _____ (2 teams)
   Trans.: 5 cars @ 10.50 ea                                 52.50
   Meals: 24 lunches @ 3.00 ea                               72.00

       _____ @ SU (2 teams)
   Officials: 2 @ 22.50 ea (double match)                    45.00
   Refreshments: 7.00                                         7.00

       _____ @ SU (3 teams)
   Officials: 2 @ 22.50 ea (double match)
              1 @ 15.00                                       60.00
   Refreshments: 7.00                                         7.00

SU @ _____ (2 teams)
   Trans.: 5 cars @ 4.00 ea                                  20.00

       _____ @ SU (2 teams)
   Officials. 45.00                                          45.00
   Refreshments: 7.00                                         7.00

SU @ _____ (2 teams)
   Trans.: 5 cars @ 7.00 ea                                  35.00
   Meals: 24 dinners @ 5.50 ea                              132.00

SU @ _____ (2 teams)
   Trans.: 5 cars @ 7.50 ea                                  37.50
   Meals: 24 lunches @ 3.00 ea                               72.00

SU @ _____ (1 team)
   Trans.: 3 cars @ 43.40 ea                                130.20
   Meals: Breakfast for 11 @ 2.50 ea                          27.50
          Lunch for 11 @ 3.00 ea                             33.00
          Dinner for 11 @ 5.50 ea                            60.50
   Lodging:
          5 doubles @ 20.00 ea                              100.00
          1 single @ 15.00                                  115.00

SU @ _____ (2 teams)
   Trans.: 5 cars @ 9.00 ea                                  45.00
   Meals: 24 dinners @ 5.50 ea                              132.00

SU @ _____ (2 teams)
   Trans.: 5 cars @ 5.50 ea                                  27.50

_____ @ SU
   Officials: 45.00                                          45.00
   Refreshments: 7.00                                         7.00
```

```
_____ @ SU
  Officials: 45.00                                45.00
  Refreshments: 7.00                               7.00

SU @ _____ (2 teams)
  Trans.: 5 cars @ 10.50 ea                       52.50
  Meals: 24 dinners @ 5.50 ea                    132.00

_____ Tournament (1 team)
  Trans.: 3 cars @ 7.00 ea                        21.00
  Meals: 11 lunches @ 3.00 ea                     33.00
         11 dinners @ 5.50 ea                     60.50
  Entry fee: 40.00                                40.00

_____ @ SU
  Officials: 45.00                                45.00
  Refreshments: 7.00                               7.00

SU @ _____ (2 teams)
  Trans.: 5 cars @ 4.50 ea                        22.50

_____ @ SU
  Officials: 45.00                                45.00
  Refreshments: 7.00                               7.00

SU @ _____ (2 teams)
  Trans.: 5 cars @ 23.40 ea                      117.00
  Meals: 24 lunches @ 3.00 ea                     72.00
         24 dinners @ 5.50 ea                    132.00

_____ @ SU (3 teams)
  Officials: 60.00                                60.00
  Refreshments: 7.00                               7.00

SU @ _____ (2 teams)
  Trans.: 5 cars @ 5.00 ea                        25.00

SU @ _____ (2 teams)
  Trans.: 5 cars @ 7.00 ea                        35.00

_____ @ SU
  Officials: 45.00                                45.00
  Refreshments: 7.00                               7.00

_____ @ SU
  Officials: 45.00                                45.00
  Refreshments: 7.00                               7.00

SU @ _____ (2 teams)
  Trans.: 5 cars @ 21.00 ea                      105.00
  Meals: 24 lunches @ 3.00 ea                     72.00
         24 dinners @ 5.50 ea                    132.00

_____ @ SU
  Officials: 45.00                                45.00
  Refreshments: 7.00                               7.00

_____ @ SU (3 teams)
  Officials: 60.00                                60.00
  Refreshments: 9.00                               9.00
```

```
SU @ _____ (2 teams)
   Trans.: 5 cars @ 9.00 ea                          45.00
   Meals: 24 lunches @ 3.00 ea                       72.00

SCWIAC Championships @ _____
   Entry fee: 3 teams @ 50.00 ea                    150.00
   Trans.: 8 cars @ 7.50 ea x 3 days                180.00
   Meals: 35 lunches @ 3.00 ea                      105.00
          35 dinners @ 5.50 ea                      192.50

WAIAW Region 8 Tournament @ _____
   Trans.: 3 cars @ 76.40 ea                        229.20
   Meals: (3) Breakfasts for 13 @ 2.50 ea            97.50
          (3) Lunches for 13 @ 3.00 ea             117.00
          (3) Dinners for 13 @ 5.50 ea             214.50
   Lodging:
          6 doubles @ 20.00 ea for 2 nights
          1 single @ 15.00 for 2 nights            270.00
   Entry fee: 75.00                                  75.00
```

```
SUMMARY
                              Entry fees         325.00
                              Officials          630.00
                              Transportation   1,170.90
                              Meals            1,961.00
                              Lodging            485.00
                              Refreshments        77.00
                                               4,648.90
```

WOMEN'S INTERCOLLEGIATE GYMNASTICS

BUDGET REQUEST FOR 1974-75

SU @ _____
  Trans.: 3 cars @ 9.00 ea 27.00
  Meals: 15 dinners @ 5.50 ea 82.50

_____@ SU
  Officials: 2 @ 20.00 ea 40.00
  Awards: 3.00 .... 3.00
  Refreshments: 7.00 .... 7.00

SU @ _____
  Trans.: Air fare for 7 @ 210.00 ea 1,470.00
       Car rental 125.00
  Meals: (3) Breakfasts for 7 @ 2.50 ea 52.50
      (3) Lunches for 7 @ 3.00 ea 63.00
      (3) Dinners for 7 @ 5.50 ea 115.50
  Lodging:
        3 doubles @ 20.00 ea for 2 nights 120.00
        1 single @ 15.00 for 2 nights 30.00

_____@ SU
  Officials: 2 @ 20.00 ea 40.00
  Awards: 3.00 .... 3.00
  Refreshments: 7.00 .... 7.00

SU @ _____
  Trans.: 2 cars @ 100.00 ea 200.00
  Meals: (3) Breakfasts for 10 @ 2.50 ea 75.00
      (3) Lunches for 10 @ 3.00 ea 90.00
      (3) Dinners for 10 @ 5.50 ea 165.00
  Lodging:
        5 doubles @ 20.00 ea for 2 nights 200.00

SU @ _____
  Trans.: 4 cars @ 23.40 ea 93.60
  Meals: 15 dinners @ 5.50 ea 82.50

SU @ _____
  Trans.: Air fare for 7 @ 150.00 ea 1,050.00
       Car rental 125.00
  Meals: (3) Breakfasts for 7 @ 2.50 ea 52.50
      (3) Lunches for 7 @ 3.00 ea 63.00
      (3) Dinners for 7 @ 5.50 ea 115.50
  Lodging:
        3 doubles @ 20.00 ea for 2 nights 120.00
        1 single @ 15.00 for 2 nights 30.00

SU @ _____ Invitational
  Entry fee: 50.00 .... 50.00
  Trans.: 5 cars @ 13.00 ea 65.00
  Meals: 21 Dinners @ 5.50 ea 115.50

_____ @ SU
  Officials: 2 @ 20.00 ea 40.00
  Awards: 3.00 .... 3.00
  Refreshments: 7.00 .... 7.00

```
SU @ _____
   Trans.: 4 cars @ 7.00 ea                        28.00
   Meals: 15 dinners @ 5.50 ea                      82.50


   _____ @ SU
   Officials: 2 @ 20.00 ea                          40.00
   Awards: 3.00                                      3.00
   Refreshments: 7.00                                7.00

Regionals @ _____
   Trans.: 2 cars @ 76.40 ea                       152.80
   Meals: (3) Breakfasts for 10 @ 2.50 ea           75.00
          (3) Lunches for 10 @ 3.00 ea             90.00
          (3) Dinners for 10 @ 5.50 ea            165.00
   Lodging:
          5 doubles @ 20.00 ea for 3 nights       300.00

"A" Finals @ _____
   Trans.: 3 cars @ 9.00 ea                         27.00
   Meals: 12 dinners @ 5.50 ea                      66.00
   Entry fee: 30.00                                 30.00

"B" Finals @ _____
   Meals: 15 dinners @ 5.50 ea                      82.50
   Entry fee: 40.00                                 40.00

SU @ _____
   Trans.: 2 cars @ 90.00 ea                       180.00
   Meals: (3) Breakfasts for 7 @ 2.50 ea            52.50
          (3) Lunches for 7 @ 3.00 ea              63.00
          (3) Dinners for 7 @ 5.50 ea             115.50
   Lodging:
          3 doubles @ 20.00 ea for 2 nights       120.00
          1 single @ 15.00 for 2 nights            30.00


SUMMARY
                              Transportation   3,418.40
                              Meals            1,864.50
                              Lodging            950.00
                              Entry fees         120.00
                              Officials          160.00
                              Awards              12.00
                              Refreshments        28.00
                                               6,552.90
```

```
                    COED INTERCOLLEGIATE FENCING

                    BUDGET REQUEST FOR 1974-75


IFCSC Dues                                              20.00
Epée Invitational @ _____
   Entry fee: 5 fencers @ 3.00 ea                       15.00
   Trans.: 1 car @ 4.50                                  4.50
Foil Open @ _____
   Entry fee: 10 fencers @ 2.00 ea                      20.00
   Trans.: 2 cars @ 21.00 ea                            42.00
   Meals: 11 Lunches @ 3.00 ea                          33.00
          11 Dinners @ 5.50 ea                          60.50
SU vs _____ and _____ @ _____
   Trans.: 5 cars @ 9.00 ea                             45.00

_____ and _____ @ SU
   Officials: 4 @ 7.00 ea                               28.00
   Refreshments: 7.00                                    7.00
SU vs _____ and _____ @
   5 cars @ 8.00 ea                                     40.00
   Meals: 21 Dinners @ 5.50                            115.50
SU vs _____ and _____ @
   5 cars @ 18.00 ea                                    90.00
   Meals: 21 Dinners @ 5.50 ea                         115.50
Conf. Round Robin @
   5 cars @ 4.50                                        22.50
   Conf. Banquet @ 2.00 per fencer                      50.00
WIFC Championships @ _____ (10 fencers and 1 coach)
   Entry fee: 21.00                                     21.00
   Trans.: Air fare for 11 @ 43.00 ea                  473.00
           Car rental                                  125.00
   Lodging:
           5 doubles @ 20.00 ea for 3 nights           300.00
           1 single @ 15.00 for 3 nights                45.00
   Meals: (3) Breakfasts for 11 @ 2.50 ea               82.50
          (3) Lunches for 11 @ 3.00 ea                  99.00
          (3) Dinners for 11 @ 5.50 ea                 181.50

WWIFC Championships @ _____
   Entry fee                                            13.00
   Trans.: Air fare for 5 @ 87.27 ea                   436.35
           Car rental                                   50.00
   Lodging:
           2 doubles @ 20.00 ea for 2 nights            80.00
           1 single @ 15.00 for 2 nights                30.00
   Meals:
           (2) Breakfasts for 5 @ 2.50 ea               25.00
           (2) Lunches for 5 @ 3.00 ea                  30.00
           (3) Dinners for 5 @ 5.50 ea                  82.50

SUMMARY
                              Transportation      1,341.85
                              Meals                 831.00
                              Lodging               455.00
                              Entry fees and
                              dues                   179.00
                              Officials              28.00
                              Refreshments            7.00
                                                  _____
                                                  2,841.85
```

COED INTERCOLLEGIATE BADMINTON

BUDGET REQUEST FOR 1974-75

February

   SU @ _____
     Trans.: 4 cars @ 9.00 ea   36.00
     Meals: 17 Dinners @ 5.50 ea   93.50

           @ SU
   Refreshments: 7.00   7.00

SU @ _____
   Trans.: 4 cars @ 7.50 ea   30.00
   Meals: 17 Lunches @ 3.00 ea   51.00

March

_____ @ SU
   Refreshments: 7.00   7.00

SU @ _____
   Trans.: 4 cars @ 21.00 ea   84.00
   Meals: 17 Lunches @ 3.00 ea   51.00
        17 Dinners @ 5.50 ea   93.50

_____ @ SU
   Refreshments: 7.00   7.00

April

SU @ _____
   Trans.: 4 cars @ 10.50 ea   42.00
   Meals: 17 Dinners @ 5.50 ea   93.50

_____ @ SU
   Refreshments: 7.00   7.00

SU @ _____
   Trans.: 4 cars @ 4.50 ea   18.00
   Meals: 17 Lunches @ 3.00 ea   51.00

May

SU @ _____
   Trans.: 4 cars @ 7.00 ea   28.00
   Meals: 17 Dinners @ 5.50 ea   93.50

_____ @ SU
   Refreshments: 7.00   7.00

SU @ _____
   Trans.: 4 cars @ 4.50 ea   18.00
   Meals: 17 Dinners @ 5.50 ea   93.50

```
SCWIAC Tournament @ _____
   Entry fee: 16 Players, 2 events @ 2.50 per event    80.00
   Trans.: 4 cars @ 21.00 ea                           84.00
   Meals: (2) Breakfasts for 17 @ 2.50 ea              85.00
          (2) Lunches for 17 @ 3.00 ea                102.00
          (2) Dinners for 17 @ 5.50 ea                187.00
   Lodging:
             8 doubles @ 20.00 ea                     160.00
             1 single @ 15.00                          15.00

Fifth _____ State Coed Collegiate Championship @
   Entry fee: 16 players, 2 events @ 3.00 per event    96.00
   Trans.: 4 cars @ 9.00 ea                            36.00
   Meals: (2) Lunches for 17 @ 3.00 ea                102.00
          (2) Dinners for 17 @ 5.50 ea                187.00




SUMMARY
                             Entry fees           176.00
                             Transportation       376.00
                             Meals              1,283.50
                             Lodging              175.00
                             Refreshments          35.00
                                                2,045.50
```

```
                 WOMEN'S INTERCOLLEGIATE BASKETBALL

                    BUDGET REQUEST FOR 1974-75


League entry fees: 2 teams @ 20.00 per team          40.00

Practice games

   Home: _____ @ SU A and B teams
            4 officials @ 15.00 ea                   60.00
            Refreshments 7.00                          7.00

            _____ @ SU A, B and C teams
            2 officials @ 15.00 ea                   30.00
            2 officials @ 26.00 ea                   52.00
            Refreshments 8.00                          8.00

            _____ @ SU C team
            2 officials @ 12.00 ea                   24.00
            Refreshments 7.00                          7.00

   Away: SU @ _____ A and B teams
            5 cars @ 9.00 ea                          45.00
            Meals: Lunch for 22 players and 2 coaches @
                   3.00 ea                             72.00

         SU @ _____ A and B teams
            5 cars @ 10.50 ea                         52.50
            Meals: Dinner for 22 players and 2 coaches
                   @ 5.50 ea                          132.00

         SU @ _____ B and C teams
            5 cars @ 3.50 ea                          17.50

         SU @ _____ C team
            2 cars @ 5.00 ea                          10.00

         SU @ _____ B and C teams
            5 cars @ 3.20 ea                          16.00

League Games

   Home: _____ @ SU A and B teams
            4 officials @ 15.00 ea                   60.00
            Refreshments 7.00                          7.00

            _____ @ SU A and B teams
            4 officials @ 15.00 ea                   60.00
            Refreshments 7.00                          7.00

            _____ @ SU A and B teams
            4 officials @ 15.00 ea                   60.00
            Refreshments 7.00                          7.00

            _____ @ SU A and B teams
            4 officials @ 15.00 ea                   60.00
            Refreshments 7.00                          7.00

            _____ @ SU A and B teams
            4 officials @ 15.00 ea                   60.00
            Refreshments 7.00                          7.00
```

```
Away: SU @ _____ A and B teams
      5 cars @ 5.00 ea                                    25.00

      SU @ _____ A and B teams
      5 cars @ 21.00 ea                                  105.00
      Meals: 24 lunches @ 3.00 ea                         72.00
             24 dinners @ 5.50 ea                        132.00

      SU @ _____ A and B teams
      5 cars @ 5.00 ea                                    25.00

      SU @ _____ A and B teams
      5 cars @ 23.40 ea                                  117.00
      Meals: 24 lunches @ 3.00 ea                         72.00
             24 dinners @ 5.50 ea                        132.00

      SU @ _____ A and B teams
      5 cars @ 7.50 ea                                    37.50
      Meals: Dinner for 22 players and 2 coaches
             @ 5.50 ea                                   132.00


Tournaments

   Holiday Tourney @ _____ A team
   3 cars @ 80.60 ea                                     241.80
   Entry fee: 75.00                                       75.00
   Meals for 3 days: 11 players and 1 coach
      (3) Breakfasts @ 2.50 ea x 12                        90.00
      (3) Lunches @ 3.00 ea x 12                          108.00
      (3) Dinners @ 5.50 ea x 12                          198.00
   Lodging: 3 nights
      6 doubles @ 20.00 ea x 3                            360.00

   SCWIAC Tourney @ _____ A and B teams
   5 cars @ 9.00 ea x 3 days                              135.00
   Entry fee: 75.00 per team x 2                          150.00
   Meals: 24 dinners @ 5.50 ea x 3 days                   396.00

   Regional Tournament @ _____ A team
   3 cars @ 48.20 ea                                     144.60
   Entry fee: 75.00                                       75.00
   Meals for 3 days:
      (3) Breakfasts @ 2.50 ea x 12                        90.00
      (3) Lunches @ 3.00 ea x 12                          108.00
      (3) Dinners @ 5.50 ea x 12                          198.00
   Lodging:
      6 doubles @ 20.00 ea x 3                            360.00


SUMMARY                          League fees               40.00
                                 Officials               466.00
                                 Refreshments             56.00
                                 Transportation          753.78
                                 Meals                 1,932.00
                                 Lodging                 720.00
                                 Entry fees              300.00
                                                       4,267.78
```

```
               COED INTERCOLLEGIATE ARCHERY TEAM

                    BUDGET REQUEST FOR 1974-75


     October

     10/18 _____ Invitational @ SU
            Entry fee: 1.50 per archer                       00.00

     10/12 SBVC FITA
            Entry fee: 2.50 @ 8 archers                      20.00
            Trans.: 2 cars 130 miles @ 10¢ per mile          26.00
            Meals: Lunch for 8 archers and 1 coach @ 3.00
                     ea                                      27.00
                   Dinner for 8 archers and 1 coach @
                     5.50 ea                                 49.50

     10/8 _____ City College Meet
            Trans.: 2 cars 120 miles @ 10¢ per mile          24.00
            Meals: Lunches for 8 archers and 1 coach @
                     3.00 ea                                 27.00

     10/29 SU-4 school meet
            Official @ 15.00                                 15.00
            Refreshments 7.00                                 7.00



     November

     11/2  SBVC FITA
            Entry fee: 8 archers @ 2.50 ea                   20.00
            Trans.: 2 cars 130 miles @ 10¢ per mile          26.00
            Meals: Lunch for 8 archers and 1 coach @
                     3.00 ea                                 27.00
                   Dinner for 8 archers and 1 coach @
                     5.50 ea                                 49.50

    *11/8 _____ Regional Championships @ _____ (SU is tri-
            host)
            Entry fee: 8 archers @ 8.00 ea                   64.00
            Trans.: 2 cars 130 miles @ 10¢ per mile          26.00
            Meals: (2) Lunches for 8 archers and 1 coach
                          @ 3.00 ea                          54.00
                   (2) Dinners for 8 archers and 1 coach
                          @ 5.50 ea                          99.00
            Lodging: 1 night for 8 archers and 1 coach
                          4 doubles @ 20.00 ea               80.00
                          1 single @ 15.00                   15.00

     11/16 SBVC FITA
            Entry fee: 8 archers @ 2.50 ea                   20.00
            Trans.: 2 cars 130 miles @ 10¢ per mile          26.00
            Meals: Lunch for 8 archers and 1 coach @
                     3.00 ea                                 27.00
                   Dinner for 8 archers and 1 coach @
                     5.50 ea                                 49.50


     *Qualifying tournaments for National Championships
```

```
*11/22 _____ Championships @ _____
         Entry fee: 8 archers @ 6.00 ea                    48.00
         Trans.: 2 cars 130 miles @ 10¢ per mile           26.00
         Meals: Lunch for 8 archers and 1 coach @
                3.00 ea                                     27.00
                Dinner for 8 archers and 1 coach @
                5.50 ea                                     49.50


   December

   12/3 _____ Meet @ State
         Trans.: 2 cars 50 miles @ 10¢ per mile            10.00
         Meals: Lunch for 8 archers and 1 coach @
                3.00 ea                                     27.00

         DGWS Postal Entry fee: 2.00 per team-2 teams       4.00


   January

   1/10 _____ Indoor Invitational @ _____
         Entry fee: 8 archers @ 5.00 ea                    40.00
         Trans.: 2 cars 15 miles @ 10¢ per mile             3.00
         Meals: Lunch for 8 archers and 1 coach @ 3.00
                ea                                          27.00

   1/24-25 _____ Open
         Entry fee: 2 teams @ 20.00 per team               40.00
         Trans.: 2 cars 600 miles @ 10¢ per mile          120.00
         Meals: (3) Breakfasts for 8 archers and 1 coach
                    @ 2.50 ea                               67.50
                (4) Lunches for 8 archers and 1 coach @
                    3.00 ea                                108.00
                (4) Dinners for 8 archers and 1 coach
                    @ 5.50 ea                              198.00
         Lodging: 3 nights for 8 archers and 1 coach
                  4 doubles @ 20.00 ea x 3                 240.00
                  1 single @ 15.00 x 3                      45.00


   February

   2/18 _____ Conference fees                        10.00

   2/25  Conference Tri-Meet @ SU
         Refreshments 7.00                                   7.00


   March

   3/4   Conference Tri-Meet @ _____
         Trans.: 2 cars 90 miles @ 10¢ per mile            18.00
         Meals: Lunch for 10 archers and 1 coach
                @ 3.00 ea                                   33.00

   3/11  Conference Tri-Meet @ SU
         Refreshments 7.00                                   7.00



   *Qualifying tournaments for National Championships
```

```
3/18   Conference Tri-Meet @ _____
       Trans.: 2 cars 45 miles @ 10¢ per mile            9.00
       Meals: Lunch for 10 archers and 1 coach @
              3.00 ea                                    33.00


April

4/1    Conference Tri-Meet @ _____
       Trans.: 2 cars 80 miles @ 10¢ per mile            16.00
       Meals: Lunch for 10 archers and 1 coach @
              3.00 ea                                    33.00

*4/8   Conference Championships @ _____
       Trans.: 2 cars 75 miles @ 10¢ per mile            15.00
       Meals: Lunch for 10 archers and 1 coach @
              3.00 ea                                    33.00

*4/18-19 _____ State Championships @ _____ (SU is tri-host)
       Entry fee: 8 archers @ 8.00 ea                    64.00
       Trans.: 2 cars 15 miles @ 10¢ per mile             3.00
       Meals: (2) Lunches for 8 archers and 1 coach
                  @ 3.00 ea                              54.00
              (2) Dinners for 8 archers and 1 coach
                  @ 5.50 ea                              99.00

4/26   SBVC-FITA
       Entry fee: 8 archers @ 2.50 ea                    20.00
       Trans.: 2 cars 130 miles @ 10¢ per mile           26.00
       Meals: Lunch for 8 archers and 1 coach @
              3.00 ea                                    27.00
              Dinner for 8 archers and 1 coach @
              5.50 ea                                    49.50

4/22   NAA Intercollegiate Mail Meet
       Entry fee: 2 teams @ 10.00 per team               20.00

SUMMARY                              Entry fees          370.00
                                     Transportation      374.00
                                     Meals             1,275.00
                                     Lodging             390.00
                                     Refreshments         21.00
                                                       2,430.00


*Qualifying tournaments for National Championships
```

APPENDIX
Example E

TO: Chairman
          Women's Physical Education Department
FROM: Director
          Women's and Coed Intercollegiate Sports
SUBJECT: Request for Supplies from Departmental Budget

ITEM	NUMBER	SPECIFICATIONS	COST PER ITEM	TOTAL
BADMINTON				
Feather Shuttlecocks	4 gross	RSL #1 Tourney-76 grain	$95.00/gross	$380.00
Equipment Carrying Bag	2	Vinyl bag and handles	25.00	50.00
			BADMINTON TOTAL	$430.00
BASKETBALL				
McGregor XL Basketballs	10	McGregor X10L	15.35	153.50
Basketball Scorebooks	6	DGWS	1.25	7.50
			BASKETBALL TOTAL	$161.00
FENCING				
Elec. Foil Blades	12	AFLA-FIE Approved 35" Flat tip comp. wired	8.50	102.00
Elec. Epée Blades	12	AFLA-FIE Approved 35" Flat tip comp. wired	8.50	102.00
Sabre Blades	12	AFLA-FIE Approved 35" Loop tip	6.75	81.00
3 Weapon Masks	6	Hot-tin dipped Castello 4 med. 2 large	15.00	90.00
Body Cords	24	Foil-Leon Paul	4.25	102.00
Body Cords	12	Epee	4.25	51.00
Practice unit for foil and sword	4	Uhlmann E262	25.00	100.00
Masking Tape	12 rolls	Two inch 7504-003-1	.65	7.80
			FENCING TOTAL	$635.80

ITEM	NUMBER	SPECIFICATIONS	COST PER ITEM	TOTAL
ARCHERY				
Hoyt Pro Flex Rest, 5 right 5 left	10	No HFR	.80	8.00
No Freeze Klicker	5	Bear No 7281	1.50	7.50
Reynolds Bowsight	5	Hooded pin #D-114	6.85	34.25
Repair of Swift Arrows including straightening	12	Arrow Manufacturing	.60	7.20
E-2 Finger Sling	12	Bear No 3535	.95	11.40
Thin-O-Fletch vanes (yellow)	36	Tofco, Inc. #175	2.95 doz	8.85
Ultra Vane	36	U-1, 1-3/4" Mini	4.95	4.95
			ARCHERY TOTAL	$82.15
GOLF				
Hoods for Woods	3	#D9517 (No. 1,3,X) Wilson	5.20	15.60
Golf Balls	6 doz	Spalding Top Flight	12.60 doz	75.60
Golf Balls	1/2 case	X-outs (Ram Golf Corp.)		75.00
			GOLF TOTAL	$166.20
TENNIS				
Tennis Balls	70 doz	Wilson Extra Duty T 1020	7.72 doz	540.40
			TENNIS TOTAL	$540.40
VOLLEYBALL				
Volleyballs	11	Rawlings V15, Japanese Leather	9.00	99.00
Volleyball nets	3	30 feet with cable, dowling supports	29.00	87.00
Volleyball nets	1	32 feet with cable, dowling supports	29.00	29.00
Volleyball scorebooks	6	DGWS	1.25	7.50
Knee Pads	12 pr.	Gold Bike #65 8 1/2 in. (6 large, 6 med)	2.95	35.40
Knee Pads	12 pr.	Natural Bike #65 8 1/2 in. (12 large)	2.95	35.40
Volleyball Antennas	2 pr.		17.95	35.70
			VOLLEYBALL TOTAL	$329.00

```
COMBINED STAFF REQUEST: ALL SPORTS

Tape                  60 cases    1½ inch, same type as in current use   16.00      960.00
Underwrap              8 cases    foam gauze                              27.00      216.00

                                              TOTAL STAFF REQUEST                 $1,176.00


SUMMARY OF SPORT BUDGET REQUESTS

Badminton              430.00
Basketball             161.00
Fencing                635.80
Archery                 82.15
Golf                   166.20
Tennis                 540.40
Volleyball             329.00
First Aid-All Sports 1,176.00

                    $3,520.55
```

Index

H

I

L

M

Magnusson, Dr. Lucille, 141
Mills College, 109

N

Naismith, Dr. James, 108
National Amateur Athletic Federation (NAAF), 112
National Association for Girls and Women in Sport (NAGWS), 11, 12, 13, 23, 24, 25, 128, 137, 138-41
National Association for Physical Education of College Women (NAPECW), 115, 119, 123, 127
  Policy on Competition for College Women, 119-20
National Athletic Conference of American College Women, 109, 144
National Federation of State High School Associations (formerly National Federation of State High School Athletic Associations), 15, 16, 27, 125, 137-38, 145-49
  Standards for Girls Sports in Secondary Schools, 118
National Joint Committee on Extramural Sports for College Women (NJCESCW), 123-24
  Policies and Procedures for the Conduct of Extramural Sports Events for College Women, 123-24
National Section on Women's Athletics (NSWA), 11, 115, 116, 117
  Standards in Athletics for Girls and Women, 116, 118

O

Ohio State University, 123
Outerbridge, Mary, 107

P

Perrin, Ethel, 115
Policies and procedures, 7, 11
  establishment of, 7
  policies, 7, 8
  procedures, 7, 8
Public relations, 97
  goals, 98
  interpersonal public relations, 103-5
  procedures and techniques, 98
    attitudes, improving, 102
    informing and interpreting, 98-100
    interest, stimulating, 101-2
    reporting, 102-3

publics, the, 97-98
Public School Physical Education Training Society of New York, 110

R

Rules and Regulations Governing Girls' Interscholastic Athletics Activities, 176-204

S

Scheduling, 34
Schoedler, Lillian, 113
Seasons, 33
Smith College, 108, 109
Stanford University, 109
Student Coordinator Handbook, 205-17

T

Thorpe, Dr. Jo Anne, 141
Title IX, 153-61
    athletics (Section 86.41), 155-56, 158
    athletic scholarships (Section 36.37), 155
    discrimination, areas of, 153-54
    suggested framework for compliance, 160-61
Transportation, 32
    travel request forms, 76
Trilling, Blanche, 109
Tripartite Committee on Golf for College Women, 123

U

United States Olympic Development Committee, 128-29
University of California, Berkeley, 109
University of Nebraska, 109
University of Wisconsin, 109

V

Vassar College, 108

W

Wellesley College, 108, 114
Women's Athletic Committee, 11, 110-12, 116
Women's Basketball Committee, 108-9, 110, 138